D1446322

The Self-Perception of Early Modern Capitalists

Margaret C. Jacob and Catherine Secretan

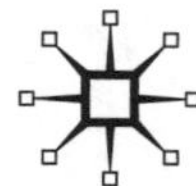

THE SELF-PERCEPTION OF EARLY MODERN CAPITALISTS

First published in 2008 by PALGRAVE MACMILLAN® in the US - a division of St. Martin's Press LLC, 175 Fifth Avenue, New York, NY 10010.

Where this book is distributed in the UK, Europe and the rest of the world, this is by Palgrave Macmillan, a division of Macmillan Publishers Limited, registered in England, company number 785998, of Houndmills, Basingstoke, Hampshire RG21 6XS.

Palgrave Macmillan is the global academic imprint of the above companies and has companies and representatives throughout the world.

ISBN-13: 978-0-230-60447-6
ISBN-10: 0-230-60447-1

Library of Congress Cataloging-in-Publication Data

The self-perception of early modern capitalists / edited by Margaret C. Jacob and Catherine Secretan.
p. cm.
Includes bibliographical references and index.
ISBN 0-230-60447-1
1. Merchants—History. 2. Commerce—History. I. Jacob, Margaret C., 1943- II. Secretan, Catherine.

HF479.S45 2008
381.09—dc22

2007052833

A catalogue record of the book is available from the British Library.

Design by Scribe Inc.

First edition: August 2008

10 9 8 7 6 5 4 3 2 1

Printed in the United States of America.

Contents

Illustrations

Acknowledgments

The editors wish to thank the Center for Seventeenth and Eighteenth Centuries Studies at UCLA and its director, Peter Reill, who made possible the conference out of which these essays emerged. Our authors have been especially diligent about the timetable we set for producing their final texts, and for that we are also very grateful. Funding for this project came from both the CNRS, and UCLA and its then dean, Scott Waugh. Finally, the editors would like to acknowledge their mutual enjoyment and enrichment from this rewarding international collaboration.

ACKNOWLEDGMENTS

Introduction

Margaret C. Jacob,
University of California at Los Angeles
and
Catherine Secretan,
Centre National de la Recherche Scientifique

Since antiquity, the handling of money and the urge to profit have generally been regarded with suspicion. Within cultures that had for so long juxtaposed material wealth to spiritual possessions only to find the first of far less merit, earthly pursuits were suspected of being inspired by greed, and merchants were seen as acting solely in their own interest. In fostering mistrust toward mercantile activity, Aristotle's *Politics*, Holy Writ, and the patristic tradition (St. Ambrose, St. Jerome) contributed greatly. Their common prohibition of usury, combined with the value that the Church attached to poverty as the Christian perfection, gave little meaning to the pursuit of riches. But there were also social stigmas associated with republican ideology, views that identified the "capitalist" as a "monster of fortune, a man with a heart of brass, and who has only metallic affection."[1] He is an architect of social inequality. How then did people who sought to make profit—striving to acquire and expand their money—view themselves? If the social utility of the *mercatores* never ceased to be asserted from medieval theology to eighteenth-century philosophy, protecting one's reputation remained a chief preoccupation among merchants.

Self-perception deserves special attention in the case of early modern "capitalists"—a term only introduced in the eighteenth century—because it concerns individuals coping with a problematical moral identity who are also living on the cusp of a fundamental transformation in the nature of the European economy. For the most part they are living before the triumph of *homo economicus*: seen as selfish, materialistic, and always imagined in modern and classical economic theory as governed by self-interest. Perhaps early modern merchants are better understood by recourse to more recent models of the economic actor. They postulate a human disposition to cooperate with others and to punish those who fail to promote that societal goal, i.e., normative constraints like self-discipline, politeness, and respectability play important roles in economic behavior.[2] If that more recent model of economic actors seeks validation, its advocates need only take a close look at the chapters before us.

The wide range of cases and contexts analyzed in these chapters offer a unique chance to place the question of moral identity in a comparative historical perspective. Topics as complex as "self perceptions"—even definitions of capitalism—can be more reliably addressed when seen from that wider perspective. At the same time, although no archetype of a merchant exists, a closer examination of each case study reveals how similarities in mentality, behavior, and self-images recur. The chapters ahead attempt to understand how early capitalists understood themselves, and each author seeks to locate similarities as well as differences. Whether we are looking at Catholic or Protestant or Jewish merchants—in Elizabethan London or eighteenth-century Amsterdam or Hamburg—we see certain patterns. Struggling with the vagaries of the market raised moral or ethical issues. All required thought and elicited emotions from fear to self-congratulation. From the medieval theologians who learnedly addressed worldly interests to a mid-eighteenth-century Leeds merchant who literally agonized about the threat posed to his salvation by his worldliness, the market fascinated and elicited thought and feeling.

Living within the framework of commercial capitalism—and eventually, by the early nineteenth century, within the ethos of industrial capitalism—was not the same thing as living with money. Money is not capital. It becomes capital when it is used to make more money, i.e., profit. Wages are not capital, but they can become capital if saved for the purpose of ventures or enterprises intended to make capital.

Having capital and *not* having capital separates the status and value of human labor, and increasingly the divisions became more sophisticated as objects were made. Commercial capitalism can cope with a fairly minimal division of labor: one person sells goods, another keeps the books, yet another may travel in search of goods or sales. By contrast, the late-eighteenth-century invention of industrial capitalism introduced greater and greater divisions of labor. The manufacturing process thrives on the efficiency of repeating small, discrete tasks that lead to the production of a finished item. By the mid-eighteenth century, foreign observers of British sites of manufacturing—even before the widespread use of power technology—thought that the complexity of their divisions of labor gave the owners a distinctive edge over their workers. Only the capitalist owner and overseer of the factory understood the entire system in a way that one worker could not. As Jochen Hoock notes, by the seventeenth century, there were some signs of protoindustrial activity, and printed surveys of mercantile life made mention of the commodities involved in these new settings.

Yet almost all the cast of characters we are about to meet lived in a preindustrial commercial universe. The relative simplicity of their divided labor—that we in hindsight may see—never dawned on them, thus it never mitigated their striving, or fear, or driving ambition, or search for ethical probity. When times were bad, generally they only had themselves and their kin to lay off or blame. Their intellectual and economic universe, and hence sense of self, was bracketed socially by two estates (with or without legal privileges): the clergy, who could be presumed to articulate probity, and the aristocracy, whose status and wealth could only be envied or emulated, but for people in commerce never taken as one's birthright. To be sure, commercial families could have servants and employees, but seldom in the numbers visible in the factories found by the 1790s in Manchester, Leeds, or Rouen. Perhaps only in the seventeenth-century Dutch republic did the wealthiest urban merchants, as presented to us by Clé Lesger, have no landed elite worthier than themselves and hence no need to emulate others. Not surprisingly, as he demonstrates, they exuded self-confidence and celebrated their wealth. Their Protestant clergymen were hardly in a position or disposition to question strongly their probity.

Was there a universal logic or code of conduct that shaped the moral ground once it entailed struggling for profit? And how much of it still fits the Weberian conceptual frame? Given our continuing fascination with a morality play where every character aspires to wealth, or at the very least comfort and profit, we can be sympathetic with Max Weber's remarkable contribution to the inquiry. Writing more than a hundred years ago, the great German sociologist thought that he had found the key to the spirit of capitalism in the ethos of Protestantism. We may respectfully disagree with many aspects of the Weberian paradigm, but it put the issue of how one lives as a capitalist forevermore on our intellectual agenda. Weber did something else. He saw that the form of economic life that had first appeared in the Italian city-states, and by the eighteenth century in the whole of Western Europe, was more complex than its generally nineteenth-century detractors imagined. Rather than being about simply greed or an unceasing desire for profit—although such impulses are seldom entirely absent—capitalism requires a self-fashioning, a set of disciplining behaviors derived from many sources to be sure. Some call them, as did Weber, "virtues" that promote at some times prudence, caution, and cooperation and at others audacity, courage, or calculation. Capitalists must negotiate not just in the market but in a set of social relations where the way one perceives others, and is perceived oneself, is critically important.[3] In addition, in most countries in early modern Europe, the aristocracy enjoyed pride of place, and the clergy, even in a resolutely Protestant country like Britain, had things to say about wealth in relation to salvation. Late in the eighteenth century the Unitarian minister (and scientist) Joseph Priestley said in Birmingham that wealth could be enjoyed provided heaven is kept firmly in mind.[4] Weber drew his examples almost entirely from the Anglo-American idiom, and as Matthew Kadane argues, his thesis retains relevance in that arena.

Looking for self-perceptions in individuals of the past—however remote or near this past may be—projects modern categories backward, where they may not always fit. As rightly noted in the essays of Matthew Kadane and Giacomo Todeschini, the notions of "self-perception" itself, as well as that of "individualism," are anachronistic. Moreover, explicit accounts of such a reality are rare, although since the Renaissance, autobiography was being developing as a genre. Hence the issue of self-perception is best approached by an "indirect route," as suggested by Clé Lesger. And indeed most of the chapters before us rely upon such varied sources as waste books, pamphlets, moral melodrama, letters disclosing social strategies or economic and financial habits, portraits and engravings, printed textbooks intended for merchants, and lexical usages. If these are not properly what Dutch and German scholars today call "ego-documents," they can nevertheless be considered as belonging to the wider sense of the category.[5] Only occasionally do we have private letters or self-revelatory diaries such as the thousand of pages of Ryder's journal that Kadane brings to light in his contribution to this volume.

In diaries and letters, the writing self often presents a calculated representation. Ryder, for example, willed his diary to posterity, suggesting that he wanted it to be read by others. More impersonal sources reveal social and cultural practices that the merchant may literally be "buying into" when he owns a pamphlet, sermon, or moral melodrama. We are suggesting that when surveyed in large quantities, such impersonal items can bring us closer to the images that merchants held about themselves. With the aid of these more impersonal sources, the essays strive to reconstruct a self-image that arguably merchants held in their minds collectively as well as individually, regardless of time or place. Such a methodological approach is all the more relevant because so many merchants viewed themselves through collective images, representations that might be normative—as in a "mirror for merchants"[6]—rather the way aristocrats or princes might validate themselves with their "mirrors." As the Hoock chapter demonstrates, there was a seemingly unending supply of merchant handbooks that told their users how to behave, as well as how to negotiate a bill of exchange.

A fairly good, if unsettling, example of such an interactive process between self and group comes from the self-images of Sephardic merchants working in several European settings. Francesca Trivellato tells us that by the early seventeenth century there were no more than fifteen thousand members of this Mediterranean diaspora living in Europe and its colonies at any one time. Yet collective stereotypes of anti-Semitic origin shaped the Sephardi's view of themselves. So compelling could these stereotypes be that, as she skilfully explains, they were even reworked by Jewish apologists to advocate the rights of their coreligionists. One of the most striking examples of such a stereotype and its persistent influence derives from the claim that Jews invented the bill of exchange. This myth was widely circulated in many editions by the work of Jacques Savary, *Le parfait négociant* (first published in 1675). It then turns up in just about every European translation and adumbration of Savary's text. In supposedly tolerant Amsterdam at the height of the financial crisis caused by the South Sea Bubble and John Law's Mississippi venture, Jews who traded as brokers on the Beurs in 1720, although a distinct minority, were blamed for the havoc the collapses provoked.[7] Although full players in the commercial life of the city, and sometimes quite prosperous, the Sephardic Jews were only marginally more accepted and integrated than their poorer Ashkenazi brethren. But at least in Amsterdam, The Hague, and Rotterdam, as in a few other European cities, they could publicly worship in their own synagogues.

The interactive process between self and group can also work on a national or collective level, as illustrated by another Dutch case drawn from the eighteenth century.[8] In a time of harsh debates about the causes of the Dutch "decline," national self-representations struggled with stark and conflicting choices between sustaining the Republic's economy and making profit for oneself by investing abroad. Dorothee Sturkenboom relies upon plays and engravings from the 1780s, as well as upon the tools made available by gender studies, to tease out artfully the anxieties of the beleaguered Dutch as they tried to find their identity and recapture their greatness—once their primacy—in a new economic reality. Holland's small area and population, and probably the absence of a strong central government, put the Dutch at a distinct disadvantage when competing with their neighbors from larger and more populous nations. Yet, as the recent book of Julia Adams amply demonstrates, in their ascendancy the Dutch had used familial identities and loyalties to forge a commercial success that lasted for many generations. Their self-perception as merchants entwined deeply with their patriarchal pride.[9]

As all the chapters make clear, in every national market, uncertainty resulting from its blind ebb and flow placed anxiety on a conscious level in the mind of all merchants. There must have been many Andrew Clows who, as Cathy Matson tells us, lost everything through no fault of their own. Anxious watching over their own performance and the vagaries of the market deeply affected mentality and behavior. For example, John Smail tellingly reveals how in eighteenth-century England the reality of uncertainty lay at the core of the advice given by parents to their sons. Uncertainty dominated economic, financial, and even meteorological events—in short, the human condition—in a capital economy. It led English merchants to hector their children, chide them for idleness, demand that they be trustworthy, and build knowingly and willfully their image of being reliable persons. As Leos Müller shows, Swedish fathers could be just as demanding. Adding the gender dimension, Smail reminds us that merchants had to be reliable men and configure a masculinity that was robust yet responsible. At the same time in Amsterdam, as Clé Lesger wisely tells us, the merchant had only himself to praise or blame for the outcome of his economic actions.

Because trust was the best weapon against the numerous instances of unpredictability, as Mary Lindemann explains, trustworthiness had to be at the forefront of the merchant's image of others and of himself. At the same time that Joseph Ryder was agonizing in Leeds, German merchants in Hamburg seemed to find ways of trusting themselves, of "settling into" the market. Indeed, Hamburg's commercial life grew by leaps and bounds. In 1720, its local governance structure enabled the city to protect merchants more effectively against the bubbles that had been so devastating in London, Paris, and Amsterdam. As Lindemann so masterfully shows, as the cities of Europe became increasingly tied to the same ebb and flow of international economic life, it became possible to think more abstractly and less personally about the meaning of speculation or prudence. With the French turmoil of the 1790s in mind, we may find it odd to think of the decade as a boom. But such was the brief good fortune of Hamburg. There was even a growing complacency at the thought of enjoying at least some luxury. In the same period, as we said, Joseph Priestley told his mercantile and early industrial clients that a degree of worldly comfort need not interfere with salvation. In the age of Adam Smith capitalism was being increasingly naturalized. If only Joseph Ryder had lived so long, what a happier man he might have been.

Closely connected to anxiety sits the ethic of hard work, an attitude differently named according to the milieu from which it came—*esercizio*, *fatica*, *industry*—but always referring to the value of tireless effort. In all places and times, merchants agreed: hard work was both a necessity and a virtue. Conveniently ignoring luck or deceit, merchants would be tempted to ascribe success to energy, business acumen, tenacity, and willpower. These were also the qualifications that Willem Usselincx, a merchant who was born in Antwerp in 1567 and settled in Amsterdam in the 1590s, cited when he argued that the rapid growth of commerce in Holland was promoted by the arrival of merchants from the Southern Netherlands like himself: "The whole of Europe feels and must admit, for your works bear witness to it, that in commerce, seafaring, knowledge of countries, cities, and almost all of the parts of the world, Your Honours are everywhere the leading, shrewdest, and most experienced men therein, who have the most and the best knowledge thereof."[10] The work ethic enhanced skill and professional knowledge and, above all, gave moral justification. Already in Florentine society from the fourteenth century we see Pegolotti, in this book analyzed by Todeschini, recommending to merchants that they look for moral legitimation by being recognized as "worthy professionals." They were worthy because of their skills at discerning values and prices and because they possessed commercial knowledge, accuracy, and precision in the keeping of their journals and accounts.

Whether Italian in the fourteenth century, or English in the age of Elizabeth, merchants could imagine themselves as a "bookish group." In a skillful linkage between numeracy, record keeping, and the work ethic in both science and mercantile life, Deborah Harkness finds in her London merchants exactly the same meaning of studied work as the one described by Leon Battista Alberti. In recalling his father, a rich merchant, Alberti tells us that he used to say, "merchants should constantly have their hands stained with ink."[11] This kind of intellectual activity accounts for their self-perception as "specialists." From the merchants' various bookkeeping practices to the increasing number of commercial manuals establishing a real "mercantile science"—as observed by Jochen Hoock—the merchants' high degree of literacy is a striking feature of their competency. But also their "speculative skill," as Lindemann notes, was a way of getting a good reputation. Harkness finds that the discipline imposed by account keeping, and by waste books and ledgers, fed into the habits and practices of naturalists, that early modern capitalism and science were closer in ethos than we might have once suspected. The relationship may actually have been long-standing, and we find that as early as the fourteenth century the experience of market and exchange impacted upon the evolving conceptual model of the natural world. Philosophers and theologians sought to measure phenomena as elusive as Christian charity or the quantity by which grace increases in the soul.[12]

The chapters in this book, combined with other sources, remind us that we should never think that professional capability and hard work kept merchants away from general knowledge and its cultivation. Trivellato tells us about the Jewish merchant, José Penso de la Vega, who even wrote an entertaining play to explain how the market in Amsterdam actually worked. Harkness and others provide striking examples of merchants participating in the exchange of natural knowledge; in writing books on learned subjects, as did the Dutch merchant Johan Rademacher with his Dutch grammar; or inviting others to enjoy their extensive libraries, as did the Rotterdam merchant Benjamin Furly, who gave vital assistance to Pierre Bayle.[13] Men engaged in commerce were both consumers and promoters of knowledge; first and foremost their learning was linked to their professional activity but then often enlarged to include general knowledge. They asserted the virtues of learning as part of the industrious behavior that was responsible, in their eyes, for their worldly success. Success was what allowed the Philadelphia merchant William Pollard to say: "I shall hold myself excusable to mankind," or to suggest, as did Willem Usselincx, ardent promoter of the foundation of the Dutch West India Company in 1621, that success was a moral reward to "the most experienced men."[14] In the same period and place Jacob Cats, famous for his moralizing short poems and "Emblems," thought that his talent and success had been decreed by God.[15]

But to what end did merchants extol success as a way of excusing oneself, a kind of special pleading? This is a crucial question and—in a way—a Weberian one. What were these merchants "guilty" of? Merchants seemed constantly in search of a moral identity, striving to get social recognition. In the eighteenth century, the growing use of the pejorative image of the "parvenu," generally applied to individuals coming from the business world, is an obvious testament that social mobility was intended to confer an honorable status. Already in sixteenth-century Italy, numerous novels and dramas pointed to those whose wealth and professional success would allow the attainment of a higher position.[16] Indeed, shift in wealth distribution brought newcomers to the noble class. But there is no possible comparison between these occasional cases of upward social mobility and what can be witnessed in the huge development of trade and manufacturing occurring in eighteenth-century England.

The prolific literary reaction that focused on these individuals branded as "nouveaux riches" reveals a general hostility—hard to refute, in the beginning, even by such a talent as Daniel Defoe—toward tradesmen and manufacturers as opposed to landed gentlemen.[17] In fact, something in the refashioning of their social status suggests that merchants might have been rather uneasy with their self-perception on this point. Just think how Florentine merchants of the fourteenth century remained concerned with finding an "honored and renowned civic identity," as Todeschini tells us, or how Jean Abraham Grill, as stressed by Leos Müller, aimed at being landed, the manager of an iron-rich estate, and how the "ever-gambling" Stephen Girard, described by Cathy Matson, chose to become a "great city landlord." In the American republic there was no titled or landed nobility to join. After years of gambling in trade Girard nevertheless gave himself a reward and became a lord over land. Through boom and bust, followed by spectacular success, Girard seems remarkably unruffled and undefensive. Could it be that a man who named his ships after the great French philosophes and deists (*Rousseau*, *Voltaire*, *Helvetius*, *Montesquieu*) had found a secular way of never having to excuse himself?

These examples reveal that only rarely did merchants cease agonizing. Among men who thought and behaved like any other humans, anxiety appears to be one—maybe the most—specific feature of the businessmen. First and foremost this was because of the nature of commercial life itself. But it was also because of the condition required for their moral identity: the delicate balance that had to be maintained between the sin of avarice and the social usefulness of merchants. That is why in such an extreme case as that of Joseph Ryder, who was "caught between two worlds," agonizing was also habitual. Perhaps guilt over one's worldliness played into the agony. Did the infamy ascribed to Jews by other merchants and even by the *philosophes* rub off a little on all merchants, if only as a guilt by distant association?[18]

Curing this posture of agonizing is precisely the aim of *Mercator Sapiens*, a famous discourse written by Caspar Barlaeus and presented to the great merchants assembled in the Illustrious School of Amsterdam, in 1632. The "philosophical merchant" is the one who, knowing that "everything in business is anxiety," will ask philosophy to be "a remedy for the soul" in the best of the Greek and Roman philosophical tradition. And here, in the precise case of profit making, the recommendation of philosophy will be to think and act in such a way that personal interest and public utility will become one and the same thing. More than a century before Adam Smith, remarkably Barlaeus opens the way to an ethic that will exonerate the merchant and his wealth.

There is something like a radical shift to be seen in the "self-perception" proposed by the *Mercator Sapiens*, a radical "change of paradigms."[19] This liberal paradigm is all the more evident if we compare—as does Clé in his essay—the discourse of Barlaeus to the one written some forty years before by the famous theologian Dirk Coornhert (himself the son of a clothier) and entitled *De Koopman*. The question presented by Coornhert was how to be both a merchant and a true Christian. How to deal with riches in front of the growing masses of poor people? One of the main differences between these two texts lies in the fact that Barlaeus's merchant is no longer described as a human placed and "monitored," so to speak, by God "on the world's stage" (*in orbis theatro positum*). On the contrary, according to the new liberal paradigm, the merchant has become a "self-acting" individual. This idea of there being a "world's stage" was a key commonplace at the time. Its origins lay with Cicero as reworked by Christian thought to convey a sense of God's providential will and so Coornhert declares, "Almighty God is the great author of this theatrical representation of the world; on the world's stage, he attributes, as he wishes, a role and a character to men from all conditions, making one a king, another a 'bourgeois,' and yet another a merchant," Barlaeus tells the merchant that thanks to his knowledge and professional skill, he is no longer a player on a stage.[20] A mere forty years later, he may now see himself as the "master and possessor of the world," as Descartes would say. Perhaps we have finally arrived at the early seventeenth-century moment when the true starting point of a capitalist's positive self-perception emerged. In 1637 Descartes tells us that urban life with its men of commerce has created in the Dutch Republic, a place of peace and security where men are "more concerned with their own affairs than curious about those of others." In such a propitious setting the philosopher said that he found peace and solitude. Perhaps so too did its merchants.[21]

It would take a century or more before Barlaeus's self-confidence and ease in the world became a commonplace in mercantile lives. Joseph Ryder's mid-eighteenth-century diary tells us that his anxieties were addressed almost weekly by the many preachers to whom he listened so intently. We must assume that they knew their audience, just as in the 1790s Priestley knew his. By that time there existed in many languages a body of economic literature that had begun to think about the market and the virtues it required on a much more abstract level than was available to individuals agonizing about their own future, either about their businesses or their souls. The lives of late eighteenth-century merchants like Grill in Sweden or Girard in Philadelphia have a secular "feel" about them.

A similar secularism surfaces in the correspondence of the family of James Watt (d. 1819) and his contemporaries and friends, the Boultons and the Wedgwoods. Commerce defined their lives; competition, invention, and the search for markets informed nearly every waking hour. Interestingly depression troubled both the Watt and Wedgwood families, as did the early death of various of their beloved children. Even in such moments of extreme distress, God is seldom invoked. Never once do they cast aspersion on their life's work or demean their callings. The market could still provoke profound anxiety, to be sure, and self-monitoring of one's virtues and those of family members had become a given. But the deity and chapel have receded to the point of almost never being mentioned. Perhaps only when capitalism had become the way of the world and its practitioners—while still anxious—largely guiltless could commentators like Saint-Simon and Marx begin to hate them.[22]

NOTES

1. Louis Sébastien Mercier, *A New Picture of Paris* (London: Symonds, 1800), 131. Translated from the French, *Le nouveau Paris* (Paris: Fuchs, 1799).

2. Herbert Gintis, Samuel Bowles, Robert Boyd, and Ernst Fehr, eds. *Moral Sentiments and Material Interests: The Foundations of Cooperation in Economic Life* (Cambridge, MA: MIT Press, 2005).
3. This point is taken up polemically but engagingly by Deirdre N. McCloskey, *The Bourgeois Virtues: Ethics for an Age of Commerce* (Chicago: University of Chicago Press, 2006).
4. Margaret C. Jacob, "Commerce, Industry, and Newtonian Science: Weber Revisited and Revised," *Canadian Journal of History* 35 (Fall 2000), 236–51.
5. On the use of "ego-documents" in history, see Rudolf Dekker, ed., *Egodocuments and History* (Hilversum: Verloren, 2002), and Mary Lindemann, "Sources of Social History," in *Encyclopaedia of European Social History* I, 6 vols. (Detroit: Scribner, 2001), 36.
6. Richard Dafforne, *The Merchants Mirrour*, quoted in Deborah E. Harkness's chapter.
7. See F. Van Cleeff-Hiegentlich, "'Eerlyke smousen, hoe zien die 'er uit myn heer?' Of hoe er in de achttiende eeuw in de Republiek der Zeven Verenigde Nederlanden over joden werd gedacht-een verkenning," Anne Frank Stichting, *Vreemd Gespuis* (Amsterdam: AMBO, 1987), 56–65.
8. See the chapter by Dorothee Sturkenboom, "Merchants on the defensive."
9. Julia Adams, *The Familial State: Ruling Families and Merchant Capitalism in Early Modern Europe* (Ithaca and London: Cornell University Press, 2005).
10. See Clé Lesger's chapter, also in this book, on "Merchants in Charge: The Self-Perception of Amsterdam Merchants, ca.1550–1700."
11. "Dicea messer Benedetto Alberti, uomo non solo in maggiori cose della terra, in reggere la repubblica prudentissimo, ma in ogni uso civile e privato savissimo, ch'egli stava così bene *al mercatante sempre avere le mani tinte d'inchiostro*," *I libri della famiglia*, R. Romano and A. Tenenti, eds. (Torino: Einaudi, 1994), 253.
12. Joel Kaye, *Economy and Nature in the Fourteenth Century: Money, Market Exchange, and the Emergence of Scientific Thought* (Cambridge, UK: Cambridge University Press, 1998), 2–4.
13. Karel Bostoen, *Bonis in bonum. Johan Radermacher de oude (1538–1617), humanist en koopman* (Hilversum: Verloren, 1998). "Anglais de nation, marchand de Rotterdam, quaker mitigé depuis quelque temps, homme d'esprit et d'érudition" ("English by birth, a Rotterdam merchant, a lukewarm quaker, a witty and erudite man"). So wrote Pierre Bayle about Furly, whose library was of great help to the author of the *Dictionnaire*. Bayle lacked the money to buy the books he needed; see W. I. Hull, *Benjamin Furly and Quakerism in Rotterdam* (Swarthmore, PA: Swarthmore College, 1941).
14. See the contributions of John Smail and Clé Lesger, in chapters 10 and 3, respectively, of this book.

15. A. Th. van Deursen, *Het kopergeld van de Gouden Eeuw*, III, Volk en overheid (Assen: Van Gorcum, 1979), 9.
16. See, for example, some of the texts in Marie-Françoise Piéjus, *Individu et société: le parvenu dans la nouvelle italienne du XVIème siècle* (La-Garenne-Colombes: Éd. de l'Espace européen, 1991).
17. See James Raven, *Judging New Health: Popular Publishing and Responses to Commerce in England, 1750–1800* (Oxford: Clarendon, 1992).
18. Margaret C. Jacob and Matthew Kadane, "Missing, Now Found in the Eighteenth Century: Weber's Protestant Capitalist," *American Historical Review* 108 (2003): 41.
19. Catherine Secretan, *Le "Marchand philosophe" de Caspar Barlaeus. Un éloge du commerce dans la Hollande du Siècle d'or*. Etude, texte et traduction du *Mercator Sapiens* (Paris: Champion, 2002).
20. Secretan, *Le "Marchand philosophe"* 97.
21. Descartes, *Discourse on the Method*, ed. and trans. George Heffernan (Notre Dame: University of Notre Dame Press, 1994), 49. On Descartes in the Republic, see Harold J. Cook, *Matters of Exchange: Commerce, Medicine, and Science in the Dutch Golden Age* (New Haven, CT: Yale University Press, 2007), chap. 6.
22. See Jerry Z. Muller, *The Mind and the Market: Capitalism in Modern European Thought* (New York: Knopf, 2002). The Watt and Boulton family correspondence can be found at the Birmingham City Library, UK; the Wedgewood papers are at Keele University, UK.

Part I

Prologue

Much of the literature on the origins of capitalism and the ethical formation of its practitioners assumes a radical disconnect between the religiosity associated with the Middle Ages and the norms and values required to make and keep profit. The following essay by Giacomo Todeschini asks us to think again. With an extraordinary grasp of the theological literature, especially that associated with the Franciscans, he synthesizes a large quantity of primary and secondary sources, much of it unavailable elsewhere to an English-speaking audience. German, Italian, and French medievalists, writing over the past twenty years, have completely revised our understanding of the mercantile impulse and its relationship to pre-Reformation Christianity. They see theologians, jurists, civic leaders, and merchants themselves assembling a new mercantile language deeply indebted to religious concerns and impulses. These new linguistic tools helped explain the life of profit and trade while offering guidance on civic status and virtuous conduct not at odds with but within Christian theological traditions. Before the mercantile assumed the importance we associate with it in the seventeenth and eighteenth centuries, its ethos had been shaped by classical as well as Christian traditions. If we now freely acknowledge the debt that the new science owed to aspects of the Aristotelian tradition, hence to medieval theology, we should not be surprised by the masterful exposition that Todeschini offers. Late medieval thinking about commercial life provided a setting where commerce and its practitioners could be integrated with the demands of civic and religious life. Eventually they could also be valorized. Before there were capitalists, we find late medieval Christian merchants who could identify themselves as pious and worthy of salvation. Their concerns were far closer to those of an eighteenth-century merchant than anything we can associate with the ethos of the modern, contemporary capitalist. The roots of early modern capitalism had been cultivated first in medieval soil.

—The Editors

Chapter 1

Theological Roots of the Medieval/Modern Merchants' Self-Representation

Giacomo Todeschini, University of Trieste

> *To be born, to labour, and to die. This is the merchandize of our country: these things here abound. To such merchandize did that Merchantman descend. And forasmuch as every merchant gives and receives; gives what he has, and receives what he has not; when he procures anything, he gives money, and receives what he buys: so Christ too in this His traffic gave and received. But what received He? That which aboundeth here, to be born, to labour, and to die, And what did He give? To be born again, to rise again, and to reign for ever. O Good Merchant, buy us. Why should I say buy us, when we ought to give Thee thanks that Thou hast bought us? Thou dost deal out our Price to us, we drink Thy Blood; so dost thou deal out to us our Price.*[1]

A systematic analysis of the self-representation, or articulated identity, found among late medieval entrepreneurs should be based on a specific survey of the standardized vocabularies utilized by these "hommes d'affaires" when they actually sought to articulate the meaning of their daily activities. Indeed, it is essential to understand the inadequacy of reading sources that concern medieval and early modern mercantile identities and imposing upon them an anachronistic individualism. From the fourteenth to the sixteenth century the writing of personal and family memoirs, or of handbooks devoted to explaining the techniques of local trading and exchange, or of catalogs of prices and exchange rates, should not be conceived as moments of purely subjective and functional expression or communication.[2] The notion of a merchant's humanism, commonplace in the historiography from Garin to Bec, has placed too much emphasis on the role of the merchant-writers as heroes of a self-centered modernity.[3] This approach consequently underestimates the linguistic complexity of the merchants' literary production. It pays no attention to the fact that the practice of self-describing and self-representing, so evident in merchants' memoirs, from the Florentine Morelli to the Ragusean Cotrugli,[4] and so hidden in merchants' manuals of *mercatura*, from Francesco Pegolotti to Giovanni da Uzzano, is deep-rooted in the conceptual syntax characteristic of the theological and canonical literature of the late Middle Ages.[5] The interpretation presented here does not suggest a mere lack of originality on the part of merchants, nor does it subvert the commonplace notion of a lay rationality expressed in the religious zeal of medieval merchants. On the contrary, this interpretation emphasizes the involvement of merchants' cultures in the cultural stream that produced, in the thirteenth, fourteenth, and fifteenth centuries, economic lexicons and discourses within clear linguistic structures that were also deeply theological.

Currently, the main problem lies in a historiography that asserts a forced and timeless separation between the lay and religious rationalities and assumes an everlasting conflict between economic and moral codes. Thus the idea of a medieval or early modern origin for the gap between "theory" and "practice" can be discarded by a close reading of the sources. They reveal a fundamental and institutional relationship between ethical and religious arguments and logical procedures aimed at defining the concept of profit or economic utility.[6] The fundamental nature of this relationship is seen in the words and conceptual grammar utilized in medieval economic treatises, questions, or manuals, but also in bureaucratic formularies. Actually all were strictly connected to the theological language of election, salvation, and spiritual profit. In many cases the same language and the same words operated in the theological as well as in the economic field. There existed a semantic potency so characteristic of many Christian economic metaphors or archetypes that it laid out strategies exploitable in the quest for heavenly treasure.

To understand this link between heaven and earthly pursuits, it is sufficient to remember the relevance of many evangelical allegories, such as the one depicted in the parable of the talents. The linguistic construction of medieval economic reflections on profit and loss and the influence exerted on theologians' and jurists' economic analysis by a widely diffused Christ's *agraphon* made it a duty for the Christian to be "similar to the skilled moneychanger"—that is, to be able to make a distinction between good or wicked actions as one would between legal or fake currencies.[7] At the same time, the core of theological speech from the Patristic age to the eleventh century demonstrates the possibility of affirming equivalence between spiritual or immaterial and economic values.[8] Ambrose, for instance, in his treatises on avarice and charity, declares without ambiguity that the foundation of a well-ordered Christian society is a balance between solidarity or friendship and utility or profit.[9] The Christian tendency to see familiar prosperity as dependent on the spiritual understanding of the bond between mutual affection and common or private good becomes the foundation of a logic that gave value and an extension (*latitudo*) of grace. At the end of the twelfth century, in consequence of the "commercial revolution" but also in consequence of the controversy about simony, theologians, canonists, and confessors intensified their analysis of the probable economic equivalence between a grace or favor or similar manifestation of friendship (*gratia*, *favor*, *amicitia*, *beneficium*) and a monetary payment or reimbursement.[10] The speculative possibility of calculating the economic value of immaterial things, or evaluating the price of manifold expressions of affection within a society founded on the polysemic notion of trust, then created the opportunity for theologians and jurists to utilize the complete textual library on that subject that had been organized during the previous centuries by the Christian West.

The compactness of this ecclesiastic economic culture was rooted in the ancient complexity of the Christian words regarding the notion of profit. The pragmatic need to manage the system of Church properties (*res ecclesiarum*) had become, in fact, from the ninth to twelfth century, even more extended and problematic in consequence of the increasing complexity of its social and religious meanings.[11] The theoretical consequence of these growing administrative complications had been the formation of a new ecclesiastical economic culture. So, from the twelfth to the thirteenth century the gap between the economic consciousness and rationality of theologians and ecclesiastical leaders and the relatively weak social role and feeble cultural presence of the "merchants" became even clearer. The word *mercatores* actually designated a very heterogeneous and gradually developing group of businessmen and traders. Actually, the culture or the linguistic mapping of this social group was far removed from the ancient economic consciousness of churchmen and newly reshaped by the Gregorian Reform.

Throughout the thirteenth century the popes Gregory IX (1234) and Boniface VIII (1296) planned a huge amplification and codification of canon law. The result of this institutional program was the increase of ecclesiastic economic thought and writings produced by the leading canonists of the century, from Sinibaldus de Fieschi (then pope Innocent IV) to Henricus de Susa, Cardinal of Ostia. The Italian, French, and English Masters belonging to the Mendicant Orders were also protagonists of this renovation. The notions of market, exchange, and merchants' civic utility, as well as the difference between forbidden usury and legal payment of interests, became a specialized section of the language commonly spoken and written by scholars, theologians, and churchmen. The jurists also, who, together with judges and notaries, formed the alphabetized and more acculturated component of the lay civil ruling class in the Mediterranean Middle Ages, were forced to acquire a new familiarity with this "holy" economic culture.[12] Actually, it is very difficult to separate the economic analysis or the economic perception produced and popularized from the twelfth to the thirteenth century by the leading Romanists from the previous and contemporary economic codification readable in economic treatises and commentaries written by the experts of Canon Law. Even though the subtle contractual analysis of credit and usury, so typical of the thirteenth-century textual stream, can be interpreted as if it were a direct and continuous dialogue between Masters of the Roman and Canon Law, the lexical and conceptual core of the discourse is based on the systematic use of the more ancient and ambiguous Christian theological vocabulary on public utility.[13] So, for instance, Romanists as well as Canonists explained the ethic and legal difference between usury and sale of rights of payment (*emptio/venditio reddituum*) on the basis of the civic and religious difference existing between the private value of money and the public (that is, civic and religious) one.[14]

From the second half of the thirteenth to the last quarter of the fourteenth century, in France, England, Spain, and Italy, the close interplay of economic and theological-juridical rationalities or vocabularies reached a final peak with the economic writings produced by the Franciscan School. The treatises or commentaries on contracts written by Peter Olivi, John Duns Scotus, Alexander of Alexandria, Guiral

Ot, Francesc Eiximenis, and other well- or lesser-known authors can be interpreted today as a coherent textual chain. This doctrinal tradition evolved then in fifteenth-century economics, as represented by, among others, Bernardino da Siena, Antonino da Firenze, Gabriel Biel, and Konrad Summenhart.[15] At the same time, in the cities of central or northern Italy and southern France—beginning in the late thirteenth century—the connection between merchants' families and Franciscan friars as confessors and leading experts on economic subjects became more and more visible. So it is easy to find in thirteenth- and fourteenth-century sources many proofs of privileged relationships between Franciscans and merchants. The private documentation from Narbonne and Montpellier shows very clearly the role of the Mendicant convents as courts where economic conflicts were resolved. Analogously, several Italian merchants' testaments written under the control or in the presence of the friars in the same period are good proof of the close relationship between friars and "merchants"—this at a time when the more reputed commercial companies flourished.[16] From the end of the thirteenth century onward, the well-known role of the Mendicant friars as confessors and judges in the tribunals enforcing the Roman Inquisition makes it easier to understand the social importance awarded to the Franciscans' economic elaborations. The authority to judge and evaluate the economic crimes represented by the word *usury* was the origin of an increasingly more accurate reflection about the meaning of legitimate economic relationships.

A similar conceptual refinement was clearly evident in the economic policies of the Holy See concerning the rights of the lords and kings to confiscate the wealth of the "usurers" and how they would be allowed to use that wealth.[17] On the whole, the close connection between the European papal finance, or the fiscal administration of the Holy See, and the growth of private banking companies managing it exerted a notable influence on the developing of an economic culture whose boundaries between "ethic" (or "sacred") and "profitable" were very ambiguous.[18]

Nevertheless, the traditional economic culture elaborated by theologians, canonists, and Romanists, was primarily reevaluated by the Franciscan Masters in light of their own representation of Christian perfection. The "Franciscan Economics" was in fact the outcome of the accurate juridical reelaboration of more ancient Christian discourses on evangelical poverty.[19] *Paupertas* as concept and praxis that shaped Christians' economic identities became the core of different procedures of using money and commodities.[20] In this perspective, the public role of a well-reputed Christian merchant and banker could be carefully separated from the one ominously played by the *notorious* usurer (*usurarius manifestus*) or monopolist.[21] From the *de contractibus* written in Narbonne by Petrus Olivi in the last decade of the thirteenth century to the textual section of the Commentary on Sentences regarding commerce and merchants exposed by John Duns Scotus in Oxford at the beginning of the fourteenth century, the social meaning of the merchant's profession became even more evident and understandable. The *mercator* was therefore recognized by the theological authority of Mendicant Masters as the main lay expert on values and prices. More exactly, he was described as a professional whose capacity to understand and analyze the current market price of money and commodities gave the reason and the moral validation of his right to get an unpredictable profit (a profit calculable in terms of probability).[22] The correct Christian way to possess wealth depended—as the Franciscan Masters wrote—on the renunciation of absolute property. It consisted in the specific understanding of the difference between necessary and superfluous amounts of wealth proportional to an individual's status. The lay Christians were to have a mindset capable of calculating this difficult balance (and so being able to evaluate the proportion of value to price). Such an ability—given the moral imperfection of the crowd—would produce less-imperfect lay individuals.[23] Because the summit of Christian perfection was "poverty"—that is a simple use of things without any sort of durable appropriation or accumulation—the ability to evaluate the economic value of things and the capacity to manage and circulate wealth could be perceived as Christian virtues. In the fourteenth and fifteenth centuries, many Mendicant theologians and confessors or jurists, Franciscans as well as Dominicans or Augustinians (Guiral Ot, Gerald of Siena, Eiximenis, Bernardino of Siena, Antonino of Florence, Johannes Nider, Gabriel Biel), elaborated upon the notion of the basic social role played within the Christian market society by the *mercatores*.[24] Actually, Franciscan economic attention was concentrated on those merchants whom Olivi defined as the more clever (*industrii in res subtiliter extimandis*), more rich (*pecuniosi*), and more renowned and trustworthy (*honorabiles et fide digni*) among the people actually present in the marketplace.[25]

Let us now consider the sources from the mid-1200s that imply or declare the visible evidence of a self-representation expressed by individuals consciously belonging to the group denoted by the Latin word *mercatores*. Until well up to the first half of the fourteenth century we have to deal with a heterogeneous mess of documents. A short catalog of these more ancient sources includes commercial letters; many official documents written by notaries; the first records of units of measurement, prices, and changes (the so-called "pratiche," like the most famous one of Francesco Pegolotti); and the first chronicles produced in Italy by men belonging to the arts and crafts societies like Dino Compagni and Giovanni Villani.[26] Then, from the 1340s it is possible to read the first manuals or memoirs relating to commerce written by Giovanni di Pagolo Morelli, Saminiato de' Ricci, and the so-called Anonymous of Florence. In the fifteenth century the Ragusean (that is, Venetian) merchant Benedetto Cotrugli then wrote a major work implying this model of the commercial manual or memoir.[27] Many renowned novelists of the Trecento, such as Sacchetti and Boccaccio, were also members or agents of commercial companies. Nevertheless, it seems inappropriate to catalog their work as typical evidence demonstrating the self-representation that the medieval and early modern groups of traders and bankers could produce in writing. The historiography today discards Pirenne's dreamy picture regarding the first medieval merchants as outlaws or adventurers; that is, poor and brave people, able to extract their capital as if by magic, from the emptiness of a depressed condition.[28] It is necessary, however, also to question the idea, clearly expressed in the fifties by Sapori, that Italian merchant culture in the Middle Ages corresponded to a homogeneous rhetoric.[29] This mercantile intellectual style would have been shaped both by its more technical written products, like merchants' memoirs or commercial letters, and at the same time by novels or political writings written by men, like Boccaccio, Sacchetti or Machiavelli, formally belonging to the merchants' rank. On the contrary, it seems essential to analyze the first textual group—letters and memoirs, "pratiche" or official records—as the written forms directly attesting the specificity of the languages consciously or unconsciously produced by medieval entrepreneurs, while the second group of sources, novels, and chronicles concerning merchants, usurers, or trade and money should be interpreted more as social representation organized by a complex system of stereotypes and rhetorical images. These often came from ancient cultural models, more than they were a source simply communicating the lexical substance of a newly developed culture that reflected an actual merchants' culture.

Before we proceed, it is essential to criticize another very common historiographical definition. It is actually crucial to state clearly that, when we read the documentation produced by medieval or early modern merchants or merchants' companies, we should make a distinction between two different styles of writing. The mercantile written sources have, in fact, a double and well-differentiated structure. On one side they have offer simple tables comparing prices and qualities of wares in different Mediterranean marketplaces. On other side they are organized books of memoirs including economic reflections, market news, and descriptions of computing techniques. The first style of writing, exemplified by the "pratiche di mercatura" of the Datini Archive in Prato, becomes very important in allowing us to analyze the first steps toward European economic rationality and to compare it to the modern one (what sometimes creates notable methodological problems).[30] Nevertheless, the second form of memoirs allows a better understanding of the growing self-perception of merchants at the end of the Middle Ages and a better opportunity to compare it to what we mean today with the word *self-perception*.

In this light, within the textual flow shaped by letters, manuals, and memoirs of the medieval and early modern merchants, it is possible to isolate some discursive elements. These aptly testify to the inner and crucial embedding of these textual forms in the previous and contemporary theological or juridical written culture. The first and more important of these semantic elements is *concordia*, clearly emphasized as social and symbolic value in merchants' memoirs, documents, and letters. It was meant to operate within the commercial company.[31] This word indicated the bond of friendship or kinship unifying the single members of the company within an economic Body. *Concordia*, and the notion of civic friendship implied in this word, recalled the concept of common and civic good. It in turn was deeply rooted in the thirteenth- and fourteenth-century communal theology of a city's mystic Body as earthly representation of Christ's Body.[32] In many commercial records that address the legal structure of the commercial and financial societies we find the visible consequence of this doctrinal complex. In the "Secret Book" written by Giotto d'Arnoldo Peruzzi in Florence around 1324, for instance, we can read that the solidarity or mutual agreement, and the total and proportional logic of subdivision of profits or losses, are the legal/religious bases of the business society. The "compagnia" is described also as a "body" whose gain, because of that harmony, will be blessed by God.

> On the whole they are seventeen companions. And these companions are concord in the agreement that, when they will make the banking account regarding the entire company, it shall be made according to the will and the opportunity of the companions (or two-thirds of them) living in Florence or in the Florentine countryside. Their decision and determination should be considered and appreciated as made by the whole company. And what our Lord God will concede to us as gain, net from expenses, damages, losses, stipends that were paid to the employees anywhere and for every reason by the company, it will

> be divided, as a net gain, among the companions and each companion will have his part in proportion to his investment in the company. And if, God save us, the company would have some loss, each companion will support it in proportion to his investment in the company. The companions acknowledge being partakers and to have to share each disbursement or gain made by the company in Florence or outside of Florence everywhere. The companions concord that, when a companion has no money to pay what he was engaged to pay when he began to participate to the company, he will make a gift to the company that will be a licit and good gain: namely a seven per cent yearly which will be blessed by God. And they concord also that, when a companion place his money in the company outside of the company's "body," the company will make as gift to him a seven per cent yearly, that will be a licit and good gain blessed by God.[33]

It is self-evident that merely the lexicon of "trust" (*fides/fiducia*) makes possible this discourse. *Fides/fiducia* is the core of each conceivable friendship, economic and familiar kinship, or civic happiness. More than the explicit and intentional meaning, the syntactic organization of the text (*di ciò che nostro Segniore Idio ci concederà di trovare guadagniato . . . E ancora sono in concordia che quale de' conpagni di questa conpagnia tengono de' loro danari in questa conpagnia di fuori dal corpo de la conpagnia che la conpagnia ne doni a que' chotali a ragione di sette per cientinaio l'anno per buono e lecito guadagnio benedetti da Dio*) and the choice of words (*concordia, corpo de la conpagnia, compagni, buono e lecito guadagnio, doni, benedetto*) indicate that the entire representation is informed by the popular doctrine of the "common good." Actually *bonum commune* was the more common theological and juridical definition of the outcome produced by the good administration of the sacred wealth belonging to an ecclesiastical institution. The prosperity of a city, however, could also be represented as *bonum commune* because of the sacred meaning attributed to the civic and communal subject.[34]

In another type of mercantile document, the contract of engagement of an administrator by the Salimbeni Company in Siena, made around 1280, the textual procedure is very similar. The new member of the commercial staff gives the leading members of the Company, Alessandro and Giovanni dei Salimbeni, his word in the form of a legal guarantee (in fact, in the form of a *iuramentum*, made by touching the Book of Gospels). By the *iuramentum* the new administrator is engaged to avoid both each form of economic deceit directly damaging the Company and each daily behavior identifying him as a wicked Christian involved in gambling and sexual crimes like adultery or fornication with virgins and nuns (and so damaging, in a different way, the reputation that is the "most precious treasure" of the Company).[35] Here, as in the example quoted above, it is easy to decode the connection between the merchants' will to be recognized as collective subjects belonging to the *Corpus civitatis* and the merchants' construction of a public renown or image: a topic afterward particularly developed by merchants' writings. It would be easy to underestimate this attention of the sources to the merchants' reputation and to define it the obvious result of an increasing market society, duly concerned for the economic trustworthiness of its members. Indeed, that would be a very reductive point of view. The value and sense of fame and renown is, in fact, a pivotal problem both from the late medieval "religious" perspective of Christian election and from that one relating to the civic and economic identity of residents in late medieval European cities.[36] To put it simply, the notion of "good reputation" (*fama*) was deeply embedded in the theological and juridical discourse that laid emphasis upon the importance that Christian individuals display in protecting carefully the purity of their civic and religious "name." Through it they would be accepted as true citizens. From the thirteenth century the notion became central in the definition of civic credibility and contractual trustworthiness. The archeology of this conceptualization is very significant. At the origin of the association between *fama* and citizenship, or trustworthiness, there were some Augustinian texts regarding the cruelty (*crudelitas*, *cruditas*), the inhuman wildness, of non-Christians (that is, infidels: *infideles*, *perfidi*) or imperfect Christians (*rudes*). Theologians and jurists represented these inadequate inhabitants of the "Christian city" as individuals paying no attention to their reputation, a consequence of their religious and cultural otherness or wickedness. Therefore, because of the incessant scandal they give to pious Christians, they actually were depicted as noncitizens or dangerous outsiders within the Christian *civitas*.[37] This notion of a social identity, dependent on a concern for personal reputation that each Christian must publicly show to confirm his right to participate in the social Body, had been widely disseminated during the high Middle Ages, largely through the hagiographic and canonistic writings. Then, from the twelfth century, it would be circulated in the commentaries on Roman law as well as in the homiletic and penitential literature. We can subsequently discover its semantic reutilization within the civic and "bourgeois" arguments of the late Middle Ages (for instance, in the perorations of the thirteenth century *advocatus* Albertano da Brescia) regarding the rules of correct citizenship. So there is great verity in the late medieval merchants' obsessive assertion of the need to have and protect each one's good reputation. It resulted from the merchants' need to be recognized as trustworthy subjects within the context of a market whose ethos and grammar was essentially Christian. The merchant's need to be accepted by his commercial partners was identical to the necessity to be identifiable by them as a real Christian member of the civic Body; namely, as an effective, trusty citizen. In this perspective there was no textual or conceptual contradiction between the functional or utilitarian identity of the merchant and the legal or religious identity of the citizen who firmly believed that Christ was the foundation of each specific and local "civic religion."[38]

From this point of view, the occasional notations relating to the utility of some commercial operations, evident also in the more elementary merchants' pragmatic sources, are not explicable in terms of a simple protocapitalist rationality. The medieval merchant's "utility" is not the obvious premise of a modern and rational intelligence of economics. For instance, we read in the *Pratica* of the administrator of the Datini Company Ambrogio de' Rocchi, at the end of the fourteenth century, that "whoever sells textiles in Valencia, and has good and well-ornamented stuff, can unworriedly store his merchandise. If, on the contrary, the gain is not sure, it will be better to unlock the hand and to get out, so that other's stuff would not be heavy on you; but above all you should sell in a secure place and to good payers."[39] It might seem absolutely clear to our "economic" and modern eye that here we have the first appearance of a "functional" and "practical" logic. But it is nevertheless essential to relate that remark to the medieval commonplace notion of "utility" and "benefit." The medieval concept of *utilitas, lucrum*, or *beneficium* was actually deeply rooted in the idea and vocabulary denoting as financially *and* politically right (i.e., virtuous) the wide circulation of money and wares (in an "antimonopolistic" or "dethesaurization" view: *largitio*). At the same time, the commercial but also moral aptitude to deal out wealth ("alarghare la mano per riuscirne") in the perspective of a future main income, or the ability to find trustworthy economic partners—that is, reliable and well-known buyers, friends, or *socii*—was commonly indicated as the ethical way to earn a good, not shameful or dishonorable, profit. *Lucrum cum mala fama dampnum est appellandum* was the most ancient and widely quoted saying.[40]

The decisive meaning of "name" and "renown" or "fame" for merchants' culture at the end of the Middle Ages is well demonstrated by the anonymous "advices on trade" (*Consigli sulla mercatura*) written in Florence at the end of the fourteenth century.[41] The author claims that the right merchant should be a rich and well-reputed man ("di netta fama"). His riches and his fame are, jointly, the foundation of his merchant's identity. By contrast, the wicked and/or ruined and notorious men ("homeni disfatti e di mala vita") should not be identified as true merchants. Similarly, at the beginning of the Pegolotti's *Libro di divisamenti di paesi e di misure di mercatantie*, written around 1330, we can find a sort of rhymed foreword that briefly but efficaciously sums up "what the real and just merchant must have inside of him" (*Quello che dee avere in sé il vero e diritto mercante*).[42] The work of Pegolotti, banker, politician, and merchant of the Bardi Company, was widely circulated and eventually came to be well known through the work of "the Florentine Chancellor of the Tithe, Gian Francesco Pagnini" in 1766. So we can appreciate the historical importance of the catalog of merchants' qualities included in the foreword. The identity of the just and authentic merchant, as well as the confirmation of his fame, results from his righteousness (*dirittura*), skill in economic prevision (*lunga provedenza*), trustworthiness (*ciò che promette non venga mancante*), good manners and honorable behavior (*bella e onesta contenenza*), a very cautious habit in buying combined with a propensity for selling (*scarso comperare e largo venda*), an irreproachably friendly attitude (*fuori di rampogna con bella raccoglienza*), regular religious practice and the practice of donating gifts in the name of God (*la chiesa usare e per Dio donare*), selling on the basis of a simple verbal engagement (*vendere a uno motto*), avoiding usury and gambling (*usura e giuoco di zara vietare e torre al tutto*), and finally, writing an accounting book without errors (*scrivere bene la ragione e non errare*). Some syntactic particulars of the text underline the correctness (*gli conviene, gli sta bene*) and at the same time the growth of "renown" (*crescie in pregio*) that the good merchant will acquire as a consequence of his social and economic or moral virtues. In light of this peremptory foreword, the following sections of Pegolotti's "pratica," regarding the itinerary toward the Near East, weights, prices, measures, commodities, and coins' relative values, can be easily read as a good example of the exhaustive, continuous, and specialized attention to the elements of the mercantile profession that the right merchant has the duty to show and to record. In this way he can be recognized as a worthy professional.

These characteristics of validation or legitimization of the merchants' identity, so evident in the earliest forms of self-representation produced by the more cultivated tradesmen, are at the same time perfectly visible (from the end of the thirteenth to the first half of the fifteenth century) in penitential or economic writings and sermons produced by the Franciscan and Dominican Schools. On the whole, the emphasis on the carefulness that (on an economic as well as on a moral level) must characterize the man who intends to be acknowledged as a merchant is common to mercantile and theological or moral writings. The Latin word *sollicitudo* or its synonym *industria* are habitually employed by theologians and preachers (Pietro Olivi, Giordano da Pisa, Bernardino da Siena, among others) to describe the right attitude of the good merchant.[43] Correspondingly, the equivalent Italian words "sollecitudine e esercitio" are commonly used by Florentine or Venetian merchants when they write their own memoirs. These cultivated entrepreneurs employ these words to emphasize their or their ancestors' skill and virtues and to explain, as Giovanni Morelli declares, how they had become typical exemplars of the "honorable citizen and good merchant" ("onorevole cittadino e buono mercatante").[44]

The caution and vigilance concerning moral, civic, as well as economic behaviors, an attitude very evident in the fourteenth century book of memoirs by Morelli, as later, during the fifteenth century, in the similar writings by Benedetto Cotrugli and Leon Battista Alberti, may not be reduced to an early manifestation of "bourgeois" spirit (as Sombart suggested).[45] It seems more appropriate to read this attitude as the product of the social and emotional transformations promoted and performed by the Christian ecclesiastic as well as civic policy in place after the fourth Lateran Council. The most visible sign of this reorganization of the social rules was shaped by the growing and imperative institutional obligation to recognize, by the reiterated and periodical confession of sins and the visible participation to public ceremonies or rituals, the correspondence between civic and religious identities. The Mass as a civic ritual denoting explicit forms of belonging to the Christian and communal group—namely, the Mass as "a social institution"— and the transformation of the confession into a recurring ritual of civic identification, by the late 1200s in all probability have much to do with the growing communication standards now in place for merchants. The diffusion inside of the Christian society of religious-linguistic techniques making possible the verbalization of the self will facilitate the growing of specific abilities to manage and record even more exactly and carefully each economic attitude, but also to consider attentively each sentiment, as well as each visible manifestation of friendship or hostility.[46] A good example of these new forms of rationality, aptly combined with religious feelings, social intelligence, and economic skillfulness, can be seen in the following passage from the Morelli's memoirs:

> The chance and his own skillfulness as well as exercise helped him. He never wasted his time, he was always careful in acquiring the love of God through alms and good deeds. Then he was provident by obtaining the friendship of good, honest and powerful men. He hobnobbed with them and exhibited to them a great love and disposition to be useful inasmuch he could. He asked their advices regarding his projects, and so he showed to have confidence and trust in them. He honored them by offering eating and other things, by assuming the role of godfather and through many other daily actions very typical of the relations among loving and affectionate people. Because of these wise and provident behaviors he turned out to be so able and prudent that in time of need, as I will report, he was helped and supported by friends and not by relatives: so that nobody could hurt him, mainly thanks to God's will and favor whose lack avoid every perfection. If we want become trustworthy Christians and friends of God, we should see His power and highest justice: but, because of our sins, we are blind and we prefer to think and believe that every prosperous or harmful thing is caused more by chance or mindlessness than by God's will; and that is not true, since everything depends on Him, but according to our merits.[47]

The factors determining the commercial as well as existential success of the subject (Pagolo di Bartolomeo Morelli, the father of the author) are the chance, namely the favor of God, but at the same time Pagolo Morelli's skillfulness (*sollecitudine*) and unexhausted activism (*esercizio*), together with an exceptional capacity to sustain hard work (*fatica*). The use of the word *sollecitudine* is not casual, since, as we have seen, this word in its Latin form *sollicitudo* was normally used by the theologians/economists from the thirteenth century to denote the carefulness and continuous mental concentration that should characterize the political leaders as well as the good merchants.[48] The concrete expression of Pagolo Morelli's economic and moral virtues is, in the text, a daily life with no wasting of time (*ché mai non perdé punto di tempo*), his habit to obtain the love and favor of God through alms and good actions, as well as his capacity to acquire by gifts and favors the friendship of worthy, respectable, and powerful men (*buoni uomini e da bene e potenti*). At this point, the author explains very clearly what he means as rational pursuit of an economic and social high standing. The financial success, he explains, is the outcome of the cleverness revealed by the merchant-citizen to be able to become friend and *socius* (that is, political and economic ally) of many praiseworthy, authoritative, and rich men. The acquaintance and friendship with these *maiores* of the city will be the starting point for the better use of the economic and psychological qualities of the hero at the center of the story. Nevertheless, building friendships (*amicitiae*) and agreements with the leading citizens, as well as gaining God's love, are not a simple task. The closeness to God results from a complicated ritual and economic practice actually made of alms, gifts to the ecclesiastic institutions, and, at the same time, charitable "donations"; that is, discounts made by the merchant to his own economic partners or customers. As Scotus writes, the reducing of a price voluntarily decided upon by a merchant, who nevertheless retains the main part of his own "right" profit, can be understood as a *donum* that the merchant offers to his partner/friend and, consequently, like a form of *charitas*.[49] The friendship with the *buoni uomini* appears, however, an even more delicate question. It is necessary to become part of a complex system of kinships, habitually described (also by Morelli) as a symbolic form of parenthood.[50] Morelli underlines as valid social strategies that belong to a member of the dominant group, both the habit of showing deference to the leading citizens (for example, by the organization of banquets and feasts, literally by offering to eat: *onoralli in dare loro mangiare e in tutte altre cose*) and the religious-familiar consanguinity derived from the fundamental role of godfather at the christening font. The final statement made by our author regards the indispensable social and religious awareness that, as the history of Pagolo Morelli's family shows, is the starting point for each professional career. The good and right merchant has to be conscious of the necessity to manage his own social life very carefully. He should look after his own business, but he should be especially concerned with his own civic reputation and with belonging to a strong social group. Finally, the understanding of the connection between, on one side, individual activism and, on the other, God's favor—in other words, the inner antifatalistic consciousness of the intimate relation between success or failure and relative individual skillfulness—seems to be the merchants' version of the increasingly commonplace theological concept of free will, the blessed principle that makes possible each civic and ethical achievement. The pious and successful businessman, in Morelli's pages, is above all a man able to penetrate the mystery posed by the divine identity of the social Body. He should understand that his own identity essentially depends from that sacred Body or superindividual community. Actually, he must realize that just his belonging to the social *Corpus*, perceived as a collective subject coalesced by many forms of kinship and repeatedly reinforced by day-by-day religious rituals, can sanctify his economic activities and identify him as a trustworthy merchant.

From this point of view, it is possible to discover a perfect and specific correspondence between the exaltation of the mercantile professionalism, represented as foundational of public happiness in the writings of the Oxonian Franciscan Scotus or the Catalan Franciscan Eiximenis, and the contemporary merchants' more or less direct self-definitions readable within texts like the Morelli memoirs, the Florentine anonymous, or Pegolotti's foreword to his *Pratica di mercatura*.[51] On the whole, the growing emphasis on the need to be watchful, seen in the Italian merchants' manuals and instructions or commercial descriptions from the fourteenth to the fifteenth century, seems interpretable as the main technical consequence of a growing identification of the merchants' groups with the cities seen as collective and sacred subjects. This trend clearly increased after the Plague. The pursuit of any form of individual profit and the participation in communal life—belonging to religious confraternities, familiar solidarities, and commercial partnerships—became even more important aspects of the same social process. Therefore, greater exactness of the accounting systems, commercial information and communication, and so a proportional multiplication of the commercial manuals was understandably the economic face of a social transformation. The social transformation related even more closely to the ritual identity of the citizen, his own ethical/religious fame, and his own economic reputation. The economic failure of a merchant's firm or the illegal nature of a transaction were commonly interpreted by the fourteenth- and fifteenth-century theologians, Eiximenis or Bernardino, as the proof and the consequence of a merchant's economic and moral loss of identity. Usury, alienation from the friendly social and religious context, hostility to the Christian society, moral disorder, and loss of reputation were the more commonplace signs of economic collapse found in the moral treatises or questions written by theologians and confessors.

At the beginning of the fifteenth century, the quoted constellation of economic and moral attitudes typical of the good merchant are represented both in the treatise on contracts written around 1430 by the Franciscan Bernardino of Siena, and in the *Libro dell'arte di mercatura* written by the merchant Benedetto Cotrugli of Ragusa in 1458. Cotrugli's treatise about navigation dedicated to the Venetian Senate in 1462 is more easily understood in light of this moral rhetoric.[52] In these works, like in the *Libro della famiglia* of Leon Battista

Alberti, the core of the discourse revolves around the necessity to display a very clear social and religious identity.[53] The problem is to be, and to appear, not simply a rich man, but primarily a devout and well-reputed citizen who is thus a man whose family and company belongs to a renowned and powerful circle of families. From this perspective, it is possible to understand the multiplication of pious foundations or confraternities established by the European merchants during the fifteenth and sixteenth centuries. A good example is offered by the School of Divinity of All Saints (Scuola della Divinità di Tutti I Santi) established around 1429 in Milan by Donato Ferrario, a middle-class merchant and landowner. Ferrario's intended to create a social and charitable institution to administrate his own properties and with the aim of providing the countless poor of the city with money and supplies.[54] Ferrario's intent was to assume a prominent and honorable civic role among a world of relevant families ruled by the Visconti family and, as Gazzini correctly underlines, to bear witness to his achieved "social standing" through the foundation of a pious institution, significant from an economic as well as symbolic point of view. It is precisely the difficult social climbing of Donato Ferrario, and so the relative weakness of his status—with the consequent lack of a public role and official appointments in fifteenth-century Milan—that explains his social and religious choice. It would be improper and anachronistic to decode this choice as a simple and clever social expedient. Actually, when Ferrario was establishing his *School of Divinity*, and so creating a charitable enterprise administrated by a well-reputed board (and not by an individual), he was acting as intellectual heir to the ethical and theological tradition that had produced from the end of the twelfth century the civic model of the righteous and saintly merchant. The main characteristic of this model citizen was his ability to distribute (*largiri*) his riches to the poor, circulating them through the institutionalization of his own wealth, though maintaining administrative control (the obvious reference was Omobono, the merchant of Cremona, who Pope Innocent III had beatified in 1199).[55] The deepest root, and the leading example of this economic and civic way of life, was represented by the religious-economic style commonly exhibited by the ecclesiastic churches and monasteries. Their riches, as the Canon Law ruled, were not individually owned by the clergy, but belonged as a collective Christian possession administrated and managed by bishops, abbots, canons, and priests. The merchant's fame and identity was therefore noticeably confirmed by his inner as well as visible participation in an economic logic with meaning that had both a sense of civic solidarity and mystic unification. Thus the welfare of the city could be represented as the achievement of the merchant's ability to transform his wealth in a public wealth.

When Bernardino da Siena, in the same years of foundation as Ferrario's *Scuola*, wrote his treatise on contracts, it was perfectly evident in his eyes that the merchants' society surrounding him was not simply an economic and religiously undisciplined crowd. As intellectual heir of the economics produced by the Franciscan School in the two previous centuries and as son of a leading merchants' family of Siena, he could easily understand that the problem was not merely to convince the merchants' community to be pious and to avoid every form of greedy behavior. On the whole, he made clear that the main goal was to communicate to his cocitizens who were merchants the duty to be rich and at the same time honorable men. This obligation was the result and the proof of their belonging to the *civitas* symbolically embedded in the universalistic Catholic *patria*. Actually, the merchant's honor is the core of Bernardino's discourse, especially when our author and preacher considers the social role of the merchant within his own neighborhood. So, it is noticeable that from Bernardino's point of view, one of the most relevant qualities of the merchant as a virtuous and Christian man, together with the abstaining from usury, liberality, and economic cleverness, is his skillfulness in distinguishing—among his own partners—the good and religious merchants from the dishonest and wicked ones. From this perspective Bernardino paints a portrait of the good merchant neatly organized by the concept of the control that the conscious merchant should exercise on his commercial neighborhood.[56] The good renown of the merchant, in other words, should be based on his ability to have a good understanding of the behaviors displayed by his commercial partners or neighbors or possible friends. The honest commercial life of the merchant, his religious habits and manifestations of belonging to the civic community, must be confirmed by his ability to detect the misbehaviors and, in total, the untrustworthiness, or infidelity, of other market participants.[57] This is a collective enterprise of watchfulness that is both internalized and communally understood and sanctified.

This care about the integrity and trustworthiness of the commercial society, so anxiously prescribed by Bernardino on the religious side, is present, too, on the secular side in a different and more daily version found in the merchants' writings of the fifteenth century. Formerly in the manual of Pegolotti it was possible to find references to the carefulness (or to the precautions regarding the suitability: *avisamento di convenenze*) that, for instance, the clever merchant should use when he is looking for a trustworthy shipmaster or shipowner.[58] The shipmaster like the shipowner, who are commercial partners of the merchant, should be considered from different points of view. So they have to be rich, able to manage and conduct the ship, skillful in ruling the sailors, and disposed to sign a paper when the merchant gives to them some money (that is, lends to them a sum, in a contract of *societas nautica*). On the whole, they must be trustworthy and well-reputed men; that is, men recognized as rightful citizens by the civic/religious community. The same problem is also at the core of some chapters found in Benedetto Cotrugli's treatise on sailing recently transcribed by Piero Falchetta.[59] The shipmaster should be sober, moderate, not a food lover, able to sustain the strain, vigorous, vital, not greedy, not young, a father of children, apt to speak properly, and well renowned (*temperato, continente, sobrio, domestico nello magnare, apto alle fatigie, acre et vivo, non avaro, non giovene, patre che agia figlioli, addire apto et ornato, de extimatione predito*).[60] At the same time the shipowner should be a good-looking, serious, and authoritative man, while it is suitable that someone who rules would have a nice and respectable appearance (the author observes that this pleasantness is typical of the Genoese shipowners). The quality of being pleasant to others (*piacievele ad ogni uno*) is very important in Cotrugli's book: the shipowner, in particular, should be agreeable to the merchants, as well as to the sailors, and, on the whole, so well disposed to each one that, as Cotrugli notes with some irony, it is commonly said that he should be similar to a whore (*lo patrone scia piecievole ad ogni uno, tanto ad marinari, vivato o mercatanti, et communemente se dicie che bisognia che lo scia come la bagascia*). This model identity is exemplary represented, according to Cotrugli, by Genoese and Venetian tradesmen. The description, with its rhetorical color, emphasizes vividly the necessity for the merchant to be very careful when he decides to organize a shipping society. At the same time, the text communicates to the reader that the catalog of the economic and civic qualities of a merchant, shipmaster, or shipowner is the codification of the complicated relationship of the subjects, as members of the merchants' universe, to the Christian market. By the middle of the fifteenth century, the "market republic," the *civitas mercatorum*, had deeply interiorized the system of civic-religious values concerning the charisma of the lay as well as ecclesiastic leaders who rule the civic communities. Also in consequence of the influence of images embedded in, and transmitted by, the classical or humanistic culture, the values become the model for each economic or social leader. At the middle of the Mediterranean fifteenth century, the good-looking presence, the seriousness, the tireless vigor, the (spiritual or physical) fatherhood, the authority, the riches, in a word, the main characteristics of each entrepreneur's renowned identity, appear as the realistic and middle-class adaptation of the notions of civic virtue, temperance, asceticism, personal charm, and, on the whole, publicly acknowledged honor. In the theological as well as juridical or homiletic writings, such men are described as the religious and political or military Christian leaders (*duces*).[61]

The semantic shift from the syntax of the charismatic holiness to the discourse regarding the ruling capacity and the civic centrality of the merchants' class is evidently made possible by a growing self-representation among merchants expressed by the vocabulary of honor and good reputation. Throughout the fourteenth century in debates about the legitimacy of the public debt of Florence and Venice, the Franciscan Scholastics had shown the correspondence between the public natures both of the Church and civic economies.[62] Similarly, during the fifteenth century Bernardino, Alberti, Cotrugli, among others, readapt a more ancient lexicon regarding the public and civic meaning of holiness and use it to describe the civic importance of the merchants. But now, this new merchants' "sanctity" is defined by the complexity of the "name" that the businessman has acquired through the multifaceted strategy of alliances, friendships, careful exchanges, and accurate participation in the ritual life of his community. The theological deepness of this identity is more than simply declared by the underlining of the merchant's religious duties, it is clearly expressed by a specific vocabulary. The ancient and typical lexicon of Christian virtues embodied by each saint, monk, or bishop becomes seemingly more appropriate to describe the daily discourse around the merchant's honor, his tirelessness, and his attitude to sacrifice. At the beginning of the so-called "commercial revolution" this model of economic and religious perfection had been well represented by the celebrated and widely discussed physical heroism of Francesco d'Assisi.

In Cotrugli's *The Book on the Merchants' Art* (1458), it is actually possible to find a final synthesis regarding the difficult professional identity of the businessmen who are *accustomed* to the practice of commerce (*usi alo exercitio della mercantia*). As we can see, the text is focused on the description of many merchants' tiring activities, and underlines that the foundation of a good merchant's identity lies in an especially strong mental and physical endurance as well as in exceptional thoroughness and patience.

> To the purpose of having a big profit, which is the goal of the merchants' profession, it is necessary to manage without worry and very

> conscientiously everything that could produce revenue and consequently improve the merchant's status; so, it is sometimes required to endure hard working night and day, to stand traveling by feet or by horse over earth and sea, hence to bear each tiring condition of buying and selling: in doing all these things, it is essential to be as careful as possible, and to put aside each other thinking not only regarding superfluous matters, but concerning also what is necessary to the maintaining of human life. Therefore it is sometimes obligatory to delay eating and drinking and sleeping: rather it is indispensable to bear hunger, thirst and wake or similar hurting and physically dangerous situations. Actually, if the merchant's body would not be well exercised like an efficient instrument, it could not endure this hard working: so, by enduring this toil obviously it would become too stressed, then it would become sick and finally it would die. The ending of the story would be that either the not exercised body could not reach the goal and obtain its fancied object, or, by trying to attain it without exercise, it would fall into sickness and death. As we should avoid both these extreme troubles, we must state and confirm that it is mainly useful and necessary to have a well-trained body namely a body right for the merchants' profession. Such a body will contribute to the goal achievement like a fit instrument: not differently from the hammer that as blacksmith's right instrument contributes to sharpen the blade.[63]

The material and immaterial merchant's wealth, represented by commodities, money, and "name," will be the desired result not only of an honored and renowned civic identity, but also of a well-exercised mind and body. Physical vigor is now especially represented as one of the most indispensable requisites of every economic achievement. The aptitude to withstand hunger, thirst, lack of sleep, and tiring journeys by feet or by horse, and the capacity to renounce not only "the superfluous things," but also the indispensable victuals, make the good and correct merchant. Beyond the representation of the merchants' identity as a skillful, ritualistic, and civic identity, the representation of the merchant's "self" becomes, in Cotrugli's text on the complicated art of trading, the description of a continuous, strenuous training (*essercitio*) whose aim is to strengthen the merchant's body, which is now perceived as the main instrument (*instrumento*) of his job. This sort of physical asceticism prepares a body that, like the hammer of the blacksmith sharpening a blade (*non altrimenti che si facci il martello che concorre come dextro instrumento del fabbro quando fabrica l'acuto*), will be molded to pursue relentlessly the merchant's prefixed goal. The mental and physical alacrity, final product of the described continuous and hard "training," will be henceforth, by the end of the

Mediterranean Middle Ages, the core of a merchants' self-representation. It implied, however, an even more elaborated definition of the control that the good businessman should exercise over his own body and mind.

When we consider the economic European situation in the second half of the fifteenth century from the point of view of the enormously growing poverty of the working and lower middle class, we can easily understand that the cultivated self-representation produced by the merchants' class was also the expression of a social process to achieve cultural and economic exclusivity. The idealized and heroic or religious representation of the businessman's mind and body silently hinted at the rising cultural insignificance and the low price and value of work, body, and mind of the outcasts or "exploited people."

NOTES

1. Augustine, Sermon 130, in *Discorsi*, *Nuova Biblioteca Agostiniana. Opere di Sant'Agostino* (Rome: Città Nuova, 1983), 130–32: "Nasci, laborare et mori. Haec sunt mercimonia regionis nostrae, ista hic abundant. Ad tales merces Mercator ille descendit. Et quoniam omnis mercator dat et accipit; dat quod habet, et accipit quod non habet; quando aliquid comparat, dat pecuniam, et accipit quod emit; etiam Christus in ista mercatura dedit et accepit. Sed quid accepit? Quod hic abundat, nasci, laborare et mori. Et quid dedit? Renasci, resurgere et in aeternum regnare. O bone Mercator, eme nos. Quid dicam, eme nos, cum gratias agere debeamus, quia emisti nos? Pretium nostrum erogas nobis, sanguinem tuum bibimus; erogas ergo nobis pretium nostrum." Translation by Rev. R. G. MacMullen.
2. Jochen Hoock and Pierre Jeannin, *Ars Mercatoria: Handbücher und Traktate für den Gebrauch des Kaufmanns, 1470–1820 or Manuels et traités à l'usage des Marchands, 1470–1820: Eine Analytische Bibliographie in 6 Bänden*, 6 vols. (Paderborn: Schöningh, 1991); Jochen Hoock, Pierre Jeannin, and Wolfgang Kaiser, *Ars Mercatoria: Handbücher und Traktate für den Gebrauch des Kaufmanns, 1470–1820 or Manuels et traités à l'usage des marchands: eine Analytische Bibliographie in 6 Bänden*, vol. 3 (Paderborn: Schöningh, 2001); Markus A. Denzel and Jean-Claude Hocquet, *Kaufmannsbücher und Handelspraktiken vom Spatmittelalter bis zum beginnenden 20. Jahrhundert: Merchant's Books and Mercantile Pratice from the Late Middle Ages to the Beginning of the 20th Century* (Stuttgart: Franz Steiner, 2002).
3. Eugenio Garin, *Prosatori latini del Quattrocento* (Milan: R. Ricciardi, 1952); Christian Bec, *Les Marchands écrivains, affaires et humanisme à Florence, 1375–1434* (Paris: Mouton, 1967).

4. Giovanni di Pagolo Morelli, "Ricordi," in *Mercanti Scrittori: Ricordi nella Firenze tra Medioevo e Rinascimento*, ed. V. Branca (Milan: Rusconi, 1986); Benedetto Cotrugli, *Il libro dell'arte di Mercatura* (Venice: Arsenale, 1990).
5. Francesco Balducci Pegolotti and Allan Evans, *La pratica della mercatura* (Cambridge, MA: Mediaeval Academy of America, 1936); Gian Francesco Pagnini, *Della Decima, e di varie altre gravezze imposte dal comune di Firenze: Della moneta e della mercatura de' Fiorentini fino al secolo Xvi T. 4, La pratica della mercatura* (Firenze 1766; Bologna: Fornie, 1967); *Saminiato* de Ricci and Antonia Borlandi, *Il manuale di mercatura* (Genoa: Di Stefano, 1963).
6. Giacomo Todeschini, *Un trattato di economia politica francescana: il "De emptionibus et venditionibus, de usuris, de restitutionibus" di Pietro di Giovanni Olivi* (Rome: Istituto storico italiano per il Medioevo, 1980); Giacomo Todeschini, "'Quantum valet?' Alle origini di un'economia della povertà," *Bullettino dell'Istituto storico staliano per il Medioevo* 98 (1992); Giacomo Todeschini, *Il prezzo della salvezza. Lessici medievali del pensiero economico* (Rome: La Nuova Italia Scientifica, 1994); Giacomo Todeschini, *I mercanti e il tempio. La società cristiana e il circolo virtuoso della ricchezza fra Medioevo ed età moderna* (Bologna: Il Mulino, 2002); Giacomo Todeschini, *Ricchezza francescana. Dalla povertà volontaria alla società di mercato* (Bologna: Il Mulino, 2004); Odd Langholm, "Economics in the Medieval Schools: Wealth, Exchange, Value, Money, and Usury According to the Paris Theological Tradition, 1200–1350," *Studien und Texte zur Geistesgeschichte des Mittelalters*, Bd. 29 (Leiden and New York: E. J. Brill, 1992); Joel Kaye, *Economy and Nature in the Fourteenth Century: Money, Market Exchange, and the Emergence of Scientific Thought* (Cambridge and New York: Cambridge University Press, 1998); Giovanni Ceccarelli, "Risky Business: Theological and Canonical Thought on Insurance from the Thirteenth to the Seventeenth Century," *Journal of Medieval and Early Modern Studies* 31, no. 3 (2001); Giovanni Ceccarelli, "Il gioco e il peccato. Economia e rischio nel tardo Medioevo," *Collana di storia dell'economia e del credito* (Bologna: Il Mulino, 2003); Avner Greif, *Institutions and the Path to the Modern Economy: Lessons from Medieval Trade, Political Economy of Institutions, and Decisions* (Cambridge and New York: Cambridge University Press, 2006).
7. A. Resch, *Agrapha: Aussercanonische Schriftfragmente, Texte und Untersuchungen zur Geschichte der Altchristlichen Literatur*, Band 30, Heft 3/4 (Neue Folge, 15. Bd., Hft. 3/4) (Leipzig: J. C. Hinrichs, 1906); Martin Florian Herz, *Sacrum Commercium. Eine Begriffsgeschichtliche Studie zur Theologie der Römischen Liturgiesprache, Münchener Theologische Studien* 2, *Systematische Abt, Bd.* 15 (Munich: K. Zink, 1958); Todeschini, "'Quantum valet?'"
8. R. Bogaert, "Changeurs et banquiers chez les Pères de l'Eglise," *Ancient Society* 4 (1973).

9. Ambrose, *Elia e il Digiuno; Naboth; Tobia* (Milan: Biblioteca Ambrosiana, 1985); Diego Quaglioni, Giacomo Todeschini, and Gian Maria Varanini, "Credito e usura fra teologia, diritto e amministrazione. Linguaggi a confronto, Sec. Xii-Xvi," *Collection de l'Ecole française de Rome* 346 (Rome: Ecole française de Rome, 2005).
10. Kaye, *Economy and Nature;* Todeschini, *I mercanti e il tempio.*
11. Robert B. Ekelund, *Sacred Trust: The Medieval Church as an Economic Firm* (New York: Oxford University Press, 1996); Convegno internazionale, *Gli spazi economici della chiesa nell'Occidente mediterraneo (secoli Xii-metà Xiv), sedicesimo convegno internazionale di studi*: Pistoia, 16–19 Maggio 1997 (Pistoia: Centro italiano di studi di storia e d'arte, 1999).
12. Raymond Adrien De Roover, *Business, Banking, and Economic Thought in Late Medieval and Early Modern Europe* (Chicago: University of Chicago Press, 1974); Langholm, *Economics in the Medieval Schools*; Todeschini, *Il prezzo della salvezza*; Todeschini, *I mercanti e il tempio*; François Menant and Odile Redon, "Notaires et crédit dans l'Occident méditerranéen medieval" (Colloques organisés à Nice et Bordighera en octobre 1996 et à Lyon en décembre 1997), *Collection de l'Ecole française de Rome* 343 (Rome: Ecole française de Rome, 2004).
13. P. Grossi, *Il dominio e le cose. Percezioni medievali e moderne dei diritti reali*, *Per la storia del pensiero giuridico moderno 41* (Milan: Giuffré, 1992); Umberto Santarelli, *La categoria dei contratti irregolari. Lezioni di storia del diritto* (Turin: G. Giappichelli, 1984).
14. Fabiano Veraja, *Le origini della controversia teologica sul contratto di censo nel Xiii secolo*, *Storia ed economia*, no. 7 (Rome: Edizioni di storia e letteratura, 1960); J. Hernando, "Quaestio disputata de licitudine contractus emptionis et venditionis censualis cum conditione revenditionis. Un tratado sobra la licitud del contrato de compra-venta de rentas personales y redimibles. Bernat de Puigcercòs, Op (Siglo Xiv),"*Acta Mediaevalia* 10 (1989); Lawrin D. Armstrong, *Usury and Public Debt in Early Renaissance Florence: Lorenzo Ridolfi on the Monte Comune* (Toronto: Pontifical Institute of Mediaeval Studies, 2003).
15. Annabel S. Brett, *Liberty, Right, and Nature: Individual Rights in Later Scholastic Thought* (Cambridge and New York: Cambridge University Press, 1997); Todeschini, *Ricchezza Francescana.*
16. S. Piron, "Marchands et confesseurs. Le traité des contrats d'Olivi dans son contexte (Narbonne, fin Xiiie-début Xive siècle)," in *L'argent au Moyen Age. Xxviiie congrès de la SHMESP* (Clermont-Ferrand, 1997) (Paris: Publications de la Sorbonne, 1998); *Nolens Intestatus Decedere. Il Testamento come fonte della storia religiosa e sociale.* Atti dell'incontro di studio, Perugia, 3 maggio 1983, Archivi dell'Umbria, 7 (Perugia: Regione dell'Umbria, 1985).
17. M. Sanchez Martinez, "El Fisc de les usures en la corona de Aragón a principios del siglo Xv," in *Credito e usura fra teologia, diritto e amministrazione. Linguaggi a confronto, sec. Xii-Xvi*, ed. Diego Quaglioni,

Giacomo Todeschini, and Gian Maria Varanini, *Collection de l'Ecole française de Rome* (Rome: Ecole française de Rome, 2005).

18. Centro italiano di studi di storia e d'arte (Pistoia Italy). Convegno internazionale.
19. Langholm, *Economics in the Medieval Schools.*
20. Todeschini, *Ricchezza Francescana.*
21. Raymond Adrien De Roover, "Monopoly Theory Prior to Adam Smith: A Revision," *Quarterly Journal of Economics* 65 (1951); Raymond Adrien De Roover, "La Doctrine scolastique en matière de monopole et son application à la politique économique des communes italiennes," in *Studi in onore di A. Fanfani* (Milan: Giuffré, 1962); De Roover, *Business, Banking, and Economic Thought.*
22. Kaye, *Economy and Nature in the Fourteenth Century*; Ceccarelli, "Risky Business."
23. David Burr, *The Spiritual Franciscans: From Protest to Persecution in the Century after Saint Francis* (University Park: Pennsylvania State University Press, 2001).
24. This word did not mean every trading man; it referred rather to the merchant bankers or the big entrepreneurs.
25. Todeschini, *Un trattato di economia politica francescana*; Todeschini, *I mercanti e il tempio.*
26. Armando Sapori, *I libri di commercio dei Peruzzi* (Milan: Fratelli Treves, 1934); Armando Sapori, *Studi di storia economica; Secoli Xiii, Xiv, Xv*, Biblioteca Storica Sansoni, Nuova Serie 5, no. 43 (Florence: Sansoni, 1955); Dino Compagni and Gino Luzzatto, *Cronica* (Turin: G. Einaudi, 1968); Giovanni Villani et al., *Cronica: con le continuazioni di Matteo e Filippo* (Turin: G. Einaudi, 1979).
27. Morelli, "Ricordi"; Ricci and Borlandi, *Il manuale di mercatura*; G. Corti, "Consigli sulla mercatura di un anonimo trecentista," *Archivio Storico Italiano* 110 (1952); Cotrugli, *Il libro dell'arte di mercatura.*
28. Henri Pirenne and Jacques Pirenne, *Histoire de l'Europe des Invasions au Xvie siècle* (Paris: F. Alcan, 1936).
29. Armando Sapori, *Le marchand italien au Moyen Age; Conférences et bibliographie* (Paris: A. Colin, 1952); Sapori, *Studi di storia economica.*
30. Cesare Ciano, "La pratica di mercatura datiniana (Secolo XIV)," *Biblioteca della Rivista Economia e Storia* 9 (Milan: Giuffrè, 1964).
31. Franz Josef Arlinghaus, "Io, Noi Und Noi Insieme. Transpersonale Konzepte in den Verträgen einer Italienischen Handelsgesellschaft des 14. Jahrhunderts," in *Bene Vivere in Communitate: Beiträge zum italienischen und deutschen Mittelalter: Hagen Keller zum 60. Geburtstag Überreicht von seinen Schülerinnen und Schülern*, ed. Thomas Scharff Hagen Keller and Thomas Behrmann (Münster: Waxmann, 1997).
32. Henri de Lubac, *Corpus Mysticum. L'eucharistie et l'Eglise au Moyen Âge. Étude historique*, 2nd ed. (Paris: Aubier, 1949); André Vauchez, *La religion civique à l'époque médiévale et moderne. Chrétienté et Islam*: Actes du

colloque, *Collection de l'Ecole française de Rome* (Rome: Ecole française de Rome, 1995); Nicholas Terpstra, *Lay Confraternities and Civic Religion in Renaissance Bologna*, *Cambridge Studies in Italian History and Culture* (Cambridge and New York: Cambridge University Press, 1995); Nicholas Terpstra, *The Politics of Ritual Kinship: Confraternities and Social Order in Early Modern Italy*, *Cambridge Studies in Italian History and Culture* (Cambridge and New York: Cambridge University, 1999); Jean-Louis Biget, Patrick Boucheron, and Jacques Chiffoleau, *Religion et société urbaine au Moyen Âge. Études offertes à Jean-Louis Biget par ses anciens Élèves*, *Publications de la Sorbonne* 60 (Paris: Publications de la Sorbonne, 2001).

33. A. Sapori, *I libri di commercio dei Peruzzi* (Milan: Fratelli Treves, 1934), 440: "E sono per tutti diciesette compagni. E i detti conpagni sono in concordia che quando voranno fare ragione de la detta conpagnia che si facia e a quelo tenpo e a' sudetti conpagni, i quali saranno ne la città e nel contado di Firenze piacerà, o a le due parti di loro che di que' cota' conpagni si ritrovasero ne la città o nel contado di Firenze, e ciò che nne faranno valia e tengha sì come per tutta la conpagnia fosse fatto; e di ciò che nostro Segniore Idio ci concederà di trovare guadagniato, netti di spese o danno che si ricievese o perdite o di ma' debiti o di salari di fattori e d'ogni altre spese che fatte fosero per la nostra conpagnia per quale che fose la cagione in qualunque parte fosse, quelo cotale guadagnio così netto si debia partire in tra' sopradetti conpagni e dame a catuno sua parte secondo la parte che ciascuno de' conpagni à ne la detta conpagnia; e se si trovase perduto, di che Dio guardi, ciascuno de' conpagni ne debia portare sua parte secondo la detta parte ch'à in questa compagnia. I sopradetti compagni riconoscono d'essere partefici e d'essere tenuti di tutto quelo che la detta compagnia dè ricievere e dè dare altrui in Firenze e fuori di Firenze in qualunque parte sia. I sopradetti compagni sono in concordia che a quale de' compagni di questa compagnia mancase danari per adenpiere quelo che dè dare per lo fornimento de la parte ch'à meso nel corpo di questa conpagnia che ne doni a la compagnia per buono e lecito guadagnio a ragione di sette per cientinaio l'anno benedetti da Dio. E ancora sono in concordia che quale de' conpagni di questa conpagnia tengono de' loro danari in questa conpagnia di fuori dal corpo de la conpagnia che la conpagnia ne doni a que' chotali a ragione di sette per cientinaio l'anno per buono e lecito guadagnio benedetti da Dio."

34. André Vauchez, *I laici nel Medioevo* (Milan: Il Saggiatore, 1985); Matthew S. Kempshall, *The Common Good in Late Medieval Political Thought* (Oxford and New York: Clarendon Press; Oxford University Press, 1999); Peter von Moos, "'Public' et 'Privé' à la fin du Moyen Âge. Le 'Bien commun' et la 'loi de la conscience'," *Studi Medievali* 41, no. 2 (2000).

35. Sapori, *Studi di storia economica.*

36. Peter Landau, *Die Entstehung des kanonischen Infamienbegriffs von Gratian zur Glossa Ordinaria* (Cologne-Graz: Böhlau, 1966); Francesco Migliorino, *Fama e infamia. Problemi della società medievale nel pensiero giuridico dei secoli XII e XIII* (Catania: Giannotta, 1985); "La renommée," monographic issue of *Médiévales* 24 (1993) (Saint-Denis, France: Presses et Publications de l'Universite? de Paris VIII); Thelma Fenster and Daniel Lord Smail, *Fama: The Politics of Talk and Reputation in Medieval Europe* (Ithaca, NY: Cornell University Press, 2003).
37. Augustine, *Sermo* 355, De moribus clericorum: "Duae res sunt conscientia et fama. Conscientia tibi, fama proximo tuo. Qui confidens conscientiae suae neglegit famam suam, crudelis est: maxime in loco isto positus, de quo loco dicit Apostolus scribens ad discipulum suum: Circa omnes te ipsum bonorum operum praebens exemplum (Tit 2, 7)"; see the juridical and semantical adaptation of these concepts in Emil Friedberg and Aemilius Ludwig Richter, "Decretum Magistri Gratiani," C. XII, q. I, c. 10, *Corpus Iuris Canonici I* (ex officina Bernhardi Tauchnitz, 1879), cc. 679–80; Giacomo Todeschini, *Visibilmente crudeli. Malviventi, persone sospette e gente qualunque dal Medioevo all'età moderna* (Bologna: Il Mulino, 2007).
38. Vauchez, *I laici nel Medioevo*; Biget, Boucheron, and Chiffoleau, *Religion et société urbaine au Moyen Age.*
39. Bruno Dini, *Una pratica di mercatura in formazione, 1394–1395* (Florence: Felice Le Monnier, 1980), 190: "Chi vende draperia in Valenza, e abi buone robe e con vaghi lavori, può ben regere la roba; ma se non è chosa avantagiosa, si vuole sapere alarghare la mano per riuscirne, chè non stenti poi la roba altrui adosso; ma sopra tuto ciedi in luogho sichuro e a buoni pagatori."
40. Albertano da Brescia, *Hic est Sermo, quem Albertanus causidicus de Sancta Agatha composuit et edidit inter causidicos brixienses, apud Fratres Minores in congregatione solita, sub anno Domini M. CC. L, in media Quadragesima*, in Sharon Lynn Hiltz, *Albertano da Brescia, De amore et dilectione dei et proximi et aliarum rerum et de forma vite: an edition* (PhD thesis, University of Pennsylvania, 1980), http://www.gmu.edu/departments/fld/CLASSICS/albertanus.html.
41. Corti, "Consigli sulla mercatura di un anonimo trecentista."
42. Pegolotti and Evans, *La pratica della mercatura*, 20.
43. Todeschini, *Un trattato di economia politica francescana*; Todeschini, *I mercanti e il tempio*; Piron, "Marchands et confesseurs"; S. Piron, "Perfection évangélique et moralité civile. Pierre de Jean Olivi et l'éthique économique franciscaine," in *Ideologia del credito fra Tre e Quattrocento: dall'astesano ad Angelo da Chivasso.* Atti del convegno internazionale, Archivio storico, Palazzo Mazzola, Asti, 9–10 giugno 2000, Barbara Molina and Giulia Scarcia, eds., *Collana del Centro studi sui Lombardi e sul credito nel Medioevo* (Asti: Centro studi sui Lombardi e sul credito nel Medioevo, 2001).

44. Morelli, "Ricordi."
45. Werner Sombart, *Der Bourgeois; zur Geistesgeschichte des Modernen Wirtschaftsmenschen* (Munich: Duncker & Humblot, 1913).
46. J. Bossy, "Blood and Baptism: Kinship, Community, and Christianity in Western Europe from the Fourteenth to the Seventeenth Centuries," in *Sanctity and Secularity: The Church and the World*, ed. D. Baker (Oxford: published for the Ecclesiastical History Society by B. Blackwell, 1973); J. Bossy, "The Mass as Social Institution 1200–1700," *Past and Present* 100 (1983); Roberto Rusconi, *L'ordine dei peccati. La confessione tra Medioevo ed età moderna* (Bologna: Il Mulino, 2002).
47. Giovanni di Pagolo Morelli, "Ricordi." In: *Mercanti e scrittori. Ricordi nella Firenze tra Medioevo e Rinascimento*, III: "Fugli favorevole la fortuna e la sua sollecitudine e esercizio, ché mai non perdé punto di tempo, sempre attento in acquistare l'amore del suo creatore Idio pelle sue limosine e buone operazioni, appresso in acquistare amicizia di buoni uomini e da bene e potenti. Riteneasi con loro, mostrando loro grande amore in servigli di quello avesse potuto, in consigliarsi con loro di suoi fatti, dove e' dimostrava fede e speranza in loro; onoralli in dare loro mangiare e in tutte altre cose; battezzare loro figliuoli, e simile cose e maggiori, come accaggiono tutto giorno nell'usare e praticare con quelle persone a chi altri vuole bene. E con questi e con altri savi e antiveduti modi e' seppe sì fare e sì provvedutamente temporeggiare, che al tempo del maggiore bisogno, come i' penso raccontare, egli ebbe degli amici, e non parenti, che l'atarono e sostennello per modo che non gli fu fatto torto, mediato principalemente l'aiuto e volere di Dio, sanza il quale non si può venire a perfezione d'alcuna cosa. E se noi volessimo essere fedeli cristiani e amici di Dio, noi vedremmo ogni giorno la sua potenzia e somma giustizia; ma noi pe' nostri peccati siamo accecati e vogliamo piuttosto giudicare e credere che le cose o prospere o dannose ci avvenghino per avventura o per indotto di più o di meno senno, che per volontà di Dio; e questo non è vero, ché tutto procede da Lui, ma secondo i nostri meriti."
48. The high economic value of the sollicitudo mentalis is described at the end of the thirteenth century by the Franciscan Olivi with these words: "ad altiora officia debite exequenda exigitur maior pericia et industria et amplior sollicitudo mentalis, et eciam quia multo et diuturno studio ac experiencia et labore, multisque periculis et expensis communiter adquiritur pericia et industria talis, et eciam quia rari et pauci sunt ad hoc ydonei, et ideo in maiori precio reputantur." See Todeschini, *Un trattato di economia politica francescana*, 57.
49. John Duns Scotus and Allan Bernard Wolter, *Duns Scotus' Political and Economic Philosophy* (Santa Barbara: Old Mission Santa Barbara, 1989); Todeschini, *I mercanti e il tempio.*
50. Françoise Héritier-Augé, and Elisabeth Copet-Rougier, eds., *La Parenté spirituelle. Textes rassemblés et présentés, ordres sociaux* (Paris: Ed. des archives contemporaines, 1995); Terpstra, *Politics of Ritual Kinship.*

51. Paolo Evangelisti, "Credere nel mercato, credere nella res publica. La comunità catalano-aragonese nelle proposte e nell'azione politica di un esponente del francescanesimo mediterraneo: Francesc Eiximenis," *Anuario de Estudios Medievales* 33, no. 1 (2003); Paolo Evangelisti, *I Francescani e la costruzione di uno stato. Linguaggi politici, valori identitari, progetti di governo in area catalano-aragonese* (Padua: EFR-Editrici francescane, 2006).
52. *BernardiniSenensisOperaOmniaStudioetCuraPatrumCollegiiS.Bonaventurae*, 9 vols. *(Ad Claras Aquas/ Firenze Quaracchi, 1950–1965)*, vol. 4, 1956; Cotrugli, *Il Libro dell'arte di mercatura*; B. Cotrugli, *De navigatione*, in Pietro Falchetta, ed., Benedetto Cotrugli, *De navigatione*, temporary transcription at http://geoweb.venezia.sbn.it/geoweb/HSL/Cotrugli.html, or available by email from falchetta@marciana.venezia.sbn.it.
53. Leon Battista Alberti, Ruggiero Romano, and Alberto Tenenti, *I libri della famiglia*. A cura di Ruggiero Romano e Alberto Tenenti (Turin: G. Einaudi, 1969).
54. Marina Gazzini, *Dare et habere. Il mondo di un mercante milanese del Quattrocento* (Florence: Firenze University Press, 2002).
55. André Vauchez, *I laici nel Medioevo* (Milan: Il Saggiatore, 1989).
56. Todeschini, *Ricchezza Francescana*.
57. *Bernardini Senensis Opera Omnia Studio et Cura Patrum Collegii S. Bonaventurae*, vol. 4, *Sermo XXXIII. De mercationibus et vitiis mercatorum*, 158–59.
58. Pegolotti and Evans, *La pratica della mercatura*.
59. Cotrugli, *De navigatione*, in Falchetta, ed., Benedetto Cotrugli, *De navigatione*.
60. Ibid., chap. V, fol. 30r.
61. Paolo Evangelisti, *Fidenzio da Padova e la letteratura crociato-missionaria minoritica. Strategie e modelli francescani per il dominio, Xiii-Xv sec.* (Bologna: Il Mulino, 1998).
62. Langholm, *Economics in the Medieval Schools*; Todeschini, *I mercanti e il tempio*; Armstrong, *Usury and Public Debt in Early Renaissance Florence*.
63. Cotrugli, *Il libro dell'arte di mercatura*, 144–45: "Però che a volere fare gran proficto per la conseghuition del fine al quale è ordinata questa arte mercantile, è necessario, posposta ogni altra cura, vacare con grande diligentia a tucte quelle cose le quali possono fare utile et giovare a tale perfectione, onde si conviene alle volte durare gran fatica di giorno et di nocte, camminare personalmente a pie et a cavallo, per mare, per terra, et così affaticarsi nel vendere et nel comperare, et usare in tucte simili facciende quanta diligentia è possibile, posponendo ogni altra cura non solamente di cose superflue, ma etiamdio di quelle che sono necessarie alla conservatione della humana vita. Et però n'occorre alcuna volta il differire il mangiare et bere et dormire, anzi è necessario di tollerare fame, sete et vigilie et simili altre cose che sono noiose et contrarie alla quiete del

corpo; il quale se non fussi acto come dextro instrumento, non potrebbe sopportare, et sopportandolo ne riceverebbe incommodità, alla quale di necessità sequirebbe infirmità et di poi morte. Onde di due inconvenienti ne sequirebbe l'uno, o veramente che non pigliando simili exercitii come si conviene non sarebbe il proposito et cet., nè verrebbe al suo desiderato fine, o che facciendolo non potrebbe per la disaptitudine del corpo perseverare et perseverando chascherebbe nella infirmità et morte. Et perché l'uno et l'altro di questi due inconvenienti extremi sono da schifare, diciamo et confirmiamo ch'egli è sommamente utile et ancora necessario l'avere il corpo in buona dispositione, acto a simile essercitio, il quale a questa opera della consequition del fine concorrerà come instrumento adacto non altrimenti che si facci il martello che concorre come dextro instrumento del fabbro quando fabrica l'acuto."

Part II

Self-Images

Chapter 2

Images and Self-Images of Sephardic Merchants in Early Modern Europe and the Mediterranean

Francesca Trivellato, Yale University

The economic role of Jews in Christian Europe changed profoundly from the Middle Ages to the early modern period. In the late sixteenth and early seventeenth centuries, Sephardic Jews—the descendents of those who had been expelled from the territories of the crown of Castile and Aragon in 1492, or of those who, after seeking refuge in Portugal, were forced to convert to Catholicism in 1497—formed increasingly stable communities in Venice, Livorno, Hamburg, Amsterdam, and London (after 1656). They were eventually tolerated in Bordeaux and other towns in southwestern France, and slowly set foot in the Dutch and English Caribbean. In the late seventeenth century, they also established small enclaves in Levantine and North African ports. Unlike medieval Jewry or other early modern segments of Jewish society in Europe, Sephardic merchants did not engage in petty credit and retail sale. Instead, many among them were largely involved—each with varying degrees of success—in long-distance trade, international finance, and the processing and manufacturing of colonial goods (especially sugar, tobacco, and diamonds). For most Sephardim, credit operations were closely linked to commerce, but for a few, such as Gabriel de Silva (ca. 1683–1763) in Bordeaux, private banking was their sole occupation.[1] Never a majoritarian force in global trade (there were, after all, no more than fifteen thousand Iberian Jews in Europe—outside Spain and Portugal—and the New World at any one time), Sephardic merchants nonetheless formed a far-reaching trading diaspora and were especially influential in certain commercial branches, including in the Dutch Atlantic and in the exchanges between Europe and the Ottoman Empire. In their daily activities, they traded with and on behalf of merchants of other denominations on a regular basis.

Did Sephardic merchants in Christian lands perceive themselves to be part of a universal "commercial society," as Adam Smith called it?[2] We search in vain for a straightforward answer in the few "ego-documents" (diaries, autobiographies, memoirs, travel accounts, personal correspondence, and the like) kept by Sephardic merchants. It is also doubtful whether they ever formulated the question in such terms.[3] And yet it seems crucial to raise the question because it goes to the heart of a cornerstone idea of the European Enlightenment, namely, that as commerce grew in size and influence over European politics and society, the solvency and trustworthiness of individual merchants became more important than their religious faith, ethnic background, or national affiliation, and that ultimately, individuals' quest for profit would overcome prejudice.[4]

If it is never possible to dissociate the images that an individual or a group have of themselves from prevalent outsiders' discourses about them, the self-perception and self-representation of Sephardic merchants also ought to be examined in relation to old and new Christian views of the relationship between Jews and money. Here, I understand the concept on which we have been invited to reflect in this volume—"self-perception"—not as synonymous with identity (a charged and slippery word), but as a lens through which to explore the power and the limits of commerce to create ever more tolerant early modern European societies.

In what follows, I do not measure if and when their religious affiliation affected the rates at which *individual* Sephardic merchants settled purchases, sales, and bills of exchange in seventeenth- and eighteenth-century Europe (I should say that as a rule, it did not). Nor do I ask how individual Sephardim integrated or failed to integrate their religious sentiments and their professional lives. Rather, I am concerned with the *collective* images and self-images of Sephardim in relation to the marketplace and, more specifically, with whether and how their economic functions, legal status, and social profile influenced their own self-perception as well as Christian representations of them in early modern Europe and the Mediterranean.

A wide range of approaches across the humanities and social sciences—microhistory, the new historicism, interactionist sociology, to name just a few—have acquainted us with notions of agency and self-fashioning. We are thus accustomed to asking about how actors escaped and manipulated the ascriptive categories to which early modern European legal systems confined them. These basic assumptions are more easily applicable to the study of individual biographies, but they can also shape the way in which we look at how collective self-perceptions and representations responded to both internal group pressures and external projections. Naturally, collective self-representations were not faithful mirrors of individual experiences. Rather, they allow us to analyze how a stigmatized group fashioned itself in relation to the opportunities and the constraints that emerged at a time when market relations eroded, but did not dismantle, ancient social, legal, and cultural barriers.

The specific ways in which Sephardic merchants were included in and excluded from European commercial society, furthermore, complicate recent approaches to the study of reputation in the organization of early modern capitalism. Economists such as Avner Greif define reputation in strictly economic terms (information about the past conduct of an individual actor on the market).[5] Historians of early modern England, in contrast, insist on the nexus between social and financial credit.[6] This varied and fascinating literature begs the question of whether collective stereotypes had an impact on the life of merchant communities. This question is central to our concern if we acknowledge, with Derek Penslar, that in early modern Europe the association between Jews and money oscillated between two opposite extremes (that occasionally overlapped): Christians saw Jews either as plutocrats and manipulative conspirators, or as parasitical paupers.[7]

How did Sephardim, burdened with such stereotypes, mingle and conduct trade with Christians? How did they preserve a reputation necessary for successful business relations? Did the new position of Sephardim in early modern Europe impact Gentile images of Jews in the marketplace? And did the self-perception of Sephardic merchants develop autonomously from stereotypes about them? In approaching these questions, I consider a diverse array of texts: business records, the so-called *ars mercatoria* (dictionaries, how-to books for merchants, treatises about commercial law and political economy, travel accounts, histories of commerce, and pamphlets on economic matters), Jewish apologetics and internal community records, diplomatic correspondence, and classics of the European history of ideas.[8] For the sake of brevity, I overlook important local variations from one Sephardic community to the other.

IMAGES AND PRACTICES

In early modern Europe, business letters were more than private statements. Although not sealed by a notary, they constituted proof of bilateral agreements or an agent's obligation in court. They were also the principal channel of communication among merchants. Thus, the few surviving collections of business letters written by Sephardic merchants (the most important ones date to the first three-quarters of the eighteenth century) open a window onto the presence and conduct of this group in European commercial society. From their business letters we know that Sephardic merchants regularly did business with non-Jews, both near and far, ranging from Huguenot bankers in Paris to Hindu traders in Portuguese India.[9]

In order to converse and maintain credible commitments with such a multifarious pool of correspondents, Sephardic merchants not only wrote their letters in several European languages, but also followed the customary etiquette of European business correspondence. This etiquette became increasingly standardized and gallant during the early modern period. It also maintained the habit, inherited from classical antiquity, of expressing commercial obligations in the form of affection, love, friendship, favor, and reciprocity. During the commercial revolution of the Middle Ages, as Giacomo Todeschini has shown, this lexicon was used to distinguish between legitimate and illegitimate profit, and thus to define membership in the Christian commercial society. A reputable merchant ought to be a good Christian and a good "citizen." Jewish moneylenders, as "infidels," were excluded (legally, socially, and rhetorically) from this virtuous community.[10]

In the course of the sixteenth century, the legitimacy of this exclusion became increasingly less self-evident. The Reformation broke the social and symbolic unity of the Christian commonwealth; the expansion of European commerce intensified cross-cultural exchanges; and Sephardic Jews were admitted to key European port-cities on the basis of new legal and social terms. It was now possible to refer to "infidels" as trustworthy merchants, and the language of business correspondence became more secular. By the early eighteenth century, we commonly find invocations of god in rhetorical formulas (for example, in greetings and salutations) rather than as expressions of spiritual conviction in business letters exchanged between merchants who worshipped different gods. Even when it contained Hebrew words or references to Jewish religious festivities, the correspondence of Sephardic merchants conformed to the growing number of printed models of letterwriting that circulated in Europe at the time.[11]

What merchants strove for was to forge a "good correspondency" (*boa correspondencia* in Portuguese or *buona corrispondenza* in Italian) with their agents.[12] A "good correspondency" indicated both a reliable letter-exchange and a dependable business relation. A Sephardic partnership in Livorno that operated between 1704 and 1746 used the expression when writing to partners in Aleppo, to other Sephardim in London and Amsterdam, to a French firm in Cyprus, and to their long-term Hindu agents in Goa.[13]

If rhetoric is a form of self-presentation, the use of this universalizing etiquette by Sephardic merchants is proof of their belonging to a European commercial society. Other sources point in the same direction. David de Castro Tartas, an Amsterdam Sephardic entrepreneur, began to produce a Spanish-language newspaper (*Gazeta de Amsterdam*) for distribution among Sephardim and New Christians in 1672, but soon had to abandon his enterprise because his gazette merely condensed information already available to its readers through local newspapers.[14] In eighteenth-century northern Europe, moreover, Sephardic scholars and practitioners authored several works with economic subjects that accorded with prevailing contemporary standards. In Hamburg, Abraham Meldola (1754–1826), the scion of an illustrious Sephardic family from Livorno, translated from German into Spanish and Portuguese one of the many manuals of business letterwriting in 1782.[15] In 1706, Gabriel de Souza Brito, an Amsterdam Sephardi, had published a book of practical and financial mathematics that copied large portions of the first Spanish treatise on double-entry bookkeeping published by a Christian author in 1590.[16]

Confusión de confusiones, an inventive play by José Penso de la Vega (ca. 1650–92), son of a New Christian exile from Cordova who settled in Amsterdam, is often cited as the first description of the inner workings of a stock exchange. Penso based his literary work on firsthand experience, and he even disclosed the ways in which Sephardic speculators traded in a specific type of shares (called *ducatones*). Written in the language and style of Spanish Baroque theater, however, the play was intended to entertain more than to instruct, and aimed least of all to represent an exclusively Jewish economic activity. Repeating a conventional cliché, Penso referred to financial speculations as the most noble and the most infamous activity that the world knows ("el mas noble y el mas infame que conosce el Mundo.")[17] Yosef Kaplan reminds us that for Penso de la Vega, the stock exchange, like other aspects of economic life, was considered to be outside the bounds of Jewish life.[18] *Confusión de confusiones* was also very much a work of its time. Confusion was at its height in the year when the play appeared. For John Wills Jr., if the play had a specific purpose, it was to incite readers to invest in the East and West India Companies and thus correct the course of the Dutch stock market in the year of its worst crash to date.[19]

Sephardic merchants, in sum, not only worked side by side and often together with Christian merchants, but also embraced the codes and the logic of dominant discourses surrounding commerce and finance in seventeenth- and eighteenth-century Europe. It would, however, be hasty to conclude that they invariably perceived themselves and were conceived as equal members of European commercial society. Hostile views of Jews persisted irrespective of the increased cooperation between Sephardic and Christian merchants. These views colored Gentile legal texts and philosophical treatises about trade, as well as day-to-day business records.

None other than David Hume, the Scottish skeptic and champion of the virtues of commerce and moderation, referred to Jews as a people "noted for fraud" in the very same essay in which he sought to debunk the existence of fixed "national characters."[20] We do not know whether Hume labored over this turn of phrase or used it casually (although we know that it appears in an essay in which he added and revised repeatedly an infamous racist footnote).[21] Whether offhand or calculated, Hume's stigmatization of Jews as fraudulent echoes a medieval discourse about Jews, and Jewish merchants in particular. Perceptions of Jews as untrustworthy were not limited to philosophical exposés. They also set the tone of legislation and peppered private correspondence.[22] While Jews were forbidden from residing in Marseille, the French crown extended diplomatic protection to Sephardic merchants in French outposts in the Ottoman Empire. In spite of the cooperation that developed among Sephardim and the French along the southeastern Mediterranean shores, a 1781 French edict regulating the office of consul in the Levant listed "the bad faith of Greeks and Jews" among the obstacles encountered by French merchants in their operations.[23]

In England, debates about the rightfulness of chartered companies' monopolies were often tinted by unwarranted fears of domination by Jewish overrepresentation, irrespective of the limited influence that Jews played in English colonial trade overall. After Sir Josiah Child became chairman of the board of directors of the East India Company in 1681, he opened up some branches of the Asian trade (and particularly the diamond trade) to Jews. In 1693, news of illegal exports of silver (an essential item in Asian trade) spurred an anti-Jewish campaign that culminated in the temporary suspension of the rights of private merchants to participate in the diamond trade with India.[24] Sephardim in England were also repeatedly accused of obstructing the release of English captives in North Africa.[25] In 1746–47, Benjamin Mendes da Costa, one of the leading Sephardic merchants and financiers in London, was tried for having insured a French ship captured at sea by the British Navy. Knowingly or not, Costa had fallen victim to a fraudulent scheme through which French merchants in Bordeaux obtained large insurance payments from London. He was now denounced for damaging British national interests.[26]

JEWS IN THE *ARS MERCATORIA*

A lot has been written about the representations of Jews in Christian political theory, literature, theater, sermons, and other genres. But how were Jews, and Sephardim in particular (if a distinction can be detected), imagined in the *ars mercatoria*? Of course, this body of literature was internally varied and not hermetically sealed from other genres. Some authors and texts, however, proved more influential than others.[27] Jacques Savary's *Le parfait négociant* was undoubtedly the best-known and most widely circulated title of the early modern European *ars mercatoria*. Written by a Frenchman who worked for Finance Minister Colbert, it was first published in 1675, and by 1800, it enjoyed twenty-six French editions. It was translated into German as early as 1676 and into Dutch in 1683. In a chapter devoted to the origin and usefulness of bills of exchange, Savary credited the Jews expelled from France in subsequent waves between the seventh and early fourteenth centuries with this invention.[28]

Merchants transferred funds from one location to the other, converted currencies, and speculated on exchange rates using bills of exchange, which were the linchpin of early modern capitalism. But in the Middle Ages, their use was also tainted by the shadow of accusation of usury. Savary's claim that Jews invented bills of exchange was thus faint praise at the very least. Moreover, although the origins of bills of exchange long remained obscured to modern scholars (we now know that merchants from northern and central Italy, not Jews, first used these financial instruments in the fourteenth century),[29] Savary's narrative was factually incoherent.

Savary distilled the story from Estienne Cleirac's *Les us et coustumes de la mer* (first printed in Bordeaux in 1647). Today largely forgotten, this work was a landmark of commercial law, containing both a compilation of European codes of commerce and an original dissertation on maritime insurance. At the opening of the section on maritime insurance, Cleirac explained that the Jews expelled from France in the Middle Ages invented both insurance policies and bills of exchange in order to salvage their goods when fleeing to Italy (Savary dropped the part about insurance policies, which others later picked up). Having found the invention highly useful, the "Ghibellines" exiled from Italy transferred it to Amsterdam.[30] To confer authoritativeness on this extravagant tale, Cleirac attributed it (without foundation) to the Florentine chronicler Giovanni Villani, who died of plague in 1348. Savary glossed over all anachronisms—in the fourteenth century, there indeed were numerous Italian merchants and bankers operating in Flanders, but Amsterdam (the world's largest entrepôt in Cleirac's and Savary's times) was barely a village.[31] Now endorsed by Savary, the fabulous conjecture about the Jewish origin of bills of exchange became a staple of the eighteenth-century literature on commerce and continued to be cited in more technical publications about maritime insurance throughout the nineteenth century.[32]

A century after its initial formulation, Montesquieu's *Spirit of Laws* (1748) gave full legitimacy to the legend.[33] The massive *Dictionnaire de commerce* compiled by Savary's two sons (one of whom was a Catholic priest) helped disseminate it among encyclopedic publications beyond the French borders.[34] In the second half of the eighteenth century, some began to doubt the validity of this story, but rehearsed it nonetheless. This was the case of Thomas Mortimer's *Dictionary* and Diderot's and D'Alembert's *Encyclopedie*.[35]

What accounts for the wide endorsement of Cleirac's and Savary's tale and its even wider dissemination? More important, why did the fable of a Jewish invention of bills of exchange emerge in the seventeenth century, when Sephardim were increasingly accepted in Europe, rather than in the Middle Ages? And what does this story tell us about early modern perceptions of Sephardic merchants? It does not seem coincidental that the legend first surfaced in mid-seventeenth-century

France. In a brief autobiographical reference in the "Preface" to *Le parfait négociant*, Savary observed that a noble pedigree ought not to impede a career in commerce. Arguably, as the legal and social barriers that had long kept the feudal aristocracy apart from mercantile groups in Europe came under attack, new symbolic barriers had to be raised against Jews, so that those among them who possessed the required means and manners would not stand on the same footing as Christian merchants. Anxieties about Sephardic participation in the local mercantile elite, moreover, were particularly intense in Bordeaux (Cleirac's hometown), where Iberian Jews were only admitted as New Christians, and thus potentially indistinguishable from French Christians, and in Marseille (Savary's adoptive town), from where Jews were expelled in 1682, but where they traded with the Levant trade in ways legal and illegal. When Montesquieu praised the usefulness of bills of exchange for the kind of commerce from which, in his view, political freedom also stemmed, he referred to their alleged inventors as "une nation . . . couverte d'infamie."[36] A few years later, Abby Coyer used the exact same expression in his *La noblesse commerçante*, which reaffirmed in even stronger terms Savary's condemnation of the legal and social impediments that barred French aristocrats from engaging in trade.[37]

The legend of a Jewish invention of bills of exchange appealed to readers for yet another reason: it blended together medieval stereotypes of Jews as usurers with contemporary (seventeenth-century) fears of their primacy in long-distance trade. In a variant of the legend, Werner Sombart attributed to sixteenth-century Sephardim the introduction in Venice of endorsable bills of exchange (the most sophisticated and influential version of this credit instrument). Consistent with his misguided identification of Sephardim with the founding fathers of modern capitalism, Sombart singled out Iberian Jews involved in international trade rather than medieval French Jews.[38] He, too, was wrong about the authors, although not about the date of this invention: bills of exchange first became negotiable in Northern Europe in the 1540s.[39]

Long before Sombart, the dominance of Jews in long-distance trade was a topos in the seventeenth- and eighteenth-century European *ars mercatoria*. The theme surfaced repeatedly with regard to the commerce between Europe and the Ottoman Empire. In revising *Le parfait négociant*, Savary introduced new accounts of Mediterranean trade, in which he claimed that Jews and Armenians controlled the majority of business in Livorno, and that French merchants were utterly dependent on them in their traffic with Izmir and other Ottoman ports—a dependence that he condemned because of the alleged "bad faith" of Jews and Armenians.[40] Savary knew the ins and outs of Marseille's commercial organization. His denunciation summarized what was both a reality (the weakness of French personnel in the Levant, and Izmir in particular, and Armenians' dominance in the export of Persian raw silk) and a fantasy (despite the scarcity of statistical data, we know that Jews and Armenians controlled some commercial niches but not all of European trade with the Ottoman Empire). English authors were no less biased. At the turn of the eighteenth century, Joseph Addison, the later coauthor of the acclaimed *Spectator*, maintained that "near Ten Thousand *Jews*" lived in Livorno (a threefold overestimation at least), and described them as "so great Traffickers, that our *English* Factors complain they have most of our Country Trade in their Hands."[41] Other commentators, later picked up by Sombart, focused more on the New World. Even Adam Smith reserved a word of exaggerated praise for "Portuguese Jews," whom he credited with having "introduced by their example some sort of order and industry among the transplanted felons [in the American colonies] . . . and taught them the culture of the sugar-cane."[42]

Benjamin Braude has unveiled the extent to which modern scholarship has relied uncritically on such narratives, especially with regard to the history of Mediterranean trade. What these narratives reveal is the persistence of Christian Judeophobic tropes and the depth of European ignorance about the Ottoman Empire (an ignorance that is also visible in the infrequent distinction made by European authors between Ottoman Jews, involved in local retail and brokerage or employed as translators, and European Sephardim, who conducted long-distance trade). According to Braude, however, some early modern Jewish apologists used stereotypical images of Jews as entrepreneurial wheeler-dealers (as opposed to peddlers) to advance the cause of toleration.[43] Rabbi Simone Luzzatto lived in the Venetian ghetto, inevitably knew most of its inhabitants in person, and was likely kept informed of population counting made by community leaders. He nonetheless inflated the size of the Jewish residents of Venice, offering a figure of six thousand against a reality of no more than half that number. On the basis of this figure, he then calculated the per capita contributions that Jews made to the impoverished coffers of the Republic in custom duties and other payments.[44] Similarly, Rabbi Menasseh ben Israel's 1655 *Humble Addresses* to Cromwell enumerated the economic reaches of Sephardim to support his plea for the readmission of Jews to England.[45]

In their self-presentation (which may or may not have corresponded to a more genuine self-perception), some Jewish leaders thus chose not to contest the exaggerated association of Sephardim with long-distance trade, but to use it to press ahead with their demands. Their arguments for toleration, it should be noted, presupposed that Jews would be recognized as Jews by Christian governments and societies. They neither entailed nor envisioned the erosion of communitarian boundaries as result of furthered economic exchanges, as predicted by Enlightenment theorists of commercial society.

SEPHARDIM, GENTILES, AND OTHER JEWS

In addition to his remarks on the Sephardim's economic prowess, In his *Humble Addresses* Menasseh ben Israel discussed four other topics that were meant to forestall negative reactions among the petition's recipients: Jews' proven allegiance to European sovereigns and peoples; accusations of ritual murder; usury; and Sephardim's "*Noblenes* and purity of their blood."[46] The last two topics are of relevance here. With regard to usury, Menasseh hastened to state that "such dealing is not the essential property of the Iews." While German Jews indeed practice it, Iberian Jews—he explained—"hold it infamous to use it"; like Christians, they invest their money in the public debt and loan at modicum interest rates.[47] In the decades following *The Humble Addresses* and the end of the Thirty Years' War in 1648, the Sephardim of northern Europe increasingly represented themselves in opposition to the growing numbers of German and Polish Jews who sought refuge from death and persecution in Hamburg, Amsterdam, and, later, London. That Menasseh claimed Sephardic superiority and distinctiveness even in matters of usury is significant in light of Gentile views that depicted Jews as invariably usurious and greedy. In his *Persian Letters* (1721), Montesquieu wrote plainly that wherever there is money, there are Jews ("où il y a de l'argent, il y a des Juifs.")[48] Half a century later, Isaac Pinto, scion of a wealthy Sephardic family of Amsterdam and noted author of several economic treatises, aimed to offset all "calumnies" that equated Jews with usurers in his scientific description of financial markets.[49]

At first sight, Menasseh's mention of "purity of blood," the very same concept that had led to the expulsion of Jews from Iberia, strikes a dissonant cord. But as Yosef Kaplan has demonstrated, once in a safe haven in the diaspora, Spanish and Portuguese exiles appropriated this concept to define their own identity in opposition to other Jews.[50] Nowhere is the idea of a noble and distinct Sephardic lineage more pronounced than in Isaac Pinto's *Apologie pour la nation juive* (first published anonymously in 1762). Encouraged by the leaders of the Sephardic community in Bordeaux to write a rebuttal to Voltaire's vicious condemnation of Jews and Judaism as sectarian and obscurantist, Pinto developed two argumentative strategies. Accusing Voltaire of failing by his own standards when he attributed derogatory characters to entire "nations" and "peoples," he pressed him to distinguish between Sephardim and Ashkenazim. For Pinto, "Spanish and Portuguese Jews . . . never mingled or joined with the crowds of the other sons of Jacob."[51] His evidence: they did not wear a beard, dressed like Christians, and were forbidden from intermarrying with non-Sephardic women; their vices (luxury, liberality, pomp, passion for women, vanity, disregard for work and commerce) were not those for which Voltaire would have reproached Jews. Internal differences among Jews were such, Pinto claimed, that "a Jew from London resembles a Jew from Constantinople as little as the latter resembles a Chinese mandarin."[52] Again, these claims projected an intra-Jewish self-perception, but also refuted Gentile images. For Montesquieu, no one resembled an Asian Jew more than a European Jew ("rien ne ressemble plus à un Juif d'Asie qu'un Juif européen.")[53]

Pinto, too, however, followed Voltaire's rhetorical tactic when he identified the general contours of the Sephardic "nation" with its richest men and families, among whom he listed some by name (the baron Belmonte, Avaro Nunes d'Acosta, the Suassos, Texeiras, Prados, Ximenes, Pereiras). In their self-presentation, in sum, Sephardim sought both to highlight the boundaries between themselves and other identifiable segments of Jewish society, and to portray their own outstanding figures (who were not only the wealthiest, but often also the most acculturated) as a synecdoche for the entire group.[54] This strategy was not entirely without effect. In a letter to Pinto, Voltaire declared to have been persuaded that some among Jews were men of great learning and thoroughly respectable; his opinion about Judaism and its superstitions, however, remained unchanged.[55] All in all, divisions between Sephardim and Ashkenazim were first and foremost part of an intra-Jewish discourse more than they became a staple of Gentile representations of Jews.

Across the Jewish world, and the Dutch Jewish world in particular, these divisions were more than figurative self-perceptions; they shaped policies and attitudes.[56] The Amsterdam Spanish and Portuguese Jewish congregation forbade marriages between Sephardim and Ashkenazim in 1671. Across the Dutch world, Sephardic communities adopted a two-tier structure that distinguished between full members (*yehidim*) and those admitted with a limited membership (*congreganten*); non-Iberian Jews as well as African converts to Judaism (usually former slaves) could only aspire to be *congreganten* and were thus excluded from the most influential governing boards and charitable associations.[57] Joseph Salvador, one of the richest and most acculturated Sephardim of eighteenth-century London, doubted the loyalty of the Levy family, Ashkenazim of considerable wealth who had arrived from Hamburg in the 1670s and attained dazzling success in the London diamond trade. From Amsterdam, another distinguished Sephardi, Abraham Lopes Suasso, also complained about the Levys in

Figure 2.1 *Ottoman Jewish Merchant in Istanbul*, in Nicholas de Nicolay, *Les navigations, peregrinations et voyages, faicts en la Turquie* (Antwerp, 1577). Beinecke Rare Book and Manuscript Library, Yale University

1749 and accused them of driving down diamond prices in Antwerp and selling at dishonorable prices ("à des prix si honteaux").[58]

While in Northern Europe Sephardim defined themselves in opposition to Ashkenazim, in the Mediterranean they marked their distance from the descendents of those Iberian exiles who had settled in Muslim lands in the sixteenth century. Initially, the two groups overlapped to a significant extent, especially in Venice. During the seventeenth century, however, migration matters, marriage alliances, and economic specialization enlarged the gulf between "Eastern" and "Western" Sephardim. This gulf was widest in the Ottoman cities where a small contingent of Sephardim from Livorno, Venice, and, more rarely, Amsterdam began to arrive in the late seventeenth century. Western Sephardim spoke Italian and Portuguese rather than Ladino (a Judeo-Spanish vernacular language) and Arabic. They engaged in long-distance trade rather than brokerage, local credit, manufacturing, and regional trade. From the point of view of Ottoman law, they were European subjects and thus exempted from wearing distinctive signs. They indeed wore wigs and dressed like Europeans, and lived in the quarters reserved to foreign merchants. They also formed separate congregations and generally worshipped according to Italian rites. For their habits, they were resented by Ottoman Jews as well as by European merchants. The chief rabbi of Aleppo is said to have wished to oblige "the Frank Jews" to comply with the precept of wearing a beard.[59] In 1690, the French consul of Aleppo decried their habit of wearing hats and wigs.[60]

Western Sephardim were most numerous in Aleppo. There, they insisted that French authorities include them in public ceremonies—a demand that would have been inconceivable in the *métropole*. Nowhere in Europe did Jews—not even the most affluent and acculturated Sephardim—appear in public ceremonies except as victims or to perform homage to sovereign authorities. In a letter of July 20, 1739, the French ambassador to Istanbul ordered that Jewish merchants under his king's diplomatic protection join the processions of the French "nation" on the occasion of its visit to local dignitaries or the entrance of a French consul. Order of appearance mattered tremendously in public ceremonies, and the ambassador prescribed that Sephardim walk after French merchants and before French artisans. French merchants in Aleppo, however, expressed their "repugnance" at the idea of marching next to Jews and claimed they would be derided by the local population (although they admitted to doing business with Jews on a daily basis and even to inviting them to their houses). When a new French consul was appointed to the post in Aleppo in 1742, a conflict ensued about the participation of Sephardim in the procession and the place they would occupy in it. In spite of protests from the "European Jewish nation" in Aleppo ("nattione hebrea europea"), the consul eventually called for the ceremony to take place on Saturday.[61]

SELF-PERCEPTION AND COLLECTIVE REPUTATION

Another important trait distinguished the conduct of Ottoman and European Sephardim in the marketplace. Unlike Ottoman Sephardim, who were most active commercially in the Eastern Mediterranean during the sixteenth and early seventeenth century, those based in Livorno, Amsterdam, Hamburg, Bordeaux, and London did not seek the advice (*responsa*) from rabbis to sort out their business disputes or establish the most ethical solution to puzzling situations.[62] They turned instead to civil and mercantile courts in the cities and states where they resided, or to the laymen (usually affluent merchants and bankers) who governed their communities and maintained varying degrees of jurisdictional autonomy (greater in Livorno than anywhere else).

The decision to sideline rabbis from direct community management reflects the Sephardim's self-perception. Among their powers, elected officials (*parnassim*) could issue a ban (*herem*, or excommunication) against members who infringed religious norms and statutory rules. Spinoza's *herem* in 1656 is only the most notorious of these pronouncements. More often, men (and rarely women) were banned temporarily for lesser transgressions, including dietary laws, sexual conduct, disparaging statements toward coreligionists, contacts with non-Jews, or improper political pronouncements.

The misbehaviors punishable by excommunication included some economic practices.[63] In Venice, in 1607, the united Jewish congregations threatened to fulminate a *herem* against those who speculated in gold and silver currencies and invested in the city's public debt.[64] The 1655 statutes of the Jewish community of Livorno punished those who dared interfere with the loading of any merchandise on board vessels that they had not freighted entirely for themselves or those who lent money to ship captains.[65] In Livorno, the list of infractions that "discredit the commerce of the Jewish Nation" later included coinage falsification, alteration of any commercial drugs, trade in false coral, and dishonest brokerage.[66]

Figure 2.2 *The Dedication of the Portuguese Jewish Synagogue in Amsterdam*, in Bernard Picart, *Cérémonies et coutumes des tous les peuples religieuses*, vol.1 (Amsterdam, 1723). Private collection.

The degree to which these measures were enforced varied form place to place. Yosef Kaplan, who first studied the *herem* as a lens through which to examine internal discipline in Sephardic communities of Northern Europe and their relations to local societies, found that excommunications exerted little deterrent power in Amsterdam, where the Sephardic population lived side by side with Gentiles and was relatively well integrated, while they proved more effective in Hamburg, where the Sephardic community was much smaller and living in a more hostile environment. In London, a sizable group of influential individuals lived as New Christians outside the community's jurisdiction. In Venice and Livorno, available records do not permit us to determine the rate at which bans were enforced, but they were not without consequences. In 1701, a Jewish merchant was excommunicated in Livorno for having loaded goods on French vessels without official registration of his cargo.[67] At the end of the War of Spanish Succession, Moses Franco and Jacob Sarmento apparently excommunicated those coreligionists who had financed the construction of some French ships.[68]

Peer pressure was likely more influential than official sanctions as a warranty against economic malpractice. The existence of the *herem* as an institution, however, was part of the Sephardim's self-perception. Upright merchants feared that excommunication would compromise their reputation inside and outside the community. Moreover, these bands bolstered the collective reputation of Sephardic merchants in contexts in which they had to manage their self-image not only against reality (were they honest or not?), but also against a catalog of accusations that were prone to surface even where Sephardic merchants were most accepted. An upsurge of anti-Semitism followed the 1688 fall of the Amsterdam Stock Exchange. To prevent similar repercussions, the London Spanish and Portuguese congregation prohibited its merchants from trading in gold and silver in 1689.[69] Even when infringed, in other words, warnings of possible excommunication betray a heightened anxiety among Sephardic leaders about their collective image in the marketplace.

CONCLUSION

By looking at the self-perception of Sephardic merchants in the ways in which I proposed here, we can revisit a thorny issue in the history of early modern Europe—the relationship between money, tolerance (as an attitude), and toleration (as a policy). We can also circumvent a disciplinary impasse—the opposition between practices and representations, between the material and the imaginary. Did Sephardic merchants see themselves as full-fledged members of a nascent, global commercial society in which profit mattered more than rank, religion, and nationality? The question, as I hope to have demonstrated, begs for a multifaceted answer that recovers the relation between images and self-images, and captures the changes and continuities in the discourses, legal prescriptions, and social attitudes about Jews in early modern Europe.

The legal position of Sephardic merchants in the few but thriving European port-cities in which they were allowed to reside differed significantly from that of earlier and other Jewish settlements. Whereas medieval Jewish communities in Christian Europe, *de lege* or *de facto*, were called to respond collectively to sovereign authorities for the economic behavior of their individual members—interest rates for moneylending activities, for example, were negotiated collectively, and the fault of one moneylender could lead to the expulsion or the curtailing of the rights of others—Sephardic merchants in early modern Europe were held to prevalent standards of individual legal responsibility (although as Jews or as foreigners, they were barred from certain economic activities). Sephardim, moreover, were immersed in Christian culture as perhaps no Jews ever before. Their merchant practices, as testified by their business correspondence and economic literature, are just one reflection of this profound acculturation.

The regime of individual legal responsibility and acculturation, however, did not erase the existence and the power of collective, often centuries-old Christian images of Jews. The self-perception of Sephardic merchants developed to a large extent in dialogue with such representations. The latter, in turn, displayed both continuity with medieval Christian discourses and new elements, as witnessed by the enduring legend of an alleged Jewish invention of bills of exchange. The most remarkable innovation was what Benjamin Braude has called the "myth of the Sephardi economic superman," that is, the distorted perception of a Sephardic dominance of long-distance trade and international finance. As Braude also insists, several Jewish leaders held on to this myth instrumentally to encourage greater acceptance of Jews in the age of European mercantilism.

If the "myth of the Sephardi economic superman" by definition recognized the existence of different groups within Jewish societies, Christian commentators (travelers, pamphleteers, political theorists, economic thinkers) often attributed essentialized characters to Jews as a whole and to their relation to money ("a people composed solely of merchants," wrote Immanuel Kant of the Jews[70]). The Pinto-Voltaire controversy epitomizes the discrepancy between Sephardic self-images, which stressed the uniqueness of this branch of the Jewish diaspora, and Christian representations of Jews, which made little distinctions between Sephardim and other Jews.

Conscious that their collective reputation for probity mattered to the conduct of economic affairs, Sephardic merchants continued to use a traditional tool of Jewish self-government (*herem*) to police their members, alongside other incentives and coercive measures such as day-to-day social control, intermarriage, and communitarian associations. Any group identified as a minority had to deal with views by outsiders. Savary scolded some French merchants whose "infidelité" compromised the reputation of the entire French nation in the Levant.[71] In 1749, the Levant Company warned its officials to avoid any association with Syrian Christians, whom the British consul in Aleppo had accused of a "spirit of bigotry and persecution"; such allegations could reflect negatively on all "Franks" in the eyes of Muslim authorities and society.[72] In eighteenth-century England, the

Society of Friends scrutinized the morality of its members who went bankrupt to avoid any negative impact on the Quakers' good name. Internal group discipline, we must emphasize, is not necessarily as a sign of an inward mentality; it can also be in trading relations with outsiders once we recognize that no commercial society is ever free of prejudice. Jacob Price writes that as a result of their scrutiny, "Quakers had very high 'credit ratings' both in dealing with themselves and with non-Quakers."[73] Sephardic merchants asserted their self-perception as full members of an increasingly tolerant commercial society, but also struggled to diminish the impact of less than sympathetic views that were meant to keep them on the margins of that very same commercial society.

NOTES

1. Jonathan I. Israel, *European Jewry in the Age of Mercantilism 1550–1750*, 3rd ed. (London-Portland, OR: The Littman Library for Jewish Civilization, 1998); Jonathan I. Israel, *Diasporas within a Diaspora: Jews, Crypto-Jews, and the World Maritime Empires, 1540–1740* (Leiden: Brill, 2002); José do Nascimento Raposo, *Don Gabriel de Silva, a Portuguese-Jewish Banker in Eighteenth-Century Bordeaux* (unpublished PhD thesis, York University, Toronto, 1989).
2. "When the division of labour has been once thoroughly established. . . . Every man . . . lives by exchanging, or becomes in some measure a merchant, and the society itself grows to be what is properly a commercial society." Adam Smith, *An Inquiry into the Nature and Causes of the Wealth of Nations*, 3 vols. (Dublin: printed for Messrs. Whitestone, Chamberlaine, 1776), 1:27 (bk. I, chap. 4: "Of the Origin and Use of Money").
3. On Jewish autobiography in early modern Europe (although with no reference to ego-documents by Sephardic merchants), see Natalie Zemon Davis, "Fame and Secrecy: Leon Modena's *Life* as an Early Modern Autobiography," in *The Autobiography of a Seventeenth-Century Venetian Rabbi: Leon Modena's Life of Judah*, ed. Mark R. Cohen (Princeton, NJ: Princeton University Press, 1988), 50–70; and her *Women on the Margins: Three Seventeenth-Century Lives* (Cambridge, MA: Harvard University Press, 1995), chap. 1.
4. Margaret C. Jacob, *Strangers Nowhere in the World: The Rise of Cosmopolitanism in Early Modern Europe* (Philadelphia: University of Pennsylvania Press, 2006), 66–94.
5. Avner Greif, *Institutions and the Path to the Modern Economy: Lessons from Medieval Trade* (Cambridge: Cambridge University Press, 2006).
6. Craig Muldrew, *The Economy of Obligation: The Culture of Credit and Social Relations in Early Modern England* (New York: St. Martin's,

1999); Margot C. Finn, *The Character of Credit: Personal Debt in English Culture, 1740–1914* (Cambridge: Cambridge University Press, 2003).

7. Derek J. Penslar, *Shylock's Children: Economics and Jewish Identity in Modern Europe* (Berkeley: University of California Press, 2001), 22.
8. For reasons of space, I omit any discussions of visual images. It has been argued that visual representations of Jews were not particularly significant until the rise of racial ideologies that linked physical appearance to alleged inner and social conditions; Ronald Schechter, *Obstinate Hebrews: Representations of Jews in France, 1715–1815* (Berkeley: University of California Press, 2003), 15. Visual representations nonetheless reveal important traits of Sephardic merchants' selective acculturation. See Richard I. Cohen, *Jewish: Art and Society in Modern Europe* (Berkeley: University of California Press, 1998), 11–16, 26–52; Michael Zell, *Reframing Rembrandt: Jews and the Christian Image in Seventeenth-Century Amsterdam* (Berkeley: University of California Press, 2002).
9. Richard Menkis, *The Gradis Family of Eighteenth-Century Bordeaux: A Social and Economic Study* (unpublished PhD thesis, Brandeis University, 1988); Raposo, *Don Gabriel de Silva*; Francesca Trivellato, "Juifs de Livourne, Italiens de Lisbonne et hindous de Goa: réseaux marchands et échanges interculturels à l'époque moderne," *Annales H,SS* LVIII.3 (2003): 581–603; and "Merchants' Letters Across Geographical and Social Boundaries," in *Correspondence and Cultural Exchange in Europe, 1400–1700*, ed. Francisco Bethencourt and Florike Egmond (Cambridge: Cambridge University Press, 2007), 3:80–103.
10. See chapter one GiacomoTodeschini's essay in this book, as well as his *I mercanti e il tempio: La società cristiana e il circolo virtuoso della ricchezza fra Medioevo ed Età Moderna* (Bologna: Il Mulino, 2002), 227–309, 393–486.
11. For a closer analysis of the language of business correspondence, see my *The Familiarity of Strangers: The Sephardic Diaspora, Livorno, and Cross-Cultural Trade in the Early Modern Period* (New Haven and London: Yale University Press), chap. 7.
12. For the expression "good correspondency" in English eighteenth-century manuals of letterwriting, see Eve Tavor Bannet, *Empire of Letters: Letter Manuals and Transatlantic Correspondence, 1688–1820* (Cambridge: Cambridge University Press, 2005), x.
13. Examples in Archivio di Stato, Firenze, *Lettere di commercio e di famiglia*, 1931, Ergas & Silvera to Fouquier Lombard & Co. in Cyprus (November 19, 1706); 1938, to Gopala and Fondu Camotim in Goa (January 12, 1722); 1939, to Isaac and Jacob Belilios in Aleppo (September 3, 1725); 1953, to Moses Cassuto in London (September 4, 1741).
14. Fragments of this publication are now preserved in the Library of the University of Amsterdam. See also Harm den Boer, "Spanish and Portuguese Editions from the Northern Netherlands in Madrid and Lisbon Public Collections," *Studia Rosenthaliana*, XXII.2 (1988): 97–143;

Henry Méchoulan, *Être Juif à Amsterdam au temps de Spinoza* (Paris: Albin Michel, 1991), 112.

15. Abraham Meldola, *Traduccion de las cartas mercantiles y morales de J. C. Sinapius: en español y portuguez* (Hamburg: Bock, 1784); Johann Christian Sinapius, *Briefe für kaufleute. Nebst einer abhandlung über wechselbriefe. Neue verbesserte aufllage* (Hamburg and Leipzig: Bey H. J. Mattheissen, 1782); J. C. Schedel, *Lettres à l'usage des négocians traduites de l'Allemand de J.C. Sinapius* (Hamburg: Chez H. J., 1782). I thank Harm den Boer for calling my attention to Meldola's work. On Abraham Meldola, see Karl-Hermann Körner, "Sobre Abraham Meldola e a sua Nova Grammatica Portugueza de 1785," in *Die Sefarden in Hamburg: Zur Geschichte einer Minderheit*, ed. Michael Studemund-Halévy (Hamburg: Helmut Buske Verlag, 1994), 375–81.
16. The first edition appears to have been printed in Amsterdam in 1706 by Cornelio Hoogenhaisen. Only a few copies of the second edition survive: Gabriel de Souza Brito, *Norte mercantil y crisol de quentas* . . . , 2 vols. (Amsterdam: Juan ten Mouten, 1769–70). Brito's model was Bartolomé Salvador de Solórzano, *Libro de caxa y manual de cuentas de mercaderes y otras personas* . . . (Madrid: En casa de Pedro Madrigal, 1590). See also Esteban Hernandez Esteve, "A Spanish Treatise of 1706 on Double-Entry Bookkeeping: 'Norte Mercantil y Crisol de Cuentas' by Gabriel de Souza Brito," *Accounting and Business Research* 15 (1985): 291–96.
17. Josseph de la Vega, *Confusión de confusiones* (Amsterdam, 1688), 17. Penso de la Vega was a prolific poet, dramaturge, and writer, whose other works did not treat economic subjects.
18. Yosef Kaplan, "The Portuguese Community of Amsterdam in the 17th Century Between Tradition and Change," in *Society and Community (Proceedings of the International Congress for Research of the Sepharadi and Oriental Jewish Heritage 1984)*, ed. Abraham Haim (Jerusalem: Mi gav Yerushalayim, 1991), 141–71 (esp. p. 167).
19. John H. Wills Jr., *1688: A Global History* (New York: Norton, 2001), 216.
20. "Where any set of men, scattered over distant nations, maintain a close society or communication together, they acquire a similitude of manners, and have but little in common with the nations amongst whom they live. Thus the JEWS in EUROPE, and the ARMENIANS in the east, have a peculiar character; and the former are as much noted for fraud, as the latter for probity." David Hume, *Essays, Moral, Political, and Literary*, ed. Eugene F. Miller (Indianapolis: Liberty Classics, 1987), 205.
21. "I am apt to suspect the negroes to be naturally inferior to the whites." Hume, *Essays*, 208n10. See also Emma Rothschild, "David Hume and the Sea-gods of the Atlantic," Paper presented at the conference *Atlantic History: Regional Networks, Shared Experiences, Forces of Integration*, Harvard University June 21–23, 2007.

22. In eighteenth-century North America, demeaning references to Jews appear in the business letters of the very same Christian merchants who did business with them; David Hancock, *Oceans of Wine: Madeira and the Organization of the Atlantic Market, 1640–1815* (New Haven: Yale University Press, 2008), chap. 7.
23. *Réglemens concernant les consulats, la residence, le commerce et la navigation des français dans les échelles du Levant et de Barbarie* (Paris: De l'Imprimerie Impériale, 1812), 161.
24. Gedalia Yogev, *Diamonds and Coral: Anglo-Dutch Jews and Eighteenth-Century Trade* (Leicester: Leicester University Press, 1978), 96–97.
25. Cecil Roth, *A History of the Jews in England* (Oxford: Clarendon Press, 1964), 191.
26. Geoffrey Clark, "Insurance as an Instrument of War in the Eighteenth Century," *The Geneva Papers on Risk and Insurance* 29 no. 2 (2004): 247–57 (esp. p. 254).
27. For a full bibliography and partial analysis of the European *ars mercatoria*, see Jochen Hoock, Pierre Jeannin, and Wolfgang Kaiser, eds., *Ars Mercatoria: Handbücher und Traktate für den Gebrauch des Kaufmanns, 1470–1820, 3 vols. (Paderborn: Schöningh,* 1991–2001). See also Jochen Hoock's chapter in this book.
28. Jacques Savary, *Le parfait négociant, ou Instructon générale pour ce qui regarde le commerce des marchandises de France et des pays étrangers* (Paris: Chez Louis Billaine, 1675), 121 (bk I, chap. 19). On Savary and his works, see Henri Hauser, "Le «parfait négociant» de Jacques Savary," *Revue d'histoire économique et sociale*, XIII (1925): 1–28; Jean Meuvret, "Manuels et traités à l'usage des négociants aux premières époques de l'âge moderne," in Id., *Études d'histoire économique* (Paris: Armand Colin, 1971), 231–50; Jean-Claude Perrot, "Les dictionnaires de commerce au XVIIIe siècle," *Revue d'histoire moderne et contemporaine*, 1 (1981): 36–67 (now in Id., *Une histoire intellectuelle de l'économie politique: XVIIe et XVIIIe siècle* [Paris: Éditions de l'École des hautes études en sciences sociales, 1992], 97–125); Jochen Hoock, "Le phénomène Savary et l'innovation en matière commerciale en France aux 17e et 18e siècles," in *Innovations et renouveaux techniques de l'Antiquité à nos jours. Actes du colloque international de Mulhouse* (septembre 1987), ed. Jean-Pierre Kintz Strasbourg: Oberlin, 1989), 113–23; Carlo M. Cipolla, "I Savary e l'Europa," in Id., *Tre storie extra vaganti* (Bologna: Il Mulino, 1994), 65–91.
29. Raymond de Roover, *L'évolution de la lettre de change, XIVe-XVIIIe siècles* (Paris: Armand Colin, 1953), 23–29.
30. Estienne Cleirac, *Us, et coustumes de la mer* (Bordeaux: Par Guillaume Millanges, 1647), 224–27. I am currently engages in a study of Cleirac and his legacy.
31. Italian merchant-bankers introduced bills of exchange and other credit instruments to Flanders in the late thirteenth century, but neither Jews

nor political expulsions from the Italian peninsula seem to have played a role in the diffusion of this invention. See Raymond de Roover, *Money, Banking, and Credit in Medieval Bruges: Italian Merchant-Bankers, Lombards, and Money-Changers: A Study in the Origins of Banking* (Cambridge, MA: Medieval Academy of America, 1948).

32. Among the first credible authors to follow Cleirac and Savary we find Jacques Dupuis de la Serra, *L'art des lettres de change suivant l'usage des plus celebres places de l'Europe* (Paris: Arnoul Seneuze, 1693), 6–7, and Samuel Ricard, *Traité general du commerce* (Amsterdam: Paul Marret, 1700), 90.
33. Charles de Secondat, baron de Montesquieu, *De l'esprit des loix* . . . , 2 vols. (Geneva: Chez Barrillot & fils, [1748]), 2:68 (bk. 21, chap. 16).
34. See entries "assurance" and "lettre de change" in Jacques Savary des Bruslons and Louis Philemon Savary, *Dictionnaire universel de commerce*, 3 vols. (Paris: J. Estienne, ca. 1723), 1:179 and 2:503. This *Dictionnaire* was reprinted in several editions and translations. For Jean-Claude Perrot ("Les dictionnaires de commerce"); 99. Considering that both Jacques Savary Sr. and Jr. died before the first edition went to press, Philémon Savary, who received theological training and had no direct experience of trade, should be considered the *Dictionnaire*'s principal author.
35. See the entry "bill of exchange" in Thomas Mortimer, *A New and Complete Dictionary of Trade and Commerce* (London: printed for the author, 1766), and the entry "Lettre de change," in *Encyclopédie ou Dictionnaire raisonné des sciences, des arts et des métiers* . . . , 17 vols. (Geneve: Paris & Neufchatel, 1751–72), 9:417–20.
36. Montesquieu, *De l'esprit des loix*, 2:123.
37. Abbé (Gabriel François) Coyer, *La noblesse commerçante* (London and Paris: Chez Duchesne, 1756), 56.
38. Werner Sombart, *The Jews and Modern Capitalism* (New Brunswick and London: Transaction Books, *[1911]* 1997), 65.
39. Roover, *L'évolution*, 83–87; John Munro, "The Medieval Origins of the Financial Revolution: Usury, *Rentes*, and Negotiability," *The International Journal Review*, XXV (2003): 505–62 (esp. p. 545).
40. Jacques Savary, *Le parfait négociant* (Paris: J. Guignard, 1679), 157 (bk. II, chap. 4) and 492–93 (bk. V, chap. 3). Savary generally has kinder words for Armenians than for Jews.
41. Joseph Addison, *Remarks on Several Parts of Italy, &c. in the Years 1701, 1702, 1703* (London: J. Tonson, 1705), 394.
42. Smith, *An Inquiry*, 2:445 (bk. IV, chap. 7: "Of Colonies").
43. Benjamin Braude, "The Myth of the Sephardi Economic Superman," in *Trading Cultures: The Worlds of Western Merchants*, ed. Jeremy Adelman and Stephen Aron (Turnhout, Belgium: Brepols, 2001), 165–94, and "Christians, Jews, and the Myth of Turkish Commercial Incompetence," in *Relazioni economiche tra Europa e mondo islamico, secc. XIII-XVIII*,

ed. Simonetta Cavaciocchi (Florence: Le Monnier, 2007), 219–39. Braude's argument builds on a hint in Salo Wittmayer Baron, *A Social and Religious History of the Jews*, 18 vols. (New York: Columbia University Press, 1937–83), 2:186.

44. Simone Luzzatto, *Discorso circa il stato degl'ebrei . . .* [1638] (Bologna: Forni, 1976); Giovanni Favero and Francesca Trivellato, "Gli abitanti del ghetto di Venezia in età moderna: dati e ipotesi," *Zakhor: Rivista di storia degli ebrei d' Italia*, VII (2004): 9–50.
45. *The Humble Addresses* in Lucien Wolf, *Menasseh ben Israel's Mission to Oliver Cromwell* (London: Published for the Jewish Historical Society of England by Macmillan, 1901), 82–89. On Menasseh's unacknowledged borrowing from Simone Luzzatto, see Benjamin Ravid, "How Profitable the Nation of the Jews Are: The *Humble Addresses* of Menasseh ben Israel and the *Discorso* of Simone Luzzatto," in *Mystics, Philosophers, and Politicians: Essays in Jewish Intellectual History in Honor of Alexander Altmann*, ed. Jehuda Rainharz and Daniel Swetschinski (Durham, NC: Duke University Press, 1982), 159–80.
46. Wolf, *Menasseh ben Israel*, 81.
47. Ibid., 100.
48. Montesquieu, *Lettres persanes*, ed. Élie Carcassonne (Paris: Éditions Fernand Roches, 1929), 127 (letter LX).
49. Isaac de Pinto, *Traité de la circulation et du credit* (Amsterdam, 1771), 201–2, 211; reprinted as *Traité des fonds de commerce . . .* (London: Chez J. Nourse, 1772), 232–33, 243.
50. Yosef Kaplan, "Political Concepts in the World of the Portuguese Jews of Amsterdam During the Seventeenth Century: The Problem of Exclusion and the Boundaries of Self-Identity," in *Menasseh ben Israel and His World*, ed. Yosef Kaplan, Henry Méchoulan, and Richard H. Popkin (Leiden: E. J. Brill, 1989), 45–62. Significantly, *The Humble Addresses* were written in Portuguese and not in Hebrew; Jonathan I. Israel, "Menasseh ben Israel and the Dutch Sephardic Colonization Movement of the Mid Seventeenth Century (1645–1657)," in *Menasseh ben Israel and His World*, 139–63 (esp. p. 161).
51. *Apologie pour la nation juive ou Reflexions critiques . . .* (Amsterdam: Chez J. Joubert, 1762), 15 (my translation). On the *Apologie*, see Baron, *A Social and Religious History*, 2:166; Léon Poliakov, *The History of Anti-Semitism* (1955–77), 4 vols. (Philadelphia: University of Pennsylvania Press, 2003), 3:4–5; Yosef Kaplan, "The Self-Definition of the Sephardic Jews of Western Europe and Their Relation to the Alien and the Stranger," in *Crisis and Creativity in the Sephardic World, 1391–1648*, ed. Benjamin R. Gampel (New York: Columbia University Press, 1997), 121–45; Schechter, *Obstinate Hebrews*, 112–19. On Voltaire's views of Jews and Judaism, see Adam Sutcliffe, *Judaism and Enlightenment* (Cambridge: Cambridge University Press, 2003), 19, 231–46.

52. *Apologie*, p. 12.
53. Montesquieu, *Lettres persanes*, 127 (letter LX). Also quoted in Schechter, *Obstinate Hebrews*, 39.
54. Pinto later defended himself from the accusation of having denied dignity to non-Sephardic Jews. See *Reponse de l'auteur de l'apologie de la nation juive* . . . (The Hague: Chez Pierre Gosse, 1766).
55. *Reponse*, 37.
56. Yosef Kaplan, *An Alternative Path to Modernity: The Sephardi Diaspora in Western Europe* (Leiden: Brill, 2000); Miriam Bodian, *Hebrews of Portuguese Nations: Conversos and Community in Early Modern Amsterdam* (Bloomington: Indiana University Press, 1997); Thomas Glick, "On Converso and Marrano Ethnicity," in *Crisis and Creativity*, 59–76.
57. Kaplan, "Political Concepts," 58–59; Robert Cohen, *Jews in Another Environment: Surinam in the Second Half of the Eighteenth Century* (Leiden: E. J. Brill, 1991), 161–74; Daniël M. Swetschinski, *Reluctant Cosmopolitans: The Portuguese Jews of Seventeenth-Century Amsterdam* (Oxford-Portland, OR: Littman Library of Jewish Civilization, 2000), 188; Jonathan Schorsch, *Jews and Blacks in the Early Modern World* (Cambridge: Cambridge University Press, 2004), 217–53.
58. Quoted in Tijl Vanneste, "Diamond Trade in the First Half of the Eighteenth Century Through the Eyes of an English Merchant: The James Dormer Network" (unpublished paper, European University Institute, 2006), 46, cited with the author's permission. On negative descriptions of Ashkenazi Jews in England, see David S. Katz, *The Jews in the History of England 1485–1850* (Oxford: Clarendon Press, 1994), 258.
59. Alexander Russell, *The Natural History of Aleppo* . . . , 2nd ed., 2 vols. (London, 1794), 2: 60.
60. Gaston Rambert, ed., *Histoire du commerce de Marseille*, 7 vols. (Paris: Plon, 1957), 5:257.
61. Archives de la Chambre de Commerce, Marseille, *Archives antérieures à 1801*, Série J, 947 (letter of the Deputies of the French Nation in Aleppo to the Chamber of Commerce in Marseille, October 17, 1739) and 908 (letter of the French consul in Aleppo to the Chamber of Commerce in Marseille, September 23, 1742); Archives Nationales, Paris, *Affaires étrangères antérieures à 1791*, B/I/83, fols 391r–394v (letter to the Minister and Secretary of State and Navy count Maurepas, September 13, 1742) and fols. 398r, 399r ("Memoire de la nation d'Alep au sujet des assistances des juifs protégés aux ceremonies publiques," September 22, 1742). See also Simon Schwarzfuchs, "La "nazione ebrea" livournaise au Levant," *La rassegna mensile di Israel* 50 (1984): 707–24 (esp. p. 717).
62. On the role of rabbinical *responsa* in the postexpulsion Sephardic world, see Matt Goldish, *Jewish Questions: Responsa on Sephardic Life in the Early Modern Period* (Princeton: Princeton University Press, 2008).

63. One author has sought to link the *herem* against Spinoza to the bankruptcy of his father rather than to the philosopher's opinions in matter of revelation; Odette Vlessing, "The Excommunication of Baruch Spinoza: The Birth of a Philosopher," in *Dutch Jewry: Its History and Secular Culture (1500–2000)*, ed. Jonathan Israel and Reinier Salverda (Leiden: Brill, 2002), 141–72 (esp. p. 149). On the recourse to such bans in the Jewish communities of late-medieval Italy as part of the self-definition and regulation of economic practices in a context in which Jews were associated with usurers and, as such, threats to Christian society, see Giacomo Todeschini, *La ricchezza degli ebrei: Merci e denaro nella riflessione ebraica e nella definizione cristiana dell'usura alla fine del Medioevo* (Spoleto: Centro italiano di studi sull'alto Medioevo, 1989), 144, 161.
64. David J. Malkiel, *A Separate Republic: The Mechanics and Dynamics of Venetian Jewish Self-Government, 1607–1624* (Jerusalem: Magnes Press, 1991), 150–51, 346–47.
65. Renzo Toaff, *La nazione ebrea a Livorno e Pisa (1591–1700)* (Firenze: Olschki, 1990), 562, 568.
66. Archivio della Comunità Israelitica di Livorno (hereafter ACIL), *Recapiti riguardanti gli Israeliti in originale nella Regia Segerteria del Governo* (hereafter *Recapiti*), no. 26. After 1740, Jews were also asked to obtain special permission from the Grand Duke to lend to non-Jews outside the regular use of bills of exchange (*Recapiti*, no. 12).
67. ACIL, *Recapiti*, no. 26.
68. The episode is reported by a Jewish informer based in Livorno to French authorities in Archives de la Chambre de Commerce, Marseille, *Archives antérieures à 1801*, Séziek, 80.
69. Israel, *Diasporas*, 453–54; Roth, *A History*, 188; Katz, *The Jews*, 171.
70. Cited in Julius Carlebach, *Karl Marx and the Radical Critique of Judaism* (London: Routledge & Kegan Paul, 1978), 152. On the fossilization of eighteenth-century Christian views of Jews as unchangeable and legalistic people, see Schechter, *Obstinate Hebrews.*
71. Savary, *Le parfait négociant* (1679), 448 (bk. V, chap. 3).
72. Public Record Office, London, *State Papers* 105/118, fol. 117.
73. Jacob M. Price, "The Great Quaker Business Families of Eighteenth-Century London: The Rise and Fall of a Sectarian Patriciate," in *The World of William Penn*, ed. Richard S. Dunn and Mary Maples Dunn (Philadelphia: University of Pennsylvania Press, 1986), 363–99 (esp. p. 386).

Chapter 3

Merchants in Charge

The Self-Perception of Amsterdam Merchants, ca. 1550–1700

*Clé Lesger, University of Amsterdam**

Introduction

In his "History of Amsterdam," first published in 1611, Johannes Isacius Pontanus boasted that during the preceding decades, Amsterdam had developed into one of the principal trade centers in the entire world.[1] While there is a large measure of exaggeration in this claim, Pontanus rightly observed that by the end of the sixteenth century, the economy of Amsterdam had entered a phase of rapid growth.[2] This is clearly demonstrated by the fact that the population of Amsterdam increased from about 25 thousand to 30 thousand in 1580 to 100 thousand inhabitants in 1622 and about 160 thousand to 175 thousand by the middle of the seventeenth century. By that time Amsterdam was among the largest cities in Europe.[3]

Although the city housed a large trading community, early modern Amsterdam's merchants have left us almost no documents in

* I am grateful to Richard Yntema, Marco van Leeuwen, Kate Delaney, and the participants at the conference in Los Angeles for their comments on earlier versions of this chapter.

which they explicitly express their worldview, or self-perception, or their anxieties regarding material wealth and salvation. Even the very extensive papers left by the merchant and regent Cornelis Pietersz Hooft are mainly comments on resolutions passed by municipal or provincial authorities and on major events that occurred during his lifetime. They contain only small bits and pieces of the very personal information that modern historians need to reconstruct the mental world that Hooft constructed and that guided his actions.[4] Because of the paucity of personal documents written by the merchants themselves, I will take a more indirect route to address the issue of self-perception as found among early modern Amsterdam merchants. Along this route, two issues that one might expect to have greatly affected their self-perception will be addressed. To what extent were Amsterdam merchants subject to restrictions and limitations in the exercise of their profession; and to what extent were they able to impose their will on others?[5]

These issues will be used to hypothesize first about the self-perception of Amsterdam merchants. Then, in the second section, these hypotheses are confronted with material expressions of self-perception in, for instance, paintings, sculpture, and architecture. I will also dwell briefly on writings in which trade and merchants are praised as the foundation of Amsterdam's wealth. Finally, section three will address the question of whether behind the façade of wealth, power, and prestige the merchants were nevertheless tormented by nagging doubts about the salvation of their souls. In the conclusion, the main findings will be recapitulated and it will be suggested that contrary to what Max Weber's thesis might lead us to think, socioeconomic change seems to have promoted the reception of Protestantism in the Netherlands rather than the other way round.

The Position of Merchants in Amsterdam Society

Although I will not defend the materialist position that the socioeconomic status of persons and groups determines their personality and perceptions, it would be foolish to say that social background and position in society are of no consequence at all. This section, which deals with the position of merchants in Amsterdam society, will offer a hypothesis on the effect the position had on merchants' perceptions of themselves and their role in society. The period under consideration includes the end of the sixteenth century and the entire seventeenth century.

Recent research has clearly demonstrated that in the early modern Netherlands, guilds were not a thing of the past, bound to disappear when the Dutch economy entered its phase of expansion. On the contrary, the number of guilds increased almost everywhere, including in Amsterdam, where the economy expanded at a much higher rate than elsewhere in the Netherlands. During the first half of the sixteenth century some twenty guilds were registered in Amsterdam, but by 1622, the number had already risen to forty-one and by 1700, the city had about fifty guilds. By that time about 70 percent of the local male workforce was directly or indirectly incorporated in the guild system.[6] A major exception was wholesale trade that was not organized in a guild and was free for everyone to enter. It was not even necessary to acquire the legal status of citizen before setting up a trading firm, and we know for a fact that many merchants never sought citizenship, or only became citizens many years after their arrival in Amsterdam. As a consequence of being outside the guild system, merchants did not have to comply with a fixed set of rules governing their business. They were free to do business as they liked, buy and sell the merchandise they thought was most profitable, and enter into partnerships if they wished to do so. Apart from the trade with the East Indies, which from 1602 onward was the privilege of the VOC (Dutch East India Company), Amsterdam merchants were also free to go and trade wherever they wanted to. Even trade with hostile states and attempts to withhold stocks and speculate on future price rises at the expense of consumers were rarely prevented. Only when merchants sold strategic goods like weapons, ammunition, and gunpowder to hostile states during wartime did authorities take action, but even then it was not hard to find ways to circumvent the prohibitions.[7]

Throughout the early modern period most skilled occupations remained under the strict control of guilds and guild-like organizations. Only crafts that were mainly practiced by Jews, like tobacco manufacturing and the cutting and polishing of diamonds, and a seasonal occupation like cotton printing that was located just outside the city gates, were free from guild control, as were sailors.[8] So it was only when merchants left the realm of wholesale trade and entered the world of retailing, inland transport, and small-scale production that they encountered the restrictions and regulations that governed the lives of the majority of the Amsterdam population. In wholesale trade, the merchant's freedom of action was almost unlimited. In his *De vroedschap van Amsterdam*, Elias writes that "as long as his actions were not too obviously criminal, or, after 1602, they did not directly violate the interests of the companies chartered by the state, the merchant was in a sense above the law."[9]

In Amsterdam, merchants did business at their own risk and with full responsibility for the outcome of their actions. If things went wrong, there was no one to blame, but if a merchant were successful, he could take full credit for it.[10] Conveniently ignoring luck and deceit, merchants would be tempted to ascribe success to energy, business acumen, tenacity, and willpower. These were also the qualifications that Willem Usselincx, a merchant who was born in Antwerp in 1567 and resettled in Amsterdam in the 1590s, cited when he argued that the rapid growth of commerce in Holland was promoted by the arrival of merchants from the Southern Netherlands like himself: "the whole of Europe feels and must admit, for your works bear witness to it, that in commerce, seafaring, knowledge of countries, cities, and almost all of the parts of the world, Your Honours are everywhere the leading, shrewdest and most experienced men therein, who have the most and the best knowledge thereof."[11] In his view, personal qualities and assets like knowledge, shrewdness, and experience make merchants successful, and his high opinion of the group to which he himself belonged undoubtedly mirrors his self-esteem.[12]

For those engaged in occupations under the supervision of guilds and guild-like organizations, success was to a much larger degree the result of collective action against people and practices that threatened their livelihoods. Especially in retail trade, inland shipping, and transportation/warehousing, it was almost impossible to expand one's business and become an entrepreneur in the Schumpeterian sense of the word.[13] For people engaged in these occupations the chances of becoming rich were extremely slim. If things were going well, it was usually because the collective to which they belonged was doing well. As a consequence, it is much less likely that they would ascribe success in business to personal qualities such as energy, business acumen, tenacity, and willpower. For merchants, on the other hand, things were very different. Success in trade was not primarily achieved through collective action with fellow merchants but in fierce competition with other merchants. That made success a personal victory over competitors rather than the outcome of collective petitioning and bargaining with municipal authorities. Moreover, merchants were not employees, and they did not have to comply with rules set by others. They made their own decisions, established their own paths, and learned to trust their own judgment.

I would therefore argue that freedom of action and the very nature of their professional activities promoted self-esteem and an individualistic attitude toward life among the merchants of Amsterdam.

Conversely, one could expect wholesale trade to be especially attractive to those with high self-esteem and individualistic in character.

It does not seem far-fetched to suppose that the extent to which people are able to impose their will on others would also affect their self-perception. This leads us to a discussion of power and the position of merchants in Amsterdam society. Here, as elsewhere in this paper, I will only deal with wholesale merchants of consequence; say, the top 10 percent to 15 percent of all those engaged in wholesale trade.[14] In the exercise of their profession, wholesalers like these usually were the dominant party in their dealings with retailers, cashiers, notaries, (sworn) brokers, shipping companies, shipmasters, warehousing companies, freighters, agents, manufacturers, and the clerks and messenger boys they employed in their offices.

This does not imply that merchants were not restricted in their dealings with these persons and institutions. As noted above, many sectors of the Amsterdam economy were subject to guild regulations, and merchants were not allowed to brush these rules aside. When their cargo had to be loaded or unloaded, they had to make use of the official lighter (or barge) men and dockworkers; for distribution within the Dutch Republic (and to some cities abroad) no one was allowed to bypass the members of the guilds engaged in inland shipping; the products of many Amsterdam industries had to be checked and approved of by many officials.[15] All these restrictions could be a nuisance, but they did not affect the fundamental imbalance of power between wealthy merchants and the people involved in the buying, selling, loading, unloading, warehousing, and transportation of their merchandise.

In politics, too, Amsterdam merchants were powerful or had access to positions of power. As a matter of fact, the commercial elite of Amsterdam not only ruled the city itself, but also had a large and sometimes controlling influence on decision making in the province of Holland and in the States General. That had not always been the case. For most of the sixteenth century, the power and influence of civic magistrates was, in fact, confined to their own towns or cities. At the provincial level they were confronted by the other estates of society (in the province of Holland only the nobility), while at the supraprovincial level they had to deal with the ruler and the central administrative, judicial, and financial organs.[16] The Revolt and the detachment of the Northern Netherlands from the Habsburg state system enormously expanded the influence of local magistrates, especially in Holland. The institutional frameworks that had taken shape in the sixteenth century remained largely intact in their main outlines, but the power relationships shifted in favor of the civic regents. While the influence of the lower strata of society had long been marginal, in the Republic, the role of the central government was also largely eliminated.[17] It was the Holland regents who now dominated local, provincial, and national government from their power bases in the cities. Amsterdam was exceptional in that such a large part of the civic patriciate was so closely involved in international trade.[18] This situation was the result of a long-running conflict within the city's elite during the sixteenth century and of the unusual wealth that wholesale trade generated.

During the sixteenth century, and for long afterward, the civic government of Amsterdam was dominated by changing groups of regents. They are often referred to as coteries or clans because their members were often closely linked by family ties as well as common interests. In the first decades of the sixteenth century the dominant faction in the city government were the related families of Boelen and Heynen. Their tolerant attitude and moderation in the enforcement of edicts against heresy gave their political opponents the opportunity to gain influence after the Anabaptist disturbances in 1535. With the support of the central government in Brussels, the opponents managed to secure their position in the city government.[19] The new party in the magistracy, known as the Hendrick Dirkists after their leader Hendrick Dirksz, was not only strictly Catholic but also less wealthy than many of the members and supporters of the deposed Boelen-Heynen clan.[20] We find the latter producing the most important merchants in the city in the 1550s and 1560s, and many of them sympathized with the Reformation.

When, in 1567, as ever-stronger rumors predicted that Alva was on his way to the Netherlands with an army to restore order, many members of the Boelen-Heynen clan found it advisable to leave for foreign parts. The result was to strengthen considerably the position of the ruling pro-Spanish oligarchy. Led by Joost Sybrandsz Buyck, this coterie remained in the saddle until 1578. Indeed, it was the exacerbation of the conflict within the city's government by these religious tensions that gave the Alteration of 1578 its radical character. In the other towns of Holland only the most pro-Spanish magistrates were forced to give up their posts, but in Amsterdam the majority of the magistrates were banished from the city.[21] Their places were taken by the merchants who had left the city to go into exile just over ten years earlier. Former exiles took all four burgomasterships and dominated Amsterdam's politics in the years after the Alteration. But even when this first generation had left the magistrates' bench, the direct relationship with wholesale trade remained. Of the forty-two men who were burgomasters one or more times between 1578 and 1630, thirty-four (81 percent) were themselves merchants or very closely involved in wholesale trade. Only eight burgomasters are not known to have had any commercial activities, but even they came largely from backgrounds in wholesale commerce.

Merchants also dominated political life in Amsterdam because of their great wealth. A recent survey of the economic elite in the Dutch Republic during the seventeenth century makes it crystal clear that the really large fortunes in Amsterdam were made in wholesale trade.[22] In particular, the decades around 1600 saw some of the most spectacular examples of commercial success. Jan Poppen, for instance, arrived in Amsterdam in the 1560s.[23] He was from a humble background and entered the service of Hans Simonsz de Oude, a wealthy grain merchant and, like Poppen, born in Holstein (present-day Germany). By the 1570s, Poppen is already conducting trade of his own account, and in 1594 he was among the initiators of Dutch trade with the East Indies and the White Sea. When the VOC was established in 1602, he subscribed no less than thirty thousand guilders and consequently became one of the directors. At Poppen's death in 1616, this very successful immigrant was buried in the prestigious choir of the Old Church. His son, Jacob Poppen, was not only an extremely wealthy merchant, but also very powerful. For many years he was a member of the city government and was appointed burgomaster no fewer than three times. At his early death in 1624, he left a fortune of one million guilders, which made him the wealthiest Amsterdammer of the age.

A career from humble migrant to burgomaster and millionaire within two generations is exceptional, but the capital base, reputations, and political careers of many of the families—among the most influential and wealthiest in Amsterdam in the seventeenth and eighteenth centuries—were formed in this period. Wealth alone was not enough to win political power and prestige, but wealth was certainly a necessary condition for marrying into the political elite of Amsterdam and paving the way for a political career. In his writings Cornelis Pietersz Hooft leaves no doubt that material wealth was a precondition for political power. In his opinion, and in this respect he mirrors the opinion of the social group to which he belonged, wealth was a reflection of one's personal qualities. The wealthiest were wise, sensible, and also the most competent.[24] So when Jacob Cats, a very wealthy and influential moralist, was appointed Grand Pensionary of Holland in 1636, he said that he would have refused the post, but for the fact that God not only called men to an office but also provided them with the talents to perform this task in a just manner.[25] Moreover, it was thought that wealthy men would not easily be bribed.

It is perfectly clear that Hooft looked down on the middle classes and lower strata of society. In the course of his lifetime this contempt intensified, reflecting the increasingly aristocratic nature of the civic government of Amsterdam. But it also reflected the increasing social and economic distance that separated the commercial elite from the rest of society. The wealthy merchants belonged to the class that ruled the city, and because of the sheer size of Amsterdam and its contribution to total tax income, they were also highly influential in provincial and national politics. Before long they refused to tolerate any interference from below (middle classes and lower strata of society) or from above (the princes of Orange). They considered themselves the backbone of the Dutch Republic and the cause of its economic prosperity.

These men were not only used to imposing their will on others in business and politics, they, and sometimes their wives, also managed the numerous institutions, both municipal and clerical, that intruded into the lives of a great many inhabitants. They held positions of power and influence not only in courts of law, but also in orphanages, hospitals, institutions of social care, prisons, and church councils. So in Amsterdam they were in charge in the economic realm as well as in politics, the administration of justice, and social affairs. It is hard not to believe that this power over their fellows would promote their self-esteem to a considerable degree. They differed enormously from their counterparts in England, where parliamentary political power continued to be the domain of the landed right up to the great reform of 1832.

A somewhat different position in society was held by merchants who did not adhere to the public (Calvinist) church and by first-generation immigrants. They were as powerful and free as any merchant in the exercise of their profession, but they were not allowed to join the ranks of regents and exercise political power. Even a moderate man like Cornelis Pietersz Hooft expressed in his writings a guild-like hatred for immigrants and strangers. For him it was unthinkable that "strangers" would wield power over those born and raised in Holland. Immigrants from the Southern Netherlands, in particular, aroused his anger. He envied the rich and successful merchants among them and he despised the clergymen, who were from more humble backgrounds and much more orthodox in religion than Hooft himself. Hooft was not the only man of his age who regarded immigrants as second-class citizens. Even Hugo Grotius wrote that immigrants should content themselves with living a quiet life in Holland and only their children, if born in Holland, might expect to have access to public offices.[26] In fact, this ascension usually took much longer. For several decades the immigrant merchants from the Southern Netherlands and native Dutch rarely intermarried, and they seem to have been two nations within one city.[27] Excluded from political power, the immigrant merchants directed their energy into business and into the management of institutions they could access.[28] However, there is no indication that these wealthy immigrant merchants felt inferior to the native population (compare the statement by Usselincx cited above). On the contrary, the successful immigrants from Antwerp seem to have looked down on the rather coarse manners and lack of refinement of the native Dutch. These immigrant merchants, too, held themselves in high esteem.

To conclude, I would like to offer the hypothesis that because of their freedom and independence in economic matters and their position of power in society, Amsterdam merchants, both natives and newcomers, held themselves in high esteem. The following section will attempt to substantiate this claim.

EXPRESSIONS OF SELF-PERCEPTION ON THE PART OF AMSTERDAM MERCHANTS

What follows is not an inventory of expressions of self-perception, but rather an impression. The work of artists, writers, and architects was used to demonstrate to the world the wealth, power, and prestige of the Amsterdam mercantile elite. As elsewhere in Europe, the Bible and classical antiquity were obvious points of reference in the arts. So Cornelis de Graeff, one of the most powerful men in mid-seventeenth-century Amsterdam, commissioned in 1652 a painting by Jan Victors in which he himself is depicted as the biblical patriarch Isaac, son of Abraham, together with his wife as Rebecca and their children representing Jacob and Esau.[29] Given his position in Amsterdam society and the widely held view that only the richest, wisest, and most honorable men could be allowed to rule the city, we should not be surprised that he had himself and his family depicted in this way. Classical antiquity and wisdom are referenced in an allegorical painting by Ferdinand Bol on education. In it Margaretha, daughter of the very rich merchant Louis Trip, represents Minerva, the Roman goddess of wisdom and knowledge, while teaching her younger sister Anna Maria Trip.[30] The high self-esteem of Amsterdam merchants is also demonstrated in a new genre of paintings. Around 1620, prominent merchants and regents had themselves painted in full-length portraits. Until then in the Low Countries such portraits were made only for sovereigns and the highest nobility. Now, "burghers" like Cornelis Bicker and his wife, Laurens Reael, and Arnoldus van Hem and his wife, had these official portraits painted and thereby demonstrated their high ambitions and the feeling that they were not socially inferior to the nobility. The genre was also practiced by Rembrandt, who in 1639 for the sum of 500 guilders painted a full-length portrait of Andries de Graeff, brother of Cornelis de Graeff.[31] Frederik Rihel, a Lutheran merchant and banker who managed the famous trading firm of Bartholotti after the death of Guillielmo Bartholotti in 1658, even had Rembrandt paint an equestrian portrait that made him look like a monarch.[32] Aristocratic values and high self-esteem were also expressed in the busts that rich merchants and regents commissioned from famous sculptors like Hendrick de Keyser and Artus Quellinus. With these busts they presented themselves in the tradition of Roman consuls, managing the Republic on the North Sea and its commercial empire.[33] The society poet Jan Vos wrote: "And thus one sees ancient Rome, being reborn in the council of IJ and river Amstel [that is the council of Amsterdam]."[34]

Architecture was another means to demonstrate wealth and prestige. During the first half of the seventeenth century, many wealthy merchants left the medieval part of Amsterdam for the more spacious locations in the canal zone and the eastern part of town. They often preferred the high returns on capital invested in trade to the security of real estate; consequently, many of them rented the houses where they lived and conducted business. However, some merchants commissioned architects to build a house, and among them we find a number of the wealthiest merchants in town. In the first quarter of the seventeenth century the richly decorated style championed by Hendrick de Keyser was very popular in Amsterdam. Wealthy merchants like Guillelmo Bartholotti and Nicolaas Sohier bought two adjoining plots of land and commissioned De Keyser to build a large, representative house.

During the 1620s, Haarlem painters like Jacob van Campen and Salomon de Bray introduced a very different architecture in Holland. They followed in the footsteps of famous Italian architects like Palladio and Scamozzi and introduced classicism into Dutch architecture. This style was particularly popular with the Stadtholder in The Hague and his circle of noble and bourgeois advisers. Before long it also became the dominant architectural style for wealthy and self-assured Amsterdam merchants like the Kooijmans brothers and the Trip brothers.[35]

Louis and Hendrick Trip made a fortune in the trade in copper, iron, cannons, ammunition, and muskets.[36] In 1660 they bought a number of houses along the Kloveniersburgwal, had them torn down, and commissioned Justus Vingboons to design a double house behind a single impressive façade. The house cost the enormous sum of 250 thousand guilders, but when it was finished it was by far the most impressive private house in Amsterdam. The house was especially noteworthy because it clearly demonstrated the pride that Louis and Hendrick Trip took in their trade. The façade is elaborately decorated with cannons and cannonballs as well as olive branches representing the peace that had been achieved through war and could be maintained only with the force of arms. Even the chimneys recalled the arms trade. They represented mortars, spitting out smoke during winter when the fire was lit. Apart from the town hall (to be discussed below), I know of no other building that so clearly demonstrates that in Amsterdam trade was not something frowned upon, but a source of wealth and pride.

In the late 1630s, the old town hall proved inadequate for the administration of the rapidly growing city. The new town hall not only had to be more spacious and more practical, but it also had to display the wealth and power of Amsterdam. After the design of Philips Vingboons was rejected by the municipality, Jacob van Campen was given the commission, and in 1648 the pile-driving started.[37] Van Campen designed a massive building in classical style, according to the principles articulated by Scamozzi. The decorations of both the exterior and interior also refer to classical antiquity, but what interests us here is the fact the new town hall explicitly glorifies trade and peace as the root and foundation of Amsterdam's wealth and power. This was clearly demonstrated in the colossal statue of the *vredesmaagd* (Maiden of Peace) on top of the building. In her right hand she holds an olive branch, in her left Mercury's staff, and at her feet the cornucopia displays its rich contents. The tympanum on the front of the building, designed by Van Campen and executed by the famous sculptor Artus Quellinus, shows Neptune and his daughters paying homage to the *stedemaagd*, the virgin symbolizing Amsterdam. All the oceans are represented. They proclaimed to all viewers that Amsterdam ruled the waves and that the city's trading network spanned the world. The message was echoed in the great "Burgerzaal" inside the town hall, where the marble-inlaid floor placed Amsterdam at the center of a map of the world. When citizens of Amsterdam took a stroll in the

Figure 3.1 Amsterdam's City Maiden (*Amsterdamse Stedemaagd*, by Reinier Vinkeles 1741–1816).

Burgerzaal, the world was literally at their feet. The tympanum on the back of the building, designed and executed by Quellinus, shows the continents bringing their merchandise and offering it to Amsterdam's *stedemaagd*. The size of the structure, the expensive building materials, and the lavish decoration made the town hall no less impressive than the palaces of monarchs elsewhere in Europe. The new town hall was an expression of the civic pride of merchants who had made the city prosper and who from their offices managed a commercial empire of unprecedented scale.

In Figure 3.1, the virgin symbolizes Amsterdam, while the humble origins of the city are represented by the fishermen on the left and the fishing nets above the throne. In the background at the right side of the picture is the town hall of Amsterdam; in the front are representations of the continents offering the "*stedemaagd*" (city's maid) their commodities. Anchors, ships, and nautical instruments are included to stress the importance of the overseas trade.

Poems also appeared intended for those who desired a more lasting impression of the new town hall. They praised it as well as the commerce that had turned the city into the warehouse of the world.[38] The poems on the occasion of the inauguration of the new town hall were not unique. Other poems about the commercial success and wealth of Amsterdam also praised the city as did plays, paintings, and hundreds of engravings and maps. No one should doubt that commerce reigned supreme in this city.

In the previous section the hypothesis was offered that Amsterdam merchants held themselves in high esteem. The material culture these men and women left to posterity supports this hypothesis and also demonstrates that trade was not something that people in Amsterdam looked down upon. On the contrary, Amsterdam merchants had created a city in which commerce was paramount and where merchants reigned like kings. In paintings, busts, architecture, and writings, they proclaimed their high self-esteem and the significance of trade. In the course of the seventeenth century some merchants became wealthy enough to leave business and live off their interest.[39] But even then they almost never lost contact with commerce, and the growth of a leisure class did certainly not depreciate the social status of merchants. However, could it be that behind the façade of wealth, power, and prestige these merchants were tormented by doubts about the salvation of their souls?

WEALTH, POWER, AND PEACE OF MIND?

Lowijs Porquin (1511–73) was born in Italy, most probably from a humble background. In the 1530s he settled in the Low Countries and made a living as a pawnbroker and moneylender.[40] He expanded his business to a number of cities and by 1556, when he moved to Bergen op Zoom, he had enough money to buy a very large and prestigious house in the Wouwsestraat. Not much would have been known of Porquin had he not written a book for his children. The book was also published and became quite popular. It was rooted in the Italian tradition of the "ricordanze," chronicles in which merchants wrote down the story of their lives with the explicit intention of instructing their children and passing on the family history.[41] Porquin's work is exceptional because it was written at the end of his life and because it also served another goal: he feared eternal damnation, confessed his sins, and hoped that God will forgive him. His fear of everlasting death is quite understandable since Porquin made his fortune by lending money at interest, otherwise known as usury. During the Middle Ages usury was regarded as a sin and consequently it was forbidden by the Church. In the fifteenth and sixteenth centuries, however, moneylenders were indispensable in the Low Countries, and Porquin was not only fully accepted among the well-to-do in Bergen op Zoom, but Charles V even raised him to a peerage. Nevertheless, Porquin feared for the salvation of his soul.

At a more general level it is clear that the economic expansion profoundly changed Amsterdam society. It created great wealth for some and considerable incomes for many more. It was only a matter of time before traditional patterns of consumption gave way to a more extravagant lifestyle and display of wealth. However, at the same time voices were heard condemning conspicuous consumption and urging people to live according to church teachings. In 1614 Jacobus Trigland, the minister of the Old Church, delivered a sermon in which he rebuked the congregation for its preference for ostentatious clothes, showiness, and lack of modesty. Since he believed that migrants from Antwerp and elsewhere in the Southern Netherlands had introduced these vices into the North, he warned the congregation that the fate of Antwerp would also fall on Amsterdam if they did not change their way of life.[42] In his *Embarrassment of Riches*, Simon Schama has welded together accounts of the material prosperity of the Dutch and concomitant criticism of luxury and ostentation; he has offered a vivid picture of Dutch culture in the Golden Age. Both the title of the book and the analysis of textual and iconographic sources demonstrate that, according to Schama, Dutch culture and the Dutch psyche were shaped by a fundamental and unresolved conflict between the enjoyment of prosperity and anxiety at its possession.[43]

In this section we will look at whether the commercial elites in Amsterdam had similar anxieties, a question not easily answered because the well-to-do merchants did not form a single, homogeneous group. Take, for instance, the contrast between Dirck Volkertsz Coornhert and Caspar Barlaeus. Each wrote a treatise on how to conduct trade in a just and honest way, both were liberal in religious matters, and their writings are clearly rooted in the humanist tradition of Erasmus. Yet in Coornhert's "De Koopman" religion is omnipresent, while in Barlaeus's "Mercator Sapiens" religion is replaced with numerous references to classical antiquity and Cicero in particular.[44] We might also expect merchants to have had very different perspectives on religion and the moral dangers of trade and material wealth. Nevertheless, it is clear from the numerous writings on the moral hazards of trade that for many, conducting trade and leading a just and honest life were not easily reconciled. We also know that merchants—and others—supported the poor and sometimes bequeathed considerable amounts of money to charitable institutions. Should this be interpreted as an indication of anxiety and fear of eternal damnation?

For seventeenth-century Amsterdam—and for the Netherlands in general—research into these questions is scarce and therefore conclusions can only be tentative. In a study on "charitable gifts" in eighteenth-century Amsterdam, Van Leeuwen rightly states that social prestige and reputation were powerful incentives to donate money to charitable institutions.[45] Some even donated enough money to found a new institution. This was, for instance, the case with the numerous "hofjes" (almshouses located around a common courtyard) in Amsterdam and elsewhere in the Low Countries. Very often the name of the founder was praised in a memorial tablet above the entrance of the hofje and usually the block of buildings also bore its patron's name. But Van Leeuwen's study also shows that less tangible motives could be involved as well. In his last will and testament, the Amsterdam merchant Octavio Francisco Tensini bequeathed in 1675 no less than sixty thousand guilders to the poor, on the explicit condition that to save his soul a mass was to be read for him every day for all eternity, a provision that neatly tied in with Roman Catholic doctrine and practice, of course. In their requests for money the governors of Catholic charitable institutions were also quite explicit in the promise that donations here on earth would be generously repaid after death in heaven. So for Catholic merchants, at least, salvation seems to have been something that to a certain extent could be bought by good works; salvation, even for the wealthiest, was not beyond reach and therefore not a source of anxiety and despair.

The curious thing is that just as Van Leeuwen observed, it was widely believed that there would be generous rewards in the afterlife for good works here below. It was also a common motive among Lutherans, Mennonites, and Calvinists. For them, too, donations to charitable institutions seem to have been investments in a better life in the next world. In 1684, for instance, the Reformed home for the elderly in Amsterdam commemorated the fact that a generous legacy by Barent Helleman had made it possible to build the massive home at the Binnen Amstel and Herengracht. In the conference room the trustees not only displayed Helleman's coat of arms, but also a poem noting that "in the hereafter the interest of their gifts awaits all."[46] And the very wealthy Calvinist industrialist and merchant Louis de Geer seems to have had a current account with God. In a letter to his children written in 1646, he mentions that he had promised God to give to the poor 200 guilders a year for each of his children as long as they would be alive. Since God had kept his part of the deal and saved De Geer's children, the merchant had yearly paid his debt to God. He then urges his children always to give to the poor and not to think that these gifts would decrease their wealth, since actually they would make their wealth grow "like seeds in fertile ground." And elsewhere in the letter De Geer wrote, "Support the poor and dejected and you and your posterity will receive God's blessing."[47] In a similar fashion, the widely read and very influential Calvinist poet and moralist Jacob Cats (1577–1660) urged his readers to donate money to the poor since that money would yield high interest and the investment was secure like "a letter of exchange issued by God himself."[48] In a text commemorating the substantial gift of Abraham Cromhuysen to the Lutheran poor relief, even the word *Hemelrente* (interest paid in heaven) is used, and Mennonites were persuaded to make donations to the orphanage with the same arguments: money given to the poor orphans is put out at interest, since God will generously repay, here on earth and in the hereafter.

Since Protestant doctrine explicitly rejects good works like donations as a means to influence God's plans with men, such "heavenly investments" are not what one would expect. In actual religious practice, Amsterdam's Catholics and Protestants were obviously much closer than religious doctrine would suggest. For both Catholics and Protestants good works were means toward obtaining God's blessing on earth and salvation in the afterlife. It seems highly improbable that, possessing such negotiable terms, the merchants of Amsterdam were consumed by anxiety and doubts about the salvation of their souls.[49]

It is not easy to explain the curious deviation between Protestant doctrine and practice in Amsterdam. Much research needs to be done, but it is already clear that the answer will probably not be found in Protestant doctrine but rather in the reception of doctrine by the congregation, including trustees of charitable institutions and possibly even clergymen. It has also been suggested that pre-Reformation views of the beneficial effect of good works lived on among Protestants in the Dutch Republic.[50] This ties in neatly with the work of historians of literature. They have argued that in the fourteenth-century Low Countries, the medieval division of society into three estates was under pressure. Especially in the southern part of the Low Countries trade, industry, and the rise of large cities had profoundly changed society. It is therefore not surprising that from the early fifteenth century, numerous literary works condemn the burgher class for being a group of usurers supported by the devil himself.[51] However, in these same years, in urban chambers of rhetoric, a new morality was being developed and propagated that criticized rich citizens for stinginess but, at the same time, provided them with information on how to save their souls and support urban society. In these circles traditional sins were being replaced by a moral philosophy that protects and supports the interests of the burgher class. Typically in their writings the traditional medieval sin of pride ("superbia") no longer occupies center stage, but has been replaced by stinginess ("avaritia").[52] High profits and great wealth were now acceptable as long as the rich cared for the poor and generously supported the urban charitable institutions.[53] Only when they violated these rules did they jeopardize the salvation of their souls. Geared to the interests of merchants—and premodern urban society in general—such a moral philosophy seems to have survived the Reformation.

CONCLUSION

In this volume a number of questions are posed regarding early modern capitalists. How did they explain themselves and how did they understand their worldly activities? How did they cope with a culture that had for so long opposed material wealth to spiritual possessions and earthly pursuits to the spiritual realm? With respect to the merchants of Amsterdam, this chapter has argued that the freedom of action they enjoyed, and the very nature of their professional activities, promoted self-esteem and an individualistic attitude to life. In addition, self-esteem was furthered by their position of power—both in their professional lives and in society at large. Especially after Amsterdam joined the Revolt and the old elite was set aside, merchants dominated the urban government as well as private and public institutions. First-generation immigrant merchants, like those from the Southern Netherlands, were not allowed to join the ranks of regents and exercise political power, but they too held themselves in high esteem. The works of art that Amsterdam merchants commissioned, their houses, and the new town hall all support the conclusion that the commercial elite had no doubt about their pivotal position in society and the crucial importance of trade for private and public welfare. In the Merchant Republic of Amsterdam, merchants were in charge.

Their self-assurance in the economic, political, and social realm seems not to have been undermined by doubts about the salvation of their souls or by embarrassment over their riches. From the early fifteenth century onward in the Low Countries, a practical moral philosophy seems to have developed that supported the interests of the burgher class and changed medieval sins into human errors that could be compensated for by good works, such as supporting urban charitable institutions. Information on charity in the seventeenth and eighteenth centuries suggests that this "commercial" morality survived the Reformation. It can be found among early modern Amsterdam Calvinists, Lutherans, and Mennonites, as well as among Roman Catholics. Amsterdam merchants were concerned about the salvation of their souls, but they most probably did not experience the agonizing uncertainty that Protestant doctrine and the work of Max Weber might induce us to expect. Judging from the contents of literary texts, hard work and thrift also seem to be rooted in the moral philosophy that came to dominate urban society in the Low Countries well before the Reformation. One cannot escape the observation that socioeconomic change in the Netherlands promoted the reception of Protestantism, rather than Protestantism promoting socioeconomic change.[54]

NOTES

1. Willem Frijhoff and Maarten Prak, eds., *Geschiedenis van Amsterdam. Centrum van de wereld 1578–1650*, II-1 (Amsterdam: SUN, 2004), 9.
2. The trade of Amsterdam is extensively dealt with in Clé Lesger, *The Rise of the Amsterdam Market and Information Exchange: Merchants, Commercial Expansion, and Change in the Spatial Economy of the Low Countries, c.1550–1630* (Aldershot: Ashgate, 2006). For a more general account of the economy of Amsterdam, see "De wereld als horizon. De economie tussen 1578 en 1650," in Frijhoff and Prak, *Geschiedenis van Amsterdam*, 102–87.
3. Population figures for Amsterdam can be found in H. Nusteling, *Welvaart en werkgelegenheid in Amsterdam 1540–1860. Een relaas over demografie, economie en sociale politiek van een wereldstad* (Amsterdam: De Bataafsche Leeuw, 1985), app.1.1 and 1.2, and for the period after 1680, in Marco H. D. van Leeuwen and James E. Oeppen, "Reconstructing the Demographic Regime of Amsterdam 1681–1920," *Economic and Social History in the Netherlands* 5 (1993), 61–102, table 9. See, for the comparison with other European cities, Jan de Vries, *European Urbanization 1500–1800* (Cambridge, MA: Harvard University Press, 1984), app. 1.
4. Cornelis Pietersz Hooft's papers have been published in H. A. Enno van Gelder, ed., *Memoriën en adviezen van Cornelis Pietersz Hooft*, Werken uitgegeven door het Historisch Genootschap, 3e serie, 48 (Utrecht: Historisch Genootschap, 1925).
5. In doing so, I follow in the footsteps of Van Gelder who, in the early twentieth century, made a very thorough study of Hooft's outlook

on life (H. A. Enno van Gelder, *De levensbeschouwing van C. P. Hooft* [Amsterdam, n.p. 1918]). For the Hooft family, see also M. van Tielhof, *The Mother of All Trades: The Baltic Grain Trade in Amsterdam from the Late Sixteenth to the Early Nineteenth Century* (Leiden: Brill, 2002), chap.1.

6. Piet Lourens and Jan Lucassen, "Ambachtsgilden in Nederland: een eerste inventarisatie," *NEHA-JAARBOEK voor economische, bedrijfs-en techniekgeschiedenis* 57 (1994), 34–62, gives an overview of guilds in the Netherlands; idem, "Ambachtsgilden binnen een handelskapitalistische stad: aanzetten voor een analyse van Amsterdam circa 1700," *NEHA-JAARBOEK voor economische, bedrijfs-en techniekgeschiedenis* 61 (1998), 121–62, describes guilds in Amsterdam.
7. See J. H. Kernkamp, *De handel op den vijand 1572–1609*, I, 1572–1588 (Utrecht: Kemink en zoon, 1931), and II, 1588–1609 (1934).
8. Lourens and Lucassen, "Ambachtsgilden binnen een handelskapitalistische stad," 147; for the organization of inland trade, see Clé Lesger, "Intraregional Trade and the Port System in Holland, 1400–1700," in Karel Davids and Leo Noordegraaf, eds., *The Dutch Economy in the Golden Age* (Amsterdam: NEHA, 1993), 185–217 (also published in *Economic and Social History in the Netherlands*, vol. 4).
9. J. E. Elias, *De vroedschap van Amsterdam 1578–1795*, 2 vols. (Haarlem: Loosjes, 1903–1905), xli. This, of course, does not imply that opportunism and deceit reigned supreme in Amsterdam. Most merchants were careful not to damage their reputation since that would make future transactions much more difficult. See Lesger, *Rise of the Amsterdam Market*, 164–65, and the literature cited there, and also Clé Lesger, "The 'Visible Hand': Views on Entrepreneurs and Entrepreneurship in Holland, 1580–1850," in Mario Rutten and Carol Upadhya, eds., *Small Business Entrepreneurs in Asia and Europe: Towards a Comparative Perspective* (New Delhi: Sage, 1997), 255–77.
10. See, for the following, also Van Gelder, *De levensbeschouwing van C. P. Hooft*, 176–200.
11. J. Briels, *De Zuidnederlandse immigratie 1572–1630* (Haarlem: Fibula-Van Dishoeck, 1978), 78.
12. In this paper I will use the term "self-esteem" to indicate confidence in one's own worth and abilities (*Oxford English Dictionary* at www.askoxford.com).
13. In the brewing industry, sugar refineries, potteries, and similar trades, large enterprises and wealthy entrepreneurs were not exceptional. See, for instance, Richard Yntema, "The Brewing Industry in Holland, 1300–1800: A Study in Industrial Development" (unpublished PhD thesis, Chicago, 1992); and Arjan Poelwijk, *"In dienste vant suyckerbacken." De Amsterdamse suikernijverheid en haar ondernemers, 1580–1630* (Amsterdam: Verloren, 2003). However, it should be noted that only a few industrialists acquired fortunes that could match those of successful

wholesale merchants. Compare the survey of the wealthiest men and women in the Dutch Republic during the seventeenth century in Kees Zandvliet (in collaboration with C. Lesger), *De 250 rijksten van de Gouden Eeuw. Kapitaal, macht, familie en levensstijl* (Amsterdam: Nieuw Amsterdam, 2006).

14. To give an impression of the size of the merchant community in Amsterdam, the archives of the Wisselbank (Bank of Amsterdam) are probably the most helpful. The obligation to pay all bills of exchange with a value of 100 pound Flemish (600 guilders) or more through the Wisselbank made it almost impossible to conduct wholesale trade and not have an account at the Bank. In the period around 1610, the earliest years for which information has survived the ravages of time, 700 to 750 account holders are registered in the ledgers of the Bank. In 1615, that number had risen to 872, and in 1627, 1,351 account holders made use of the services of the Wisselbank. By the end of the seventeenth century that number had doubled (see Lesger, *Rise of the Amsterdam Market*, chap. 4 and app. B; and J. G. van Dillen, ed., *Bronnen tot de geschiedenis der Wisselbanken* (Amsterdam, Middelburg, Delft, Rotterdam), Rijks Geschiedkundige Publicatiën, 59–60 (Grote Serie) (The Hague: Nijhoff, 1925).
15. See, for instance, Van Tielhof, *The Mother of All Trades*, chap. 8.
16. Hugo de Schepper, "De burgerlijke overheden en hun permanente kaders 1480–1579," *Algemene Geschiedenis der Nederlanden* 5 (Haarlem: Fibula-Van Dishoeck, 1980), 312–49; and J. E. Elias, *Geschiedenis van het Amsterdamse regentenpatriciaat* (The Hague: Martinus Nijhoff, 1923), 2.
17. See D. J. Roorda, "Het Hollandse regentenpatriciaat in de 17e eeuw," in C. B. Wels e.a., eds., *Vaderlands verleden in veelvoud* I (The Hague: Nijhoff, 1980), 221–40; and A. Th. van Deursen, "Staatsinstellingen in de Noordelijke Nederlanden 1579–1780," *Algemene geschiedenis der Nederlanden* 5 (Haarlem: Fibula-Van Dishoeck, 1980), 350–87, in particular the section on the Holland regents.
18. Roorda, "Het Hollandse regentenpatriciaat," 238–39.
19. S.A.C. Dudok van Heel, "Oligarchieën in Amsterdam vóór de Alteratie van 1578," in Michiel Jonker, Leo Noordegraaf, and Michiel Wagenaar, eds., *Van stadskern tot stadsgewest. Stedebouwkundige geschiedenis van Amsterdam* (Amsterdam: Verloren, 1984) 35–61.
20. Elias, *De vroedschap van Amsterdam*, xxxvii.
21. Roorda, "Het Hollandse regentenpatriciaat," 235–36.
22. Zandvliet, *De 250 rijksten van de Gouden Eeuw.*
23. The following story is based on Elias, *De vroedschap van Amsterdam.*
24. Van Gelder, *De levensbeschouwing van C. P. Hooft.*
25. A. Th. van Deursen, *Het kopergeld van de Gouden Eeuw*, III, Volk en overheid (Assen: Van Gorcum, 1979), 9.
26. Van Gelder, *De levensbeschouwing van C. P. Hooft*, 44–45, 125.

27. Niek Al and Clé Lesger, "'Twee volken . . . besloten binnen Amstels wallen'? Antwerpse migranten in Amsterdam omstreeks 1590," *Tijdschrift voor Sociale Geschiedenis* 21 (1995), 129–44.
28. For the economic success of immigrant merchants from the Southern Netherlands, see Lesger, *Rise of the Amsterdam Market*, chap. 4.
29. Frijhoff and Prak, *Geschiedenis van Amsterdam*, 270.
30. Zandvliet, *De 250 rijksten van de Gouden Eeuw*, 210.
31. Ibid., 79.
32. Ibid., 16.
33. Ibid., xxxi, 78, and 337, and also Frijhoff and Prak, *Geschiedenis van Amsterdam*, 272.
34. "Zo ziet men 't oude Room; Herboren in de raad van IJ en Amstelstroom.'" Cited in Willem Frijhoff and Marijke Spies, *1650. Bevochten eendracht, Nederlandse cultuur in Europese context* (The Hague: Sdu uitgevers, 1999), 452.
35. Koen Ottenheym, *Philip Vingboons (1607–1678) Architect* (Zutphen: Walburg Pers, 1989), chap. 1.
36. For the business of the Trip family, see P. W. Klein, *De Trippen in de 17e eeuw. Een studie over het ondernemersgedrag op de Hollandse stapelmarkt* (Assen: Van Gorcum, 1965).
37. For Van Campen and the town hall of Amsterdam, see Jacobine Huisken, Koen Ottenheym, and Gary Schwartz, eds., *Jacob van Campen. Het klassieke ideaal in de Gouden Eeuw* (Amsterdam: Architectura & Natura Pers, 1995); see also Simon Schama, *The Embarrassment of Riches: An Interpretation of Dutch Culture in the Golden Age* (London: Fontana, 1991), chap. 4.
38. Frijhoff and Spies, *1650. Bevochten eendracht*, 449–54.
39. The literature on the "aristocratisation" of the merchant class is extensive. Useful are Joop de Jong, "De regenten, de Republiek en het aristocratiseringsproces: een terugblik," in Guido Marnef and René Vermeir, eds., *Adel en macht. Politiek, cultuur, economie*, Publicaties van de Vlaams-Nederlandse Vereniging voor Nieuwe Geschiedenis 1 (Maastricht: Shaker Publishing, 2004), 5–15; and J. L. Price, "De regent," in: H. M. Beliën, A. Th. van Deursen, and G.J. van Setten, eds., *Gestalten van de Gouden Eeuw. Een Hollands groepsportret* (Amsterdam: Bert Bakker, 1995), 25–62.
40. M. Greilsammer, *Een pand voor het paradijs. Leven en zelfbeeld van Lowys Porquin, Piemontees zakenman in de zestiende-eeuwse Nederlanden* (Tielt: Lannoo, 1989), part I, chap. 2.
41. Ibid., 13.
42. Trigland's sermon is quoted in Briels, *De Zuidnederlandse immigratie*, 65–66. In 1655, the very strict Amsterdam burgomaster Nicolaas Tulp and a number of sympathizers in the city council issued an order setting a limit on expenditures for weddings and even for meals in inns (Frijhoff and Spies, *Bevochten eendracht*, 30).

43. Schama, *Embarrassment of Riches.* Jan Steen's painting *The Burgher of Delft and His Daughter*, on the cover of Schama's book, has become an icon of the embarrassment of riches. Recently, the identity of the man (Adolf Croeser) and his daughter (Catharina) has been established as well as a plausible motive for commissioning the painting; see Frans Grijzenhout and Niek van Sas, *De burger van Delft. Een schilderij van Jan Steen* (Amsterdam: Rijksmuseum/Nieuw Amsterdam, 2006). Their research does not support Schama's thesis of embarrassment.
44. Caspar Barlaeus, *Mercator Sapiens. Oratie gehouden bij de inwijding van de Illustere school te Amsterdam op 9 januari 1632; met Nederlandse vertaling en inleiding uitgegeven door dr. S. van der Woude* (Amsterdam: Universiteitsbibliotheek, [1632] 1967), 15. See also Catherine Secretan, *Le "Marchand philosophe" de Caspar Barlaeus. Un éloge du commerce dans la Hollande du Siècle d'Or* (Paris: Champion, 2002).
45. Marco H. D. van Leeuwen, "Liefdadige giften in Amsterdam tijdens de achttiende eeuw," *Tijdschrift voor Sociale Geschiedenis* 22 (1996), 417–42, 427. The following story is largely based on this article and on S. Groenveld, "'Geef van uw haaf een milde gaaf ons arme weesen.' De zorg van wezen tot 1800 als onderdeel van de armenzorg," in S. Groenveld, ed., *Daar de orangie-appel in de gevel staat. In en om het weeshuis der doopsgezinde collegianten 1675–1975* (Amsterdam: Stichting De Oranjeappel, 1975), 9–51.
46. "Elk wacht van zijn Talent de Renten 't zijner tijt," cited in Van Leeuwen, "Liefdadige giften in Amsterdam," 428; and Jan Wagenaar, *Amsterdam, in zyne opkomst, aanwas, geschiedenissen, voorregten, koophandel, gebouwen, kerkenstaat, schoolen, schutterye, gilden en regeeringe* (Amsterdam: Isaak Tirion, 1760–67), part 2, 326–27.
47. Van Leeuwen, "Liefdadige giften in Amsterdam," 432. Among the richest Dutchmen in the seventeenth century, Louis de Geer, also known as the father of Swedish industry, ranks number 4 out of the top 250. At his death in 1652, he left a fortune of about 1.5 million guilders (Zandvliet, *De 250 rijksten van de Gouden Eeuw*, nr. 4).
48. "Ghy hebt een wissel-brief van Godes eygen handt," cited in Groenveld, "Geef van uw haaf een milde gaaf," 38.
49. Of course, that did not prevent them from being acutely aware of the uncertainties of trade and early modern life in general. Daniel van der Meulen, an immigrant merchant from Antwerp, referred to this uncertainty with the Franco-Italian phrase "l'instabilité della fortune" (cited in Luuc Kooijmans, *Vriendschap en de kunst van het overleven in de zeventiende en achttiende eeuw* [Amsterdam: Bert Bakker, 1997], 53).
50. Groenveld, "Geef van uw haaf een milde gaaf," 38–39, and Van Leeuwen, "Liefdadige giften in Amsterdam," 432.
51. Herman Pleij, *Het gilde van de Blauwe Schuit. Literatuur, volksfeest en burgermoraal in de late middeleeuwen* (Amsterdam: Meulenhoff, 1983), esp. chap. 4; and see also Herman Pleij, "Inleiding: op belofte van profijt," in Herman Pleij, ed., *Op belofte van profijt. Stadsliteratuur en*

burgermoraal in de Nederlandse letterkunde van de middeleeuwen (Amsterdam: Prometheus, 1991), 8–51. R. Künzel, *Beelden en zelfbeelden van middeleeuwse mensen. Historisch-antropologische studies over groepsculturen in de Nederlanden* (Nijmegen: SUN, 1997), chap. 4, argues that in contrast to theological and scholastic texts, medieval *vitae* and *miracula*, which probably better reflect the clergy's perception of society, display little disdain for merchants and trade in general. However, like the "official" texts, they were very critical of the political and legal ambitions of the burgher class.

52. Pleij, *Het gilde van de Blauwe Schuit*, 144.
53. The works on "the merchant" by Coornhert and Barlaeus, mentioned before, seem to fit perfectly in this tradition. See also the analysis of the texts presented at the famous *rederijkerslandjuweel* (contest of chambers of rhetoric in Brabant) held in Antwerp in 1561, in Karel Bostoen, "Zo eerlijk als goud: de ethiek van de wereldstad," in Pleij, *Op belofte van profijt*, 333–46. On the chambers see Arjan van Dixhoorn, "Writing Poetry as Intellectual Training. Chambers of Rhetoric and the Development of Vernacular Intellectual Life in the Low Countries between 1480 and 1600," in Koen Goudriaan, et.al., *Education and Learning in the Netherlands, 1400-1600 (Leiden:Brill, 2004), 202–22.*
54. See J. C. Riemersma, *Religious Factors in Early Dutch Capitalism* (The Hague: Mouton, 1967), 85–86; and see also J. A. Aertsen, "Burger en beroep in de middeleeuwen. Enkele kanttekeningen bij Max Webers beeld van het middeleeuwse 'Wirtschaftsethos,'" *Economisch-en Sociaal-Historisch Jaarboek* 41 (1978), 23–85. It should be noted that Weber in "Die protestantische Ethik und der Geist des Kapitalismus" restricted the scope of his theory to the Puritans and related groups in seventeenth-century England. Others have argued that the Protestant Reformation of the sixteenth century also contributed to a cultural environment promoting economic expansion.

Chapter 4

Merchants on the Defensive

National Self-Images in the Dutch Republic of the Late Eighteenth Century

*Dorothee Sturkenboom, Roosevelt Academy Middelburg, Utrecht University**

During most of their famous seventeenth century, the merchants of the Dutch Republic had every reason to be proud of themselves. After all, at the same time that the United Provinces of the Netherlands fought their war of liberation with Spain (1568–1648) they also rapidly developed into the leading commercial economy in the world that for a short period outstripped all its neighboring countries in economic, maritime, and military power. The ambitions and activities of the Dutch merchant class had played no small part in this development. It was difficult for anyone at the time not to be aware of that.[1]

This chapter, however, does not deal with the Golden Age of the Republic when its merchants were "in charge" of their firms, their republic, and the oceans.[2] It focuses on a later stage in history when Dutch merchants were losing their leading position in international commerce and the Dutch Republic was perceived to be spiraling toward a state of cultural decline and economic ruin. Although

* This chapter has its origins in a joined writing project with Henk Reitsma, my former roommate at VU University Amsterdam. I wish to express my thanks for the different ways in which he contributed to my knowledge on this subject over the years.

economic historians tend to disagree about the actual degree of that decline (because of the flourishing of other economic sectors such as financing and traditional crafts), contemporaries who witnessed the growing army of unemployed paupers were convinced that there was "something rotten" in the state of the Dutch Republic.[3] The last decades of the eighteenth century consequently saw the birth of a radical political movement that, partly inspired by progressive Enlightenment ideas of reform and partly by conservative ideas of restoring the golden past, sought to redress the balance in economic, political, and cultural respect—both internally and internationally. The reformists called themselves "Patriots." If their plans to restore the Republic to its former grandeur were to succeed, they needed the support of people with capital. What had thus been an individual and moral dilemma for merchants in the seventeenth century—that is, the question of how to invest or spend their accumulating fortunes—had now become a national and political issue with relevance for all Dutchmen and—women.

This chapter therefore employs a different angle on the theme of early capitalists' self-perceptions than most of the other contributions to this book. In lieu of approaching the subject on the level of personal self-esteem, individual ethics, or professional rationality, it tackles the subject of self-perception on the level of the nation by asking, How did a wealthy nation of capitalists perceive itself when confronted with a succession of crises that threatened to put it out of business? I will argue that on this national level, economic self-perceptions are as much the product of interaction with others as they are negotiated on an individual level. Whether capitalist or not, the way in which nations picture themselves is in large measure the upshot of a subtle play of challenge and response between outsiders and insiders who form their images neither autonomously nor in complete dependence of each other.[4] In this chapter I intend to highlight two elements in this dynamic and imaginative process. First, the role of gender as a crucial signifier in the assessment of economic acts, and second, the common strategy of transferring disagreeable parts of one's (economic) reputation to others.

ECONOMIC SPECTACLES

Let me start my argument with a case study of the *Toneelspel in twee afdeelingen* (*Play in Two Acts*), a peculiar Dutch pamphlet of forty-eight pages written by a nameless author who mysteriously identified himself as "a Friend of the Fatherland."[5] Fortunately, we do have the name of the Amsterdam publisher, Dirk Schuurman, who published the text in 1780 on the eve of the Fourth Anglo-Dutch War (1780–84). Although title and form presented the text as a theater play, it was probably never performed onstage.[6] We may even question whether it was ever intended to be performed as it has all the characteristics of similar Dutch "drama pamphlets." These were written in those politically turbulent years as sociopolitical critiques and only styled as plays to make them more appealing to the reader.[7] The *Toneelspel*, moreover, was explicitly presented as a further explanation of two graphic prints that had been brought on the market earlier that year. They were part of a steady stream of political prints that likewise commented upon the unstable political and economic situation of the Dutch Republic.[8] The two prints were published without a title, but each featured a Dutch "capitalist," and they were fitted with the epithet "economic" in the national print collection in which they survived.[9] Since both the anonymous pamphleteer and his publisher Schuurman believed there was a market for the *Toneelspel*, we may deduce that the economic prints were a commercial success.[10]

The prints have been reproduced several times since 1780. As a result, they are no strangers in Dutch historiography.[11] Due to the disciplinary borders between historical specializations, however, the fictitious *Toneelspel* has hitherto gone unnoticed in Dutch historical research. Yet the text offers the opportunity for a deeper and more

Figure 4.1 First economic print. Atlas van Stolk, *Engelsche kraam etc.*, no. 4318, Stichting Atlas van Stolk, Rotterdam.

Figure 4.2 The World of the Great. Detail from Atlas van Stolk, *Engelsche kraam etc.*, no. 4318, Stichting Atlas van Stolk, Rotterdam.

detailed understanding of the two prints. Studied together, they provide us with a fascinating historical narrative about the lures of foreign commodities and the schemes of needy foreign financiers who were after the honest and hard-earned money of Dutch capitalists. When the prints were first published in 1780, they were printed with elaborate legends that already helped to explicate several details of the pictures. The extensive title of the *Toneelspel* claimed nevertheless that this was a work "highly necessary to arrive at a true understanding of the plates mentioned and of the Dutch interests." Although the claim may have been a sales stunt, the pamphleteer lived up to his words. He offered an extended moral analysis of his country's economic and social problems by the words of one of his characters, Petrus, a Dutch retail trader and obviously the alter ego of the author.[12]

We see Petrus at the right corner of the first economic print (Figure 4.1) in front of his stall with solid Dutch goods that he offers to a young Dutchman, seated on a richly filled money chest that is in the process of being pulled away from Petrus. The young man, called Klaas in the play—a name often used for fools in Dutch[13]—is rejecting Petrus's products. He prefers to lend his money to an English banker. The banker, ominously called Master John Always Short, can hardly wait to take the money out of the chest. He poses as a friend to the Dutchman, promising a steady interest for the loan without the risks that come with investments in commercial or industrious undertakings and without the hard work that such investments entail. Klaas, who did not earn the money himself but inherited it from his father, a virtuous Dutch merchant of the old school, is obviously rather taken with the prospect of not having to work and nevertheless receiving a guaranteed income. As are his three female companions to the left, who expect to share in this income if they succeed in persuading Klaas to plunge himself into an easy life full of Luxury, Lechery, and Lust for Liquor—the vices the women personify.

This would be the life that we see depicted at the left side of the print (Figure 4.2), the life of what is called "The World of the Great" in the play and the legend of the print. It is the life that aristocratic elites are understood to lead, full of superficial temptations (banquets, cards, duels, adultery) that attract people who lack a strong moral compass to tell them what is right and what is wrong. Charles Always Something Foolish is making inviting gestures already, but before Klaas can pass the broad archway and make a successful entry to this world, he has to take off his simple Dutch merchant's suit and learn

Figure 4.3 Klaas as would-be gentleman. Detail from Atlas van Stolk, *Engelsche kraam etc.*, no. 4318, Stichting Atlas van Stolk, Rotterdam.

how to dress himself as a true gentleman, a Man of Birth, the scene in the middle of the print (Figure 4.3). Here Jean Poli and other Frenchmen enter the picture. Better than anyone else they know how to "dress for success"—at least that is the impression they succeed in transmitting to the naive Klaas. Hence the various "Modes de Paris," the French fashions that Klaas has to make himself familiar with if he wishes to pass for an important man—and Haughtiness and Foolishness, the two male, yet not very masculine, figures who are pulling his chest in the direction of the archway, are certainly in the midst of leading him to that goal (Figure 4.1).

It is up to Petrus to talk sense into Klaas, an undertaking in which he sadly fails. In the play he tries to draw Klaas's attention to the smirking Fool's mask, to the monkey with the French feathered hat, to Mr. Grub and his flourishing stall of earthenware and other English products that drive the Dutch out of the market thanks to Klaas's ill-considered financial decisions, and finally to the English privateers who attack Dutch ships in the Channel, proving that the English cannot be trusted. Recall it is 1780, at the end of which year the English would declare war on the Dutch, their former allies, for supporting the Americans in their War of Independence. In spite of all these bad omens, Klaas refuses to listen. He cannot be bothered with the ramshackle state of the Republic of the Seven United Netherlands, represented by the seven pillared temple at the right of the

Figure 4.4 Second economic print. Atlas van Stolk, *Eerwaardigen Nederlander*, no. 4322, Stichting Atlas van Stolk, Rotterdam.

Figure 4.5 Patriotic citizens following Reason. Detail from Atlas van Stolk, *Eerwaardigen Nederlander*, no. 4322, Stichting Atlas van Stolk, Rotterdam.

print. The construction, badly maintained by Carelessness, is under attack. The Dutch Virgin has fled to its roof. Klaas, however, expects that the building will last. He flatly refuses to show any interest in the products from Petrus's stall. Because he intends to pose as a gentleman, he foolishly gets himself involved in a fatal duel and loses his life at the end of the first act. Petrus has no choice but to admit his defeat and start considering the liquidation of his business.

However, in the second act of the play and in the second economic print (Figure 4.4), the mise en scène has drastically changed. Again we find ourselves at the Dutch "free" seaside, a longtime symbol for Dutch liberty.[14] But this time the central character is not a foolish young man who lends his ears too easily to foreigners, but a mature and honorable citizen who has heard of Petrus's adversities and realizes his country is at risk. This Burgerhart—the name literally means "Citizen's Heart"—is aware of the dishonesty of the foreigners who try to win his friendship whereas in reality they are only interested in his money. Next to Master John Always Short, who tries to sell him English bonds, we see a bowing Frenchman (Jean Poli), an eager Spaniard (Don Sebastian), and a subservient German (Hans). They all have spectacular new plans for investments and promise the highest profits to the Dutchman if he is willing to buy their stocks.

Burgerhart, however, bluntly rejects all of them. He makes clear that he prefers to invest his capital in the various industrial, agricultural, and reclamation projects with which three of his industrious Dutch fellow citizens, in the middle of the picture, plan to reanimate the Dutch economy—though, of course, only after he has scrutinized the solidity of their business plans. While Burgerhart does not invest directly in Dutch commerce, the vast merchant fleet at sea shows the beneficiary effects that his wise policy is believed to bring to all branches of Dutch economy. As Petrus comments in the play, it will be thanks to this citizen's example, demonstrating the bold decisions, patriotism, and spirit of enterprise asked for, that the flock of lost compatriots will come to its senses and commit itself to the common good of the Dutch Republic again. Reason, the female figure at the head of the procession, armed with the attributes of the goddess Athens, will lead them back to the Republic and the process of renovation. The Dutch lion will successfully chase off the English dog, as the dog has already enough trouble to fight off the French cock, let alone the much more awe-inspiring lion—or so Petrus confidently claims. And if other well-to-do Dutchmen are still not persuaded by this heart-warming and promising spectacle and led to invest their money in Dutch projects, then they are in need of an aid to clarify their vision: hence the box at the left with a great many "economic spectacles," free to test for any capitalist who needs them.

Dutch Reformist Societies and Economic Patriotism

While the two economic prints and companion drama pamphlet were unique in their artistic arrangements, they were far from unique in the ideas and feelings they conveyed. The same sentiments were expressed in other reformist responses to the economic and political crisis that the Republic was experiencing in those years, at least in the perception of its inhabitants. The viewpoints taken by Petrus and Burgerhart were therefore precisely what could be expected from the reformist milieu where the anonymous drawings and *Toneelspel* appear to have originated. The official dedication in the legends of the prints, and the title and contents of the pamphlet, indicate that both the graphic artist and the pamphleteer—assuming they were not the same person[15]—had a strong affinity to the objectives of the "Vaderlandsche Maatschappy van Redery en Koophandel" (National Society of Shipping and Commerce) and the "Oeconomische Tak der Hollandsche Maatschappy der Wetenschappen" (Economic Branch of the Holland Society of Sciences), two reformist societies established at Hoorn and Haarlem, respectively.

Haarlem was an industrial town near Amsterdam that had suffered greatly from the national decline in trade and industry, and the same was true for Hoorn, a more northerly seaport, also in the province of Holland. The appeal of both societies, however, surpassed the location of their foundation. Thanks to their economic and patriotic ideals, they attracted participating members from all over the country and from all walks of life. Soon after its formation, the Economic Branch had nearly 3,000 members and local departments in more than fifty Dutch towns and villages. The National Society of Shipping and Commerce, set up by Cornelis Ris, a Mennonite clergyman, followed another formula: members became stockholders and were obliged to invest at least 100 Dutch guilders. Five days after its inaugural meeting the society had 268 registered participants.[16]

The National Society of Shipping and Commerce and the Economic Branch were both founded in 1777 by reform-minded citizens actively involved in designing economic plans intended to put the Republic back on a firm footing. Participating members included well-to-do city councilors, wholesale merchants, and shipowners, as well as intellectuals, clergymen, retail merchants, and educated craftsmen. Their analyses and solutions for the economic situation in the Republic differed according to their background, but what all members shared was the profound conviction that the Dutch Republic was in great trouble and action was required. Although we cannot rule out the possibility that several of these economic patriots had personal investments in foreign stocks, the overall conviction in this milieu was that having Dutch capital channeled abroad, and therefore not invested in its own economy, was an important part of the Republic's problem. The discussions furthermore zeroed in on the question of whether the Dutch nation should try to regain its leading position in international commerce, and if so, how to realize that end. The issue entailed a reorientation toward industrial development and agricultural production in order to combat the omnipresent pauperism. In the years around 1780 it was not a foregone conclusion that Dutch international trade would never regain its former supremacy.[17]

Social and political discussions about the different paths to a flourishing economy were not reserved to the Dutch at the time. In Great Britain and all over continental Europe, people were debating—from different viewpoints—the elements that constituted the wealth of nations.[18] Concerned citizens tried to identify the causes that were hampering the further growth of trade, industry, and agriculture in their own countries. Mercantilists, industrialists, physiocrats, and Kameralists pursued the same goals, even if they did not opt for the same strategies. Rather than going into that broader international debate, however, I will concentrate on the Dutch part of it, as present in the prints and pamphlet at hand.[19]

Regarding the first economic print and the first act of the play, the pursuits and ideals of the National Society of Shipping and Commerce call for our attention. It cannot be a coincidence that the commodities that retailer Petrus had for sale at his stall (stockings, gloves, hats, cloth, baize, wallpaper, and, still in their packings, stoneware and carpets) were all products of the new factories set up by the National Society of Shipping and Commerce. Evidently, this society did not restrict its activities to shipping and commerce in order to stimulate the local economy and help the unemployed to a job. Petrus's express animosity toward British and French commodities was representative of a widespread sentiment among Dutch manufacturers about these unwanted competitors at the Dutch market. A number of patriotic authors believed that import duties could solve the problem, but for the time being the ruling elite, which had made its fortune in wholesale trade, obstructed this solution. It should be noted that no member of the cast in the prints and play advocated the remedy of a levy on imports. Instead, a plea was made for a more patriotic attitude among Dutch consumers and capitalists. The National Society of Shipping and Commerce had, furthermore, fitted out a whaling vessel and two ships for lumber trade. Not yielding enough profit, however, the ships were sold within five years after their purchase. A special "Konst-Schilder-en Behangselfabriek" (Art, Painting, and Wallpaper Factory) was one of the other projects. It had a number of graphic designers and painters in employment, thus providing us with several possible candidates for the anonymous hand that drew the economic prints.[20]

The contents of the second economic print and the second act seem more directly connected to the ideas of the Economic Branch. Modeled on the society instituted in London for the Encouragement of Arts, Manufacturers, and Commerce in 1754, the Economic Branch likewise issued essay competitions and prizes for practical solutions to economic problems. It even owed its own formation in 1777 to an earlier essay competition that the "Hollandsche Maatschappy voor Wetenschappen" (Holland Society of Sciences) at Haarlem had issued in 1771, asking what were the foundations of Dutch commerce, what were the causes of its decline, and what were the best means to improve its present condition.[21] Three of the thirteen essays that were sent in were awarded a medal and published in the *Transactions* of 1775. The prizewinning essay, written by Hendrik Herman van de Heuvel, registrar at the Court of Justice of Utrecht, suggested that the government should, on the one hand, offer the greatest possible liberty to Dutch transit trade and, on the other hand, protect the Dutch industry. Even more important, he argued for the encouragement of patriotic fervor among his fellow countrymen. He therefore proposed to transform the Holland Society of Sciences into a patriotic society, aiming first and foremost to stimulate the applied sciences and economic practices that would benefit the whole nation. This was one step too far for the (elite) directors of the Holland Society, who tended toward a more elevated and conservative approach of scientific matters at the time.[22] They did consent, however, to the formation of a separate branch that would concentrate on the new goal. From its start, members of the Economic Branch disagreed about the relative importance of the various economic sectors in their country. In time, its main initiator, Van de Heuvel, would distance himself from the belief, popular with the ruling commercial elites, that trade could play a key role in the resurrection of the Dutch economy. He increasingly emphasized the need for investments in agriculture and industry. The reclamation of heath lands, the resuscitation of porcelain and textile factories, and the impoldering of the Haarlemmermeer (a huge lake situated between Amsterdam, Haarlem, and Leiden)—all projects favored by Burgerhart in the *Toneelspel*—became part and parcel of a new ideology that appealed in particular to the middle-class members of the Economic Branch.[23]

The Economic Branch and the National Society of Shipping and Commerce were not the only Dutch reformist societies formed in those years, but together they represent the winds of change blowing through the Republic. Typically, the Dutch adjectives in the name of the two societies ("economisch" and "vaderlandsch") were virtually interchangeable at the time and almost identical to the adjectives used for the pairs of spectacles, offered to the myopic countrymen in the second economic print. While the inscription on the chest named them *economische brillen* (economic spectacles), the legend spoke of *inlandsche brillen* (native or national spectacles). This overlapping terminology is characteristic of the interaction of meanings found in the semantic field of the Dutch word *economisch* at the time: the word not only referred to economic matters in the strict sense of the word, but it was also used for other phenomena of a national, native, or domestic nature that were all seen as intricately related.[24] This brief excursion into Dutch conceptual history confirms that, by 1780, economic decisions about financial fortunes were no longer considered a private matter. Instead, they had become a matter of national discussion and interest.

THE TWO-SIDED AND GENDERED FACE OF THE DUTCH CAPITALIST

Small wonder, then, that the allocation of the accumulated "national" capital, symbolized by the money chest in both prints, was seen as a source of conflict between different parties, brilliantly represented by the cast of characters surrounding the chest in the prints and play. In the perception of concerned Dutchmen for whom Petrus acted as spokesman, Klaas and Burgerhart represented two different kind of rich men or *kapitalisten*.[25] On the one hand, Klaas embodied the short-sighted, careless egoistical rentier who put his money in foreign (government) bonds with a fixed interest, which he subsequently spent on luxury items imported from abroad. On the other hand, Burgerhart exemplified the visionary and yet prudent patriotic entrepreneur who reinvested all his capital in various Dutch ventures.[26] Whether these stereotypes carried any relation with economic reality of the time is not the issue here. Rather, the issue is what kind of role these contrasting images played in national self-representations of the Dutch. This particular case indicates that at the end of the eighteenth century, the Dutch capitalist carried a Janus face in Dutch national self-perceptions. A further analysis of this two-sided face from a gender perspective may help us to a deeper understanding of how patriotic Dutchmen perceived and represented the effects of capitalism in their country.

The second scene is dominated by the figure of Burgerhart, explicitly characterized as "honorable" in both the pamphlet and the legend of the print, standing his ground to foreign bankers and financiers. His pose is mirrored by the brave lion, a natural leader, defending his country. The lion, all skin and bones, has apparently gone through a rough time but is back in form and on top again. Similarly, the patriotic Burgerhart is in full control of the situation. He is setting the example to his fellow men, courageously investing his capital in native projects that reinforce Dutch economy. The central character in the first scene, on the other hand, is a far cry from a man in control. Klaas has no command over the course of his money chest, nor of his life, for that matter. Of middle-class birth he may be, but he prefers to imitate the polished and idle lifestyle of the French or frenchified aristocracy, including its conspicuous consumption, often dubbed effeminate in Dutch moral discourse at the time.[27] His mimicry, vanity, and inertia are mirrored by the sitting monkey of indefinite sex, holding a fashionable French feathered hat. Jean Poli and John Always Short encounter no difficulties in taking advantage of his youthful naiveté. At the same time Klaas also displays a youthful recklessness in sharp contrast to the manful maturity of Burgerhart. Klaas's refusal to behave in a responsible way is demonstrated in many details, but most revealingly in the duel that he—as a would-be gentleman—gets caught up in at the end of the first act.

This duel is a telling detail. The practice of dueling had been losing ground in Dutch culture for some time by then, as had the corresponding notion of honor, which equated male honor with readiness to defend one's name with the sword and keeping up outward appearances.[28] Both prints and pamphlet delivered a satirical commentary on the love that some men had for swords, and notably, hardly the manliest of the men present. In this they followed earlier Dutch theater plays from about 1720 that had juxtaposed the unreliability of swaggering wind-traders with their twisted sense of honor, symbolized in an ostensible fondness for the duel, which, naturally, the wind-traders always backed out of in the end.[29] Thus, the *Toneelspel*'s mocking of this particular notion of honor confirmed a development that was already present on different fronts. The satire also served to emphasize the more prudent character of Burgerhart, whose manners were taken to be more reflective of Dutch bourgeois standards. Burgerhart's honorability clearly represented a different notion of male honor, that of the merchant whose honor was defined by reason, integrity, and financial dependability—as the Dutch said: *een man een man, een woord een woord* ("an honest man's word is as good as his bond").[30]

The contrasting financial decisions of Klaas and Burgerhart were thus displayed in a gendered frame of reference, in which two different models of masculinity competed: the aristocratic model of the polite gentleman reminiscent of the noble knight, and the bourgeois model of the dependable merchant. The figures of the rentier and entrepreneur have been grafted onto this existing pair of opposing characters.[31] In the visual rhetoric of the prints and the textual dramatization in the pamphlet, the first got disqualified as superficial whereas the second was idealized as the good guy. Stereotypical ideas about gender, age, class, and national differences were used, furthermore, to present the entrepreneur as the true Dutchman and to reject the rentier as a degenerate.

Meanwhile, by wishfully emphasizing the honorability, courage, and patriotism of Burgerhart, the *auctores intellectuales* of print and pamphlet responded not only to a national economic crisis but also to internationally held unfavorable opinions of the commercial character of the Dutch. In early modern political and ethnographic discourse we can observe a strong current that depicted commercial societies as solely driven by a passion for profit that overtook all other passions, including the passions for honor, valor, or the fatherland. To be sure, this perception was especially strong in the Atlantic tradition of civic republicanism and contested by other authors.[32] But the notion that commerce threatened to make men immoral, weak, even effeminate, had existed since antiquity and was still very influential in anthropological works published around 1780.[33]

In the seventeenth and eighteenth centuries, elements of this ancient thinking had permeated travel accounts, letters, and histories voicing the opinion that Dutchmen have "little sense of honor, governing themselves more by the rules of profit and advantage, than of generosity and decorum," to quote, for instance, Sir Francis Barnham writing in the seventeenth century.[34] The Dutch were also said to lack in courage, preferring peace to war.[35] When in war, they left it to their allies and mercenary troops to defend them.[36] Dutchmen did not attach much value to military glory or national honor; divided among themselves, they seemed afraid of everything, concluded a disappointed John Adams when visiting the Republic in search of support for the American Revolutionary War.[37] And according to Johann Gottfried Herder, the behavior of the Dutch illustrated "how the spirit of commerce . . . neutralizes or diminishes the spirit of valor."[38] In Caesar's *De Bello Gallico* (50 BCE) and in Tacitus's *De origine et situ Germanorum* (ca. 100 CE) the ancient inhabitants of the Low Countries had still been courageous fighters, but their descendants had lost this strength of character.[39] As Sir William Temple had written in his *Observations upon the United Provinces of the Netherlands* in 1673: "not only the long disuse of arms among the native *Hollanders* (especially at land), and making use of other nations chiefly in their milice [military], but the arts of trade, as well as peace, and their great parsimony in diet . . . may have helpt to debase much the ancient valour of the nation."[40]

Obviously, according to the background of the authors and the moment of their writing, opinions would differ. As longtime neighbors, "disowned" allies, and rivals at sea, the English were not the only critics of the Dutch, though they certainly were the fiercest. In the seventeenth century they coined expressions such as "Dutch defense" for a treacherous surrender and "Dutch courage" for the pot-valor of a drunk. This was typically the only valor one could occasionally observe among the Dutch, the English would claim.[41] Authors of other nations often expressed more favorable views, at least as far as Dutch militarism was concerned.[42] Dutch greed was another matter.[43]

More Dutch Responses

There are striking similarities between this characterizing of the Dutch and the portrait of Klaas or, in the same category, the character of the egoistic and spineless rentier omnipresent in other Dutch writings. By contrast, the portrait of Burgerhart or, similarly, the overall image of the enterprising merchant in Dutch discourse had nothing in common with this unflattering portrait of the Dutch character. Quite the contrary. Burgerhart and his fellow entrepreneurs, whether mercantile or industrial, were generally presented as genuine Dutchmen who were true to the original Dutch character that was asserted to be essentially honorable, bold, and patriotic. Clearly, Dutch authors, wishing to restore the strength and self-confidence of their nation, were not impervious to the accusations of national dishonor, weakness, and pusillanimity. Let us listen to a few more Dutch voices from the period.

Take, as an example, Simon Stijl, son of a Frisian fur shipper and author of a historical work about the Dutch Republic published in 1774. He acknowledged that the Dutch had not always acted as manfully as they could have. To say that they generally lacked courage, however, seemed disproportionate to him. Obviously, a trading republic had to seek a balance between peaceful coexistence and the readiness to fight when needed. Stijl conceded that perhaps on land the militancy required had sometimes been insufficient, but at sea the Dutch had amply proved their courage. Dutch history had also shown how commercial power and war power could mutually reinforce each other. If matters had changed lately, Stijl argued, it was because affluence had introduced haughtiness, splendor, and luxury to the Republic. Misled by the international standard of (false) politeness, the Dutch had started to develop despicable preferences. A change in educational goals should provide the remedy to this imitation of alien manners.[44]

Another Dutchman, Engelbertus Engelberts, believed that the international animadversions were inspired by jealousy. In 1763, this reformed clergyman at Hoorn, member of the prestigious Holland Society of Sciences, had published a laudatory pamphlet on the Dutch character defending it against what he considered unjust British criticism during the Seven Years' War when the Republic had remained uncommitted.[45] Engelberts claimed that the British were inconsistent, illogical, and historically unjust in their accusations. As the clergyman contended, the British might wish that *they* could boast the bravery the Dutch had demonstrated in their history. Indeed, it was part of the Dutch system to avoid war if it would damage their commerce and prosperity. But the Republic deserved praise and not scorn for the fact that it did not immediately take up arms at every trifle.[46]

When Engelberts published a second edition in 1776, however, he added an extensive epilogue in which he expressed more ambivalent words about the Dutch character. If he had neglected the weaknesses of the Dutch too much in the first edition, he explained, he had done so for didactic reasons. Better to emphasize virtues than to expand on vices that might give the youth the wrong ideas. Engelberts would not deny that in some respects the Dutch were not in the same league as the British, the Germans, the French, or the Italians. Especially politeness was not one of their strengths, even if his countrymen and women had become more polite and soft over the course of time, a consequence of the sustained freedom, peace, commerce, affluence, and interaction with other nations, particularly with the French who were masters of politeness. But, the clergyman asked rhetorically, were they a better kind of people for that? Better than the genuine Dutchman, who "coupled his imagined coarseness to an honest nature, pure morals, dignified behavior . . . a noble longing for liberty, bold actions, unfailing loyalty, prudent consideration of receipts and expenses, generous hospitality, and a caring charity to the needy?" In his opinion politeness should not be confused with true virtue, and therefore the lack of it could not be considered a Dutch shortcoming. Rather, Engelberts thought that luxury and the recent adoption of foreign manners and ideas were at the heart of the present problems of the Dutch Republic.[47]

And then there was the publisher and book trader Elie Luzac, who in the years 1780–83 wrote and published the four-volume *Hollands rijkdom*, an adaptation of *La richesse de la Hollande* written by Jacques Accarias de Sérionne and published by Luzac in 1778. In this work Luzac defended commercial society in general, and the Dutch in particular, against classical republican criticisms. Influenced by Montesquieu's idea of *le doux commerce*, he stated that merchants were men of multiple skills whose competition and activities led to prosperity, sociable people, and peaceful relations between nations. However, as the merchant was driven by his desire for profit, Luzac argued, one could not expect him to act from benevolence, patriotism, or any other moral principle. As much as the manufacturer, the scholar, and the soldier, the merchant had to be looked upon as a specialist. Specialization had narrowed the merchant's personality, made him less courageous and less charitable, Luzac was ready to acknowledge. Still, as long as the merchant's income provided the means to keep up a standing army and a strong navy, his country was not necessarily at risk. It was the task of the government to organize a commercial state's defense and to promote its general interest. As a defender of the political institution of the stadholderate and genuine believer in the blessings of luxury, Luzac differed in opinion from his Dutch patriotic fellow countrymen in more than one respect. But he shared their belief that contemporary Dutch values had changed, and not for the better. According to Luzac, the true spirit of commerce was threatened by ubiquitous desire for social status, which expressed itself among the sons of merchants in contempt for hard and honest work, in conspicuous consumption, and in imitation of French morals and manners.[48]

The writings of Stijl, Engelberts, and Luzac make clear that the portrait of the young merchant's son Klaas that we came across in the economic prints and pamphlet was constructed from fixed elements, easy to recognize for contemporaries who were familiar with the debate on Dutch decline. This debate had been going on for at least half a century by that time, chiefly taking place in the Dutch "spectatorial press," which was made up of dozens of moral weeklies in the tradition of the famous *Spectator* (1711–12), written by Steele and Addison.

The Dutch moral weeklies consistently blamed the economic and political decline on a national decay of morals. The decay was believed to have started at the end of the seventeenth century when wealthy Dutchmen and women had started to give in to the temptations of luxury. While most Dutch intellectuals expressed the belief that luxury caused moral weakness and decline, they did not see luxury as the inevitable side effect of successful commerce. They did not make the connection between commerce and the corruption of morals that was made elsewhere. After all, notwithstanding their wealth, their seventeenth-century ancestors had been more famous for making of money than spending it.[49] Neither did Dutch spectatorial authors perceive the Dutch merchants as solely driven by a passion for money that overtook all other passions, including the passions for honor, valor, or the fatherland. Rather, they glorified the Dutch merchant as one of the main pillars of the Republic, with well-developed sentiments of human and civic responsibility. Unfortunately, in the course of the eighteenth century those virtuous merchants had become rarer and rarer in the Republic. Copying foreign customs and manners, the spectatorial authors contended, the Dutch too had started to develop a propensity for aristocratic, arrogant, artificial behavior.[50]

CONCLUSION

This intellectual environment, complemented by the reformist societies, produced the economic prints and companion pamphlet, and they artistically expressed the patriotic economic ideas that were in vogue at the moment. Concurrently, they struck back at other European countries that were felt to be sneering at the plain style and commercial mind of the Dutch and still wanting to take advantage of the Republic's accumulated riches. If lately the younger Dutch generations, personified by Klaas, had stopped following traditional national standards, pictures and text suggested, it was because of the greediness of foreign bankers and investors who were after the Dutch money, the cheap products of British manufacturers who ruined the market for trade in Dutch top-quality products, and the misleading manners of the effeminate French who posed as the cultural masters of the universe. The anonymous maker(s) of the economic prints and drama pamphlets, nevertheless, wishfully claimed that there were still wealthy Dutchmen who could ánd would make the difference—men such as Burgerhart who paired patriotism and honor with an authentic Dutch spirit of enterprise, boldly and yet prudently investing in Dutch ventures, giving the national economy the financial injection that it needed. If trade was perhaps not the best route to economic success anymore, the former merchants could transform themselves into industrial and agricultural entrepreneurs.

Thus, Dutch patriotic economic discourse was not only idealizing the glorious commercial past of the Republic, and still identifying the genuine Dutch character with the character of the Dutch merchant, but it was also blaming foreigners for Dutch moral and economic weaknesses, and transferring disreputable economic behavior to other groups of economic agents such as bankers and rentiers.[51] In the past decades modern economic historians have, of course, produced more factual and sophisticated analyses of the Republic's economic problems.[52] More interesting in relation to the self-perceptions of early modern capitalists, however, is the conclusion that economic acts were presented in a gendered frame of reference with two competing, class-biased standards of male honor. The classical and aristocratic idea, popular abroad, that commercial states were crowded with dishonorable men who shunned confrontation, was countered by the bourgeois invention of the Dutch merchant/entrepreneur as a deeply honorable, bold, and socially responsible capitalist. The problem of the two conflicting self-perceptions of Dutch capitalism was dealt with by simply eliminating the most troubling one, the rentier, as a native capitalist model.

NOTES

1. See Jonathan Israel, *Dutch Primacy in World Trade, 1585–1740* (Oxford: Clarendon, 1989), and Jonathan Israel, *The Dutch Republic: Its Rise, Greatness, and Fall, 1477–1806* (Oxford: Clarendon, 1995); Jan de Vries and Ad van der Woude, *The First Modern Economy: Success, Failure, and Perseverance of the Dutch Economy, 1500–1815* (Cambridge: Cambridge University Press, 1997); Julia Adams, *The Familial State: Ruling Families and Merchant Capitalism in Early Modern Europe* (Ithaca, NY: Cornell University Press, 2005).
2. See the contribution of Clé Lesger to this book.
3. For the changes in distribution of economic surplus, see Jan Luiten van Zanden, *The Rise and Decline of Holland's Economy: Merchant Capitalism and the Labour Market* (Manchester: Manchester University Press, 1993).
4. See Willem Frijhoff, "Het zelfbeeld van de Nederlander in de achttiende eeuw, een inleiding," *De Achttiende Eeuw* 24 (1992): 5–28, esp. p. 12.
5. *Toneel-spel in twee afdeelingen, ziende op de twee konstplaaten, toegewyd aan alle de leden van de loffelyke Vaderlandsche Maatschappy te Hoorn, en van den Oeconomischen Tak der Hollandsche Maatschappy te Haarlem. Waar in alle de persoonen, in de gemelde plaaten voorkomende, spreekende ingevoerd worden. Zynde een werkje, ten hoogste noodzakelyk, om een waar denkbeeld van gemelde plaaten en Neêrlands belangen te krygen. Als mede van de kunstplaat, tot tytel voerende: De Tyd geeft Verandering. Door een Vriend des Vaderlands in de smaak der schrandere Graave van Nassau la Leck en de Heere Schatz [sic] in een vloeibare en aangenaame styl geschreeven* (Amsterdam: Dirk Schuurman, 1780).
6. I am very much indebted to Henk Gras and Klaartje Groot who checked the archival sources in Rotterdam and Amsterdam (1774–1811) for me. The play is also not recorded in the playing list in Paul Bordewijk, ed., *Wat geeft die Comedie toch een bemoeijing! de Leidse schouwburg 1705–*2005 (Amsterdam: Boom, 2005), nor in Henny Ruitenbeek, *Kijkcijfers: de Amsterdamse schouwburg 1814–1841* (Hilversum: Verloren, 2002).
7. J. A. Worp, *Geschiedenis van het drama en van het toneel in Nederland* (Rotterdam: Langerveld 1903–7), 2:179–82.
8. See, for Dutch print culture at the time, N.C.F. van Sas, "Eigen en vreemd. Internationale verhoudingen en prentcultuur rondom 1800," Bram Kempers, ed., *Openbaring en bedrog. De afbeelding als historische bron in de Lage Landen* (Amsterdam: Amsterdam University Press, 1995), 147–68.
9. Collection of prints Atlas van Stolk, Rotterdam, nos. 4318 and 4322.
10. Another indication of their popularity is the fact that these two prints were among the fifteen selected prints that were redrawn and collectively reproduced in one large assembled engraving, the "Algemeene

Staatkundige Konstplaat van 't Jaar 1780," Atlas van Stolk, no. 4329. For this engraving, see Van Sas, "Eigen en vreemd," 147–50.

11. Clé Lesger, "Stagnatie en stabiliteit. De economie tussen 1730 en 1795," W. Frijhoff and M. Prak, eds., *Geschiedenis van Amsterdam. Zelfbewuste stadstaat 1650–1813* (Amsterdam: SUN, 2004), 219–65, reproduction at p. 226; J. J. Kloek, "Letteren en landsbelang," F. Grijzenhout, W. W. Mijnhardt, and N.C.F. van Sas, eds., *Voor vaderland en vrijheid. De revolutie van de patriotten* (Amsterdam: De Bataafsche Leeuw, 1987), 81–97, reproduction at p. 81; W. Fritschy, "De patriottenbeweging in Nederland. Een verzetsbeweging tegen een financiële oligarchie?" Th.S.M. van der Zee, J.G.M.M. Rosendaal, and P.G.B. Thissen, eds., *1787. De Nederlandse revolutie?* (Amsterdam: De Bataafsche Leeuw, 1988), 52–69, reproduction at p. 67.

12. Our informed guess is that the text was written by Nicolaas François Hoefnagel (1735–84), a hack who linked his career to the Patriots' cause when their reformist campaign started to gather momentum. He published numerous political and economic-political pamphlets with publisher Dirk Schuurman, including some drama pamphlets. He also wrote more than one national plan of reform, including the *Plan ter verbetering van Neêrlands Zee-weezen* (Amsterdam: Dirk Schuurman), which figured prominently in the *Toneelspel* where it was praised abundantly. On Hoefnagel, see A. J. Hanou, "Een 18e-eeuws broodschrijver: Nicolaas François Hoefnagel (1735–84)," *Spektator* 2 (1972–73): 62–81, 535–48. His bibliography was published by Hanou in *Documentatieblad Achttiende Eeuw* (1973) 18:21–43, and 21:15–38.

13. See *Woordenboek der Nederlandsche Taal* (The Hague: Nijhoff, 1882–1998), entry "Klaas," meaning B3b.

14. See Bram Kempers, "Assemblage van de Nederlandse leeuw. Politieke symboliek in heraldiek en verhalende prenten van de zestiende eeuw," Bram Kempers, ed., *Openbaring en bedrog. De afbeelding als historische bron in de Lage Landen* (Amsterdam: Amsterdam University Press, 1995), 60–100, esp. p. 94.

15. Nicolaas Hoefnagel, possibly the author (see note 12), started his career as a painter and was still occasionally publishing political pictures in 1782. See Hanou, "Een 18e-eeuws broodschrijver," 69–70, and Hanou, "Een dood van Klaas Hoefnagel," *Mededelingen van de Stichting Jacob Campo Weyerman* 27 (2004): 35–36.

16. See J. Bierens de Haan, *Van Oeconomische Tak tot Nederlandsche Maatschappij voor Handel en Nijverheid, 1777–1952* (Groningen: Tjeenk Willink, 1952), 10–11; H.F.J.M. van den Eerenbeemt, *Armoede en arbeidsdwang. Werkinrichtingen voor "onnutte" Nederlanders in de Republiek, 1760–1795. Een mentaliteitsgeschiedenis* (The Hague: Nijhoff, 1977), 102–3.

17. W. W. Mijnhardt, *Tot heil van 't menschdom. Culturele genootschappen in Nederland, 1750–1815* (Amsterdam: Rodopi, 1987), 106–16; Bierens

de Haan, *Oeconomische Tak*, 28, 31, 50. On the actual size of the capital drain at the time, see De Vries and Van der Woude, *First Modern Economy*, chap. 4.3 and 4.4.

18. See Margaret C. Jacob, *Scientific Culture and the Making of the Industrial West* (New York and Oxford: Oxford University Press, 1997), 131–64.
19. For a broader discussion of the development of Dutch economic thinking, see Ida J. A. Nijenhuis, "De ontwikkeling van het politiek-economische vrijheidsbegrip in de Republiek," E.O.G. Haitsma Mulier and W.R.E. Velema, eds., *Vrijheid. Een geschiedenis van de vijftiende tot de twintigste eeuw* (Amsterdam: Amsterdam University Press, 1999), 233–52.
20. See Eerenbeemt, *Armoede en arbeidsdwang*, 98–113.
21. See J. G. de Bruijn, *Inventaris van de Prijsvragen uitgeschreeven door de Hollandsche Maatschappij der Wetenschappen, 1753–1917* (Groningen: Tjeenk Willink, 1977), 44.
22. De Bruijn, *Inventaris*, passim. See also Jacob, *Scientific Culture*, 147.
23. See Bierens de Haan, *Oeconomische Tak*, 1–16, 24–76; and Mijnhardt, *Tot heil*, 109–10.
24. See Kloek, "Letteren en landsbelang," 85, 88, 90, and Ellen Krol, "Over 'den Meridiaan des huisselyken levens' in *Sara Burgerhart*," *Spektator* 20 (1991): 237–44, esp. pp. 237–40.
25. The word *kapitalist* (or "capitalist" in ancient Dutch spelling) was used as early as 1673 in the Dutch periodical *De Hollandsche Mercurius* (1651–91) to denominate in a neutral sense a man of great fortune. See *Woordenboek der Nederlandsche Taal* (The Hague: Nijhoff, 1882–1998), entry "kapitalist." An early example of the word as a term of abuse for a rentier in Dutch can be found in the legend of the political print "De tyd geeft verandering," dated 1780, from the collection Atlas van Stolk, Rotterdam, no. 4319.
26. This juxtaposition has a forerunner in late medieval economic thought that opposed the social inutility or sinfulness of uninvested wealth to the social or civic utility of circulating money. See Giacomo Todeschini, *I mercanti e il tempio. La società cristiana e il circolo virtuoso della ricchezza fra Medioevo ed Èta Moderna* (Bologna: il Mulino, 2002), 311ff., and Odd Langholm, *Economics in Medieval Schools: Wealth, Exchange, Values, Money, and Usury According to the Paris Theological Tradition, 1200–1350* (Leiden: Brill, 1992), passim.
27. See Dorothee Sturkenboom, *Spectators van hartstocht. Sekse en emotionele cultuur in de achttiende eeuw* (Hilversum: Verloren, 1998), 209–14.
28. See Herman Roodenburg, *The Eloquence of the Body: Perspectives on Gesture in the Dutch Republic* (Zwolle: Waanders, 2004), 93–99; and Pieter Spierenburg, *Written in Blood: Fatal Attraction in Enlightenment Amsterdam* (Columbus: Ohio State University Press, 2004), 17–18.
29. See Dorothee Sturkenboom, "Staging the Merchant. Commercial Vices and the Politics of Stereotyping in Early Modern Dutch Theatre," *Dutch Crossing* 30 (2006): 211–28.

30. For the professional roots of this notion of honor, see L. Kooijmans, "De koopman," H. M. Beliën, A. T. van Deursen, and G.J. van Setten, eds., *Gestalten van de Gouden Eeuw. Een Hollands groepsportret* (Amsterdam: Bakker, 1995), 65–92, esp. pp. 70, 78–83; G. Verhoeven, "Het vertrouwen geschonden. Ondernemerscultuur van de Antwerpse uitgevers Moretus en Verdussen (1665–1675)," *De Zeventiende Eeuw* 21 (2005): 375–95, esp. pp. 391–95; Mary Poovey, "Accommodating Merchants: Accounting, Civility, and the Natural Laws of Gender," *Representations* 8, no.3 (1996): 1–20, esp. pp. 13–14; John Smail, "Credit, Risk, and Honor in Eighteenth-Century Commerce," *Journal of British Studies* 44 (2005): 439–56, esp. pp. 446–52.
31. See, for the same juxtaposition in other contexts and from more socially informed perspectives, the papers of John Smail and Leos Müller in this book.
32. See, for example, J.G.A. Pocock, *Virtue, Commerce, and History: Essays on Political Thought and History, Chiefly in the Eighteenth Century* (Cambridge: Cambridge University Press 1985), 101–123; Tjitske Akkerman, *Women's Vices, Public Benefits: Women and Commerce in the French Enlightenment* (Amsterdam: Spinhuis, 1992), 18–21; Harold Mah, *Enlightenment Phantasies: Cultural Identity in France and Germany, 1750–1914* (Ithaca and London: Cornell University Press, 2003), 19–25; Daniel Tröhler, "Switzerland and the Netherlands in the Eighteenth Century. The Republican Discourse of Public Virtues," *De Achttiende Eeuw* 37 (2005): 90–104. See also Martin van Gelderen and Quentin Skinner, eds., *Republicanism: A Shared European Heritage* (Cambridge: Cambridge University Press, 2002), vol. 2, part III: "Republicanism and the Rise of Commerce."
33. See André Liquier, *Discours qui a remporté le prix de l'Academie de Marseille, en 1777, sur cette question: "Quelle a été dans tous les temps l'influence du commerce sur l'esprit et sur les moeurs des peuples?"* (Marseille: Brebion, 1778), 1, 24–26; William Falconer, *Remarks on the Influence of Climate, Situation, Nature of Country, Population, Nature of Food, and Way of Life on the Disposition and Temper, Manners and Behaviour, Intellects, Laws and Customs, Form of Government, and Religion of Mankind* (London: Dilly, 1781), 409–12, 514–18; Azémor, *Considérations sur l'influence des moeurs dans l'état militaire des nations* (Londres: 1788), 278–79.
34. Quoted in John Ray, *Travels Through the Low Countries, Germany, Italy, and France, with Curious Observations, Natural, Topographical, Moral, Physiological &c.* (London: Hughs, [1673] 1738), 47. See also William Temple, *Observations upon the United Provinces of the Netherlands* (London: A. Maxwell, 1673), 164; R. Murris, *La Hollande et les Hollandais au XVIIe et au XVIIIe siècles vus par les Français* (Paris: Champion, 1925), 63, 67; A.C.J. de Vrankrijker, *In andermans ogen* (Utrecht: Spectrum, 1942), 44.
35. See, for example, Barnham, quoted in Ray, *Travels*, 46; John Reresby, *The Memoirs and Travels of John Reresby* (London: Jeffery and Rodwell,

1813), 159. Owen Felltham, however, maintained that the Dutch were war-minded, but in their hearts cowards; see his *A Brief Character of the Low Countries under the States* (London: Henry Seile, 1652), Graeme Watson, ed., *Dutch Crossings* 27 (2003): 89–141, esp. pp. 118, 120.

36. See Falconer, *Remarks on the Influence*, 407; *An Exact Survey of the Affairs of the United Netherlands* (London: Thomas Mabb, 1665), 175–80; Denis Diderot, *Voyage en Hollande* [1773–1774], Yves Benot, ed. (Paris: Maspero, 1982), 56–57; Charles Pierre Coste d'Arnobat, *Voyage au pays de Bambouc, suivi d'observations intéressantes sur les castes indiennes, sur la Hollande, et sur l'Angleterre* (Brussels: Dujardin, 1789), 173–81, 229–32.

37. John Adams, for example, in his letter to the Continental Congress of America of May 16, 1781, and letter to Abigail Adams of September 15, 1780. See for the first letter *The Revolutionary Diplomatic Correspondence of the United States, edited by Francis Wharton* (Washington: 1889) IV, 420; for the second letter *The Book of Abigail and John: Selected Letters of the Adams Family, 1762-1784, with an introduction by L.H. Butterfield, Marc Friendländer, Mary-Jo Kline* (Cambridge: Harvard University Press, 1975) 270.

38. See Johann Gottfried Herder, *Journal meiner Reise im Jahr 1769*, *Pädagogische Schriften*, Rainer Wisbert, ed., series *Werke*, vol. 9/2 (Frankfurt am Main: Deutscher Klassiker Verlag, 1997), 76 (my translation). See also Liquier, *Discours*, 15, 19, 72–73; Coste d'Arnobat, *Voyage*, 179–184; Azémor, *Considérations*, 140; and finally the Swiss Johann Heinrich Füssli, quoted in Tröhler, "Switzerland and the Netherlands," 92–93.

39. See, for example, Christian Kirchner, *Holland oder Beschreibung der Sieben Vereinigten Niederländischen Provintzen* (Leipzig: Kirchner 1672), 3, 6.

40. See Temple, *Observations*, 158–59.

41. See Reresby, *Memoirs and Travels*, 159, and *Exact Survey*, 180, 182–83.

42. See, for example, Lodovico Guicciardini, *Descrittione di tutti i Paesi Bassi, altrimenti detti Germania Inferiore*, 3rd ed. (Aversa: 1588), 39–40; J. N. Jacobsen Jensen, ed., "Moryson's reis door en zijn karakteristiek van de Nederlanden," *Bijdragen en Mededelingen van het Historisch Genootschap* 39 (1918): 214–305, esp. pp. 286–87; John Andrews, *A Review of the Characters of the Principal Nations in Europe* (London: Cadell, 1770), 2:127–32, 148, 245; Carlo Antonio Pilati di Tassulo, *Lettres sur la Hollande* (La Haye: Munnikhuizen and Plaat, 1780), 120–22; Pierre-Sylvain Maréchal, *Costumes civils actuels de tous les peuples connus, dessinés d'après nature, gravé et coloriés [par J. Grasset de Saint Sauveur]. Accompagnés d'une notice historique sur leurs coutumes, mœurs, religions, &c.&c.* (Paris: Knapen and Fils, 1788), 1; Azémor, *Considérations*, 163–64. For other French and German authors of this opinion, see also Murris, *La Hollande*, 80, and Anja Chales de Beaulieu, *Deutsche Reisende in den*

Niederlanden. Das Bild eines Nachbarn zwischen 1648 und 1795 (Frankfurt am Main: Peter Lang, 2000), 207, 213–14.

43. See Julia Bientjes, *Holland und der Holländer im Urteil Deutscher Reisender 1400–1800* (Groningen: Wolters, 1967), 225–26; and Madeleine van Strien-Chardonneau, *Le voyage de Hollande: récits de voyageurs français dans les Provinces-Unies 1748–1795* (Oxford: Voltaire Foundation, 1994), 257.
44. See Simon Stijl, *Opkomst en bloei van de Republiek der Vereenigde Nederlanden, voorafgegaan door eene verhandeling over de opkomst en den ondergang van oude en hedendaagsche Republieken* (Amsterdam and Harlingen: Petrus Conradi and Folkert van der Plaats, 1774), 497–98, 537–619, 663–64, 676–88.
45. N.C.F. van Sas, "De vaderlandse imperatief. Begripsverandering en politieke conjunctuur, 1763–1813," N.C.F. van Sas, ed., *Vaderland. Een geschiedenis vanaf de vijftiende eeuw tot 1940* (Amsterdam: Amsterdam University Press, 1999), 275–308, esp. pp. 279–83.
46. E. M. Engelberts, *Verdediging van de eer der Hollandsche natie*, 2nd ed. (Amsterdam: Yntema and Tieboel, 1776), 24–25, 33–34, 42, 59–60, 64–66.
47. Engelberts, *Verdediging*, 59–62, 89–111, quotation taken from p. 89 (my translation).
48. See Wyger R. E. Velema, *Enlightenment and Conservatism in the Dutch Republic: The Political Thought of Elie Luzac (1721–1796)* (Assen and Maastricht: Van Gorcum, 1993), 114–43.
49. See Irma Thoen, *Strategic Affection: Gift Exchange in Seventeenth-Century Holland* (Amsterdam: Amsterdam University Press, 2006), 17.
50. See Sturkenboom, *Spectators van hartstocht*, 201–14, 309–13; and Wijnand W. Mijnhardt, "The Dutch Enlightenment: Humanism, Nationalism, and Decline," Margaret C. Jacob and Wijnand W. Mijnhardt, eds., *The Dutch Republic in the Eighteenth Century: Decline, Enlightenment, and Revolution* (Ithaca/London: Cornell University Press, 1992), 197–223, esp. pp. 205–11. For Dutch ideas about luxury, see also Ida Nijenhuis, "De weelde als deugd?" *De Achttiende Eeuw* 24 (1992): 45–56.
51. Some Dutch authors were fair enough to recognize that in the past, Dutch commerce had greatly benefited from the flow of immigrants into the Republic. Even Engelberts acknowledged this fact, although it would not change his opinion in the end. See his *Verdediging*, 55, 88–89. See furthermore J. Le Francq van Berkhey, *Natuurlijke historie van Holland* (Amsterdam: Yntema and Tieboel, 1769–1778), 3:422–28.
52. See, for example, Jan Luiten van Zanden and Arthur van Riel, *The Strictures of Inheritance: The Dutch Economy in the Nineteenth Century* (Princeton, NJ: Princeton University Press, 2004). See also Adams, *Familial State*, 137–63, for a more sociological and gender-informed analysis.

Part III

Capitalism as Normative

Chapter 5

"Merchants" and "Gentlemen" in Eighteenth-Century Sweden

Worlds of Jean Abraham Grill

Leos Müller, Uppsala University

A merchant is accustomed to employ his money chiefly in profitable projects; whereas a mere country gentleman is accustomed to employ it chiefly in expense. The one often sees his money go from him, and return to him again with a profit; the other, when once he parts with it, very seldom expects to see any more of it. Those different habits naturally affect their temper and disposition in every sort of business. The merchant is commonly a bold, a country gentleman, a timid undertaker. The one is not afraid to lay out at once a large capital upon the improvement of his land, when he has a probable prospect of raising the value of it in proportion to the expense; the other, if he has any capital, which is not always the case, seldom ventures to employ it in this manner. If he improves at all, it is commonly not with a capital, but with what he can save out of his annual revenue. Whoever has had the fortune to live in a mercantile town, situated in an unimproved country, must have frequently observed how much more spirited the operations of merchants were in this way, than those of mere country gentlemen. The habits, besides, of order, economy, and attention, to which mercantile business naturally forms a merchant, render him much fitter to execute, with profit and success, any project of improvement.

Adam Smith[1]

INTRODUCTION[2]

Adam Smith made a clear distinction between the entrepreneurial "merchants" and country "gentlemen." The quotation indicates clearly on which side his sympathy lay: the first elite was favorable for economic development, whereas the second one was not. Smith's dichotomy between entrepreneurial merchants and spending gentlemen reflects his view of commerce as a dynamic economic sector, and the men of commerce as men valuable to the whole society. This view, however, was not uncontested. The early modern history of economic thought is full of controversies on the role of commerce and merchants. Classical mercantilist thought perceived commerce—especially foreign trade—as an important source of ready money that should be supported. Overseas commerce was easy to control and tax; in addition, it could rapidly expand. But commerce could also draw on the country's resources, not least silver, if the luxury imports were to be bought.

Smith's view of merchants as important actors for wealth creation goes back to the beginning of the eighteenth century, when we may notice a rising diversity in the views on commerce, merchants, and consumption of luxury goods. For example, Daniel Defoe expressed similar views to those of Smith about stagnant agriculture and beneficial commerce. Agriculture, according to Defoe, was a stable and secure but not very dynamic sector. Thus, if a state wished to increase its wealth—and revenues—it should support foreign trade.[3] But expansion of foreign trade meant also increasing consumption of luxuries. The traditional bullionist view of trade was hostile to imports.[4] This view influenced mercantilist perception of imports of luxury commodities and their consumption patterns. But this traditional thinking came under contest in the eighteenth century. In Britain, the most controversial contribution to the debate was Bernard de Mandeville's famous *Fable of the Bees* (1714). But even rather backward and poor Sweden, which is the focus of this chapter, had similar discussions in the mid-eighteenth century on the benefits and harm of consumption. In 1741, Anders Johan von Höpken published his *Speech About the Luxury's Benefit*, in which he defended Mandeville's ideas.[5]

Beneficial or harmful effects of consumption and the roles of dynamic trade and stagnant agriculture have puzzled scholars since Defoe's and Smith's time. Recently, historians of the consumer revolution have stressed consumption's role in the transition to an industrial society. The authors of *Birth of a Consumer Society* have argued that a consumer revolution had to precede industrial revolution. Thus, the better way of understanding the shift to the sustainable economic growth is the study of consumption, in particular the question how and why early modern consumption had increased.[6]

Also Smith's dichotomy between merchants and gentlemen survived to be emulated. At the beginning of the twentieth century, the Italian sociologist Vilfredo Pareto made a similar distinction between entrepreneurs and rentiers in his analysis of elites. However, Pareto primarily stressed entrepreneurs' willingness to take risks and to make change. According to him, entrepreneurs are "adventurous souls, hungry for novelty in the economic as well as in social field." Rentiers are afraid of change. They invest carefully, preferring safety before profitability.[7] Economic development was not important for Pareto, and so he did not characterize entrepreneurs in a more favorable light than rentiers. The two represented for him just different elite strategies of upholding power and status in different historical situations. One strategy was more appropriate in one situation, while the other was probably more successful in another situation. In the long run, according to Pareto, there was a functional equilibrium between the two elites.

British historian Peter Burke applied Pareto's dichotomy in his classical study of merchant elites in Venice and Amsterdam, and he stressed the connection between the preferred strategies and the specific historical circumstances of Venice and Amsterdam. The majority of the Venice merchant elite behaved as rentiers—or "country gentlemen," in Smith's words—because this behavior was the best strategy in the stagnating world of seventeenth-century Venice. Amsterdam, in the same period, was the center of expanding European and world trade and thus a place in which more risky entrepreneurial behavior was to be preferred. The behavior of the Amsterdam urban elite, which earned its income mainly from trade, was entrepreneurial. However—and this is interesting in relation to the discussion about a consumer revolution—both groups marked their elite status by consumption.

I suggest that to overcome Smith's dichotomy between merchants and gentlemen we should employ the concept of social reproduction as the general motive of entrepreneurial behavior in early modern period. This concept points at the rather plain fact that the major aim of any early modern economic activity, as Julia Adams has shown, was the survival of the family. In this sense a merchant firm did not differ from a craftsman's or peasant's household. The concept asserts that the modern division between family and firm is inadequate for the early modern period. Social reproduction includes, in addition to biological reproduction, also a social and cultural reproduction, the transfer of values, ideas, knowledge, and status between generations. In other words, this might be expressed as continuity or improvement of the family's wealth, power, and prestige.[8]

The concept of social reproduction may be perceived as too general. The statements that men build families and that parents support their children are hardly revolutionary. However, the concept is useful for our understanding of entrepreneurial behavior of the early modern family firm, the predominant form of business organization in the period. The logic of the family business does not strictly follow the premise of classical economics, with profit as the dominant motive of economic activity, because the long-term survival of the family is more important than the short-term profitability of the firm.[9]

Motives of entrepreneurial behavior of an early modern merchant are also much more complex than the logic of profitability suggests. This chapter enlightens the complexity of early modern entrepreneurial behavior with the example of Jean Abraham Grill (1736–92), a Swedish merchant and supercargo in the service of the Swedish East India Company, and eventually a land and ironworks owner. I will look at his self-perception, career choices, and career and family life through the above-discussed dichotomy, and I will show how he could play different roles depending on specific situations in his life, so that during one part of his life he might be described as a risk-taking merchant/entrepreneur, while during another period he might be characterized as a typical country gentleman/rentier—a Swedish nabob.

The following account of Grill's business career and family life is based mainly on the copybooks in his personal archives, and it roughly follows the three phases of Jean Abraham's life: the period of the "French exile" (1756–60), the period in the service of the Swedish East India Company (1761–69), and the life of a country gentleman after the company service (1769–92). The focus is mainly on the correspondence with his close relatives because these letters show more private and personal sides of the letterwriter.[10] But first I have to present the man and his family and put him in the context of Sweden's eighteenth-century history.

JEAN ABRAHAM GRILL'S FAMILY AND BUSINESS CAREERS

Jean Abraham Grill belongs to a well-established Swedish mercantile family, with Dutch-German, perhaps even Italian roots. According to the family tradition, the Swedish and Dutch Grills were related to the well-known medieval Genoese family Grillo.[11] However, the first known records about the family relate to the Augsburg wine merchant Andreas Grill in 1571. By 1600, the Grills, like many other German merchants, moved to Amsterdam, and in 1659 the first member of the family, Anthony Grill, settled in Stockholm. Thus, after 1700, the family began its rise to prominence in Sweden.

In the decades after the end of Great Northern War (1721), which ended Sweden's short "great power" period, the Grill family belonged among the leading Stockholm merchants. They were Sweden's leading iron exporters in the 1730s and 1740s, and they also played a very important role as bankers.[12] Considering the fact that iron made over a half of Sweden's foreign trade and the Grill family was one of the seven biggest iron exporters in the country, we have to see the Grills as true tycoons of Sweden's early modern trade. Their economic position was reflected in their influence on economic policy of the period. The leading members of the family, Claes and his half-brother Johan Abraham Grills, took part actively in shaping many of the mercantilist institutions of the period, and this political influence also explains the family's engagement in Sweden's foremost mercantilist project—the Swedish East India Company.

The political situation in Sweden after 1721 opened doors for these mercantile families. The end of the Great Northern War did not only terminate the great power period, it also entailed a remarkable shift in Sweden's political history. The absolute royal rule of the late seventeenth century was replaced by the rule of Swedish Estates (*riksdag*) in a kind of protoparliamentary regime, which is why the period 1721–72 in Swedish history is called the Age of Liberty. The Swedish Estates were dominated by political protoparties, the so-called Hats and Caps, with adversary preferences in foreign and economic politics. For example, the Hats were pro-French and mercantilist, while the Caps were pro-Russian (and pro-British) and criticized heavily the Hat mercantilist policy, which did not mean that they did not apply mercantilist thought when they could. The Hats dominated the Estates from the late 1730s to the mid-1760s and shaped Sweden's economic policy in these decades.

The Grills were one of those mercantile families that hugely benefited from the Hats' mercantilist policy. The leading member of the family was Claes Grill (1705–67), the head of the Stockholm merchant house Carlos & Claes Grill and Jean Abraham Grill's uncle. The connection to this powerful man played a crucial role in the business career of young Jean Abraham. Jean Abraham's father and Claes Grill's brother Abraham began his career as a Swedish consul in Elsinore in Denmark, yet he settled soon in Gothenburg, Sweden's second trading city and the headquarters of the Swedish East India Company. The Grill brothers had a close relationship to the company. Brothers Claes, Abraham, and Johan Abraham became the company directors—so did even Jean Abraham, at the end of his business career.

This close relationship between the company and the family explains why Jean Abraham was able to enter the company service already in 1753, at the age of seventeen, and he was allowed to follow on his first voyage to China in 1755, as supercargo assistant. After his return to Sweden he began a grand tour of France, which unexpectedly stretched to five years. In 1756 we find him at Montpellier in the office of the Swedish consul Kristian Holm, and in 1758 at the Marseilles firm of Mallet & Blancheney. The years of his "French exile" between 1756 and 1760 are well covered in his copybooks and will be used for an analysis of his thoughts, self-perception, and career choice. They show in a personal way his career dreams, his doubts, and his dependency on his father and family network.

In France, he aspired to the position of supercargo aboard a Swedish ship to China and after years of waiting, in autumn 1760, he got the desired message—appointment as the third supercargo on the Swedish East Indian ship *Fredric Adolph.* He returned quickly home and at the beginning of 1761 entered the voyage to Canton. In September 1761, *Fredric Adolph* was shipwrecked near the Chinese coast. Fortunately, the crew, including Jean Abraham, survived. Instead of returning home with a next vessel, Jean Abraham Grill decided to stay in Canton and established a partnership with the Swedish merchant Michael Grubb. Their firm worked partly on the Swedish company's account, partly in private trade. Much of their business was carried on in a shady and profitable zone of "country trade."

Jean Abraham Grill stayed in Canto and Macao for seven years, first working together with Michael Grubb and, after Grubb's return to Sweden in 1764, with Jacob Hahr, another supercargo placed in Canton. With the agreement of the company, Grill returned to Sweden in 1769.

Undoubtedly, his stay in China was very profitable but appeared also to infect his relationship with the company. In contrast to many other supercargoes, Grill left the company service directly after his return and settled in Stockholm. He seemed also to be having problems with the transfer of his money from China to Sweden. Yet in 1772 his financial situation apparently improved. The same year he married Lovisa Ulrica Lüning from a well-known merchant family in Stockholm and three years later he became a country gentleman. He acquired from the De Geer family the ironworks and estate Godegård in central Sweden. The Grills were not a noble family, which made the transfer of the estate complicated, but by the end of the year Jean Abraham Grill was registered as the owner of Godegård, and he spent the remaining seventeen years of his life on his estate as a gentleman. He continued to expand the estate and the iron production. He continued also to keep his Chinese contacts, but at a much reduced level. He was appointed director of the Swedish East India Company in 1778. The family expanded, too, for Jean Abraham Grill had fathered nine children before his death in 1792. After this short review of Jean Abraham Grill's history, we will look closely at the papers preserved from the different stages of his career and family life.

THE PERIOD OF "FRENCH EXILE" (1756–60)

Between 1756 and 1760 Jean Abraham Grill made his grand tour of France, working in the firms of the family's business friends. Apparently this stay abroad turned out to be longer than he wished. He seems to have wanted to continue his career in the company, but this choice did not entail a simple continuation of what he done before the grand tour. As his chances of appointment in the company appeared shrinking, he seriously considered settling in France.

The correspondence covering his years in France gives a detailed account of his thinking. Letters were frequently addressed to family members—father, brother Lorentz, cousin Jacob, and sister Christina Maria—confirming his dependence on the family. Jean Abraham naturally adopted his writing to the addressee.

His correspondence with his father was rather formal. Frequently it concerned his appointment in the company service, and he appeared indirectly to blame his father for the lack of success in that issue.[13] Via the mediation of the Swedish consul Holm in Montpellier, Jean Abraham received a job at the house of Mallet & Blancheney, first in Montpellier and then, in 1758, in Marseilles. After two years in France he was losing hope for an appointment in the company and began to prepare himself for a career in Marseilles. In March 1758, he was writing to father about his plans to establish a business firm in France. In the letter, interestingly, he argued that the supercargo career might be too sluggish for making money and that it would take many years in the company service before he could be appointed the first supercargo, the best-paid position. So a career in France was to be preferred.

Apparently he tried to convince himself that the company career was not the best option for him. As regards his father's firm in Gothenburg, he supposed that brother Lorentz could take over and so he, Jean Abraham, was not necessary in the family's business in Sweden. Instead, he might use the family network for his career in Marseilles. Yet it must be stressed that at the same time he noted in the letter that these career thoughts must not be revealed to the company directors, so as not to diminish his chances for an appointment. It is also difficult to say how serious his plans for settling in France were. It seems that argumentation partly was his way of putting pressure on his father.[14] But also in a letter from 1757, to a close friend Samuel Schütz, he expressed his doubts about a supercargo career. The company trade was a risky business, and supercargo appointment was no guarantee of wealth and no guarantee that a man should learn more about trade.[15]

When at the end the message about the appointment as supercargo arrived, Jean Abraham was not convinced. In a letter to his father (February 1760), he again argued about benefits and shortcomings of a supercargo career. Once again he pointed out the risks of being in the company service and the long time that the voyages took. This letter also unveils clearly that he perceived the supercargo career only as a means, for a limited period of time, for making money before establishing a proper gentlemanly life in Sweden. According to his uncle Claes Grill, he needed five years as supercargo to make sufficient money "to settle down."[16]

His letters to his father show only one side of this young man. They were written in a style addressing a father's expectations for a son in a merchant's career. Yet the father's letters to the son, and sometimes his sour comments, show that the young Jean Abraham was not a perfect merchantman.[17] The father pointed out that the son should return home from the French grand tour with wisdom and understanding, instead of new dress and knowledge of "whistling." This apparently was a hint about Jean Abraham's interest in nice clothes and music; he was all his life an avid flute player.

Jean Abraham's letters to his brother Lorentz and sister Christina Maria are of another character. The correspondence with the sister shows a very different side of this young man. Concerned mainly with his wardrobe and contemporary fashion, his letters provided her with detailed instructions about which clothes she should send to him in

France, and which she should sell and repair. In detail he noted what is out of date in France and what he still could use.[18] Obviously Jean Abraham Grill was very concerned about his appearance, a quality not really corresponding with the view of a hardworking and conscientious merchant, revealed in his letters to the father.

His letters to brother Lorentz and cousin Jacob concern both business—Jacob was living at the house of the Amsterdam family branch, Anthony & Johannes Grill—and private and family affairs. Not least they discussed love affairs of brothers and sisters; such gossip never appeared in the letters to father.

In February 1758, Jean Abraham writes an open-minded letter to Jacob in Amsterdam. He is twenty-one and has just begun his employment in the firm Mallet & Blancheney in Marseilles.

> If my beloved brother saw me now he should never say that I am the same person as in the time of Caissa Kijk in Gothenburg, then I was a *petite maitre* and I had no other pleasure than with girls, now I am going in fine dress and I have my greatest pleasure in the office, I have all opportunity in the world to go here both in the best and most pleasant companies if I wish, but I do not see any pleasure in the former because I do not play cards, and in the latter, with which my brother well understand what I mean, because they are against my temper and because they are dangerous here in this place.[19]

The letter says perhaps more about Jean Abraham's past than about his present, and it may partly explain why the company directors were unwilling to employ him. Jean Abraham discusses also the sister, Christina Maria's suitors, and her marriage with Gustav Tham, a close family friend and supercargo in the company. The letters to relatives and friends in the same generation expose a world that in many ways reminds us of present-day youth. In his early twenties, Jean Abraham had so many choices and opportunities that it was difficult to make a decision. But eventually he appeared to be fulfilling familial and societal expectations of career and family building. Looking back on his career and family life, he probably felt that freedom of choice appeared rather limited. The letters also show his awareness of the Grill family's privileged situation in Sweden and the obligations such status entailed.

By the late 1750s, still in his twenties, Jean Abraham Grill already appeared to focus first on making money in the company business, and second on settling in Sweden as a country gentleman.

THE YEARS IN CHINA 1761–68

Jean Abraham Grill's voyage to Canton ended in 1761 with the shipwreck of vessel *Fredric Adolph*. Fortunately, the crew was saved, as well as the valuable cargo of silver necessary for the company's trade in Canton. Instead of returning home with another Swedish vessel, *Riksens Ständer*, Jean Abraham decided to stay in Canton as an associate of Michael Grubb (1728–1808), a Swedish merchant who arrived to China some years earlier and had a trading firm. Grill and Michael Grubb knew each other from Sweden. The Grubb family belonged to the same Stockholm mercantile elite as the Grills. Grubb was related to Niclas Sahlgren, the powerful director of the Swedish East India Company, as well as to other leading mercantile families: the Totties, the Thams, and the Kijks.

The establishment of a Swedish firm in Canton was a new step in development of the Swedish company trade with China, and Grubb and Grill were the first Swedes staying in China for a longer period. Yet their relation to the company was ambiguous. Grill and Grubb stayed in the company's factory but they did not receive any salary. Instead they carried on their private trade in Asia and mediated in the company purchases in Canton. First in 1764 the relationship between the two associates and the company was clearly defined. That year the company established a capital fund in Canton that was used for purchases of the company cargoes. The two Canton representatives carried out these operations. Undoubtedly, the company's intention with the fund was reduction of its dependency on silver cargoes and better employment of the credit market in Canton and Macao.[20]

At the same time the company was attempting to draw clear lines between the company's and the associates' trade in China. It was important to avoid competition between the private trade and the company's monopoly trade. Thus, the associates were forbidden to establish any affairs, on their or on their business friends' accounts, in competition with the company's charter. The trade was strictly divided between the inter-Asia "country trade," which was open for them, and the monopolized company trade between Canton and Gothenburg in Sweden.

Jean Abraham Grill's correspondence shows that the two associates were deeply engaged in extensive trade from Canton. Grill and Grubb appear to work as intermediaries between Portuguese and other foreigners in Macao and the capital market in Canton. They invested the money typically in two ways: either in the form of bottom loans in Canton's junk trade, or in the form of loans to Chinese merchants.

Bottom loans combined insurance with credit and so were rather risky. However, the risk could be reduced by investments in many different junks, and return (interest rate) was fairly large, normally 40 percent on the invested money. During the 1760s, Jean Abraham Grill himself invested in thirty-seven different junks that were going between Canton and different destinations in southeast Asia, a substantial share in Canton's total junk trade.[21] A large number of these vessels were destined to Batavia, Manilla, and present-day Vietnam and Cambodia.[22] The second way of investment, employed by Grill and Grubb, were loans to Cantonese merchants. Even in this case the sums were large and the Chinese merchants engaged belonged to the *hong*, the Canton monopoly company for trade with foreigners.[23]

To conclude, the two Swedes profited on channeling of credit between rich financiers (Portuguese, British, Armenian, and other merchants) in Macao and Chinese merchants in Canton. There is strong evidence of European dominance of the credit market in Macao and Canton, which might be explained by the supply of cheap money from India—so-called remittance capital. Yet an interesting question is why the two Swedes, with very limited experience of Asia trade, could enter this credit market and play such a prominent role in this business. The reason appears to be the loose relation between them and the Swedish East India Company. The big companies, such as the Dutch and English East India Companies, simply did not allow their employees such activities.[24] The Swedish company, however, was comparatively small and with insignificant control over its employees in Canton. Moreover, as mentioned above, Grill and Grubb formally were not the company's employees until 1764.

The intermediary position that Grill and Grubb succeeded in keeping was extremely lucrative. Already in 1761, the year of Grill's arrival, a bookkeeper of the Swedish company in Gothenburg wrote to a Scottish investor, Charles Irvine,

> Young Grubb has made a great fortune in a short time by venturing considerable cargoes in Jonks to Manilla & Japan. They say that he never minds to Lay any safe or reasonable schemes, but ventures upon the most desperate undertakings, for he is sure to be prosperous. He's worth now above 30 thousand Taels [equal to about 130,000 Swedish dollars silver money].[25]

Obviously the trade with Grill was carried on in the same style. In 1764 Michael Grubb returned to Sweden, but the association with Grill continued even during his absence in Canton. Letters of the company's bookkeeper show that by his return, Grubb's wealth was estimated at six hundred thousand dollars silver money, a huge sum in contemporary Sweden.

The same year the company promised Jean Abraham Grill a position as the second supercargo on a forthcoming return voyage, but again, he was passed. Instead of returning home he continued in the country trade, now in cooperation with Jacob Hahr who replaced Michael Grubb in Canton. At the same time he continued to transfer Michael Grubb's Canton money to Sweden.

The transfer of wealth made in intra-Asian trade to Europe was one of the greatest problems for European traders. Because the trade between Asia and Europe was largely monopolized, it was difficult to transfer the money in the form of commodities—it would infringe on the companies' monopoly. This was an especially large problem for the private English merchants in India. A solution was to transfer money through other companies or via Canton and as remittances. In this way the intra-Asian trade financed Europeans with a supply of cheap money. From the 1760s onward, the intra-Asian trade in turn began to finance the return cargoes of European companies, including the Dutch and not least the Swedish.[26] This means that the significance of silver sent to Asia diminished. The following letter to English merchant George Smith at Forth St. George (November 1768) shows clearly how this remittance business might be organized:

> As to the Sum you intend to send home by our Company if you are contented with Five shillings per Spanish Dollar for bills on 3 or 4 months sight, drawn on the Company agent in London, please do advise Mrs. Chambers & Hahr thereof by the first opportunity, as otherwise what is want may be taken up. As to the Sum you intend to remit home by the way of Canton in the year 1770, the best you can do, is to write about it to Gottenburg, by the homeforbound Ships this year from Madras or other places, and then you may get an answer in time . . . You know that your friends Sandberg & Grubb [Michael] are both Directors of the Oost-Indian Company, or if else you choose to employ your humble servant you may depend on my best endeavours[27]

It is apparent that the country trade of Grubb, Grill, and Hahr was a part of this business. Yet it is also clear that the transfer of their profits to Sweden was no easy task. Grill was rather successful in the late 1760s when transferring Grubb's money from Canton to home. Yet for Jacob Hahr, who replaced Jean Abraham Grill in Canton, it took four years to transfer a substantial part of Grill's money to Sweden.

First, in 1772, Grill received a substantial part of his Chinese capital, yet still by the late 1780s, the contacts that Jean Abraham Grill had with China concerned his old claims on Cantonese merchants.[28]

The Canton years are very well covered in Jean Abraham Grill's correspondence. For example, the letter exchange between him and Michael Grubb survives. This partly is the outcome of the special situation. The Swedes had two offices, one in Macao and one in the Swedish East India Company's factory in Canton, and much correspondence was running between Canton and Macao. Moreover, Grill's papers provide a detailed picture of contacts with other European merchants in Canton and Macao. There were many British, Portuguese, and Spanish, and a few French, correspondents, which reflects the character of Grill and Grubb's country trade.

Nevertheless, the letters provide few traces of more private information or self-perception of these men. In spite of a close relationship over many years they write mostly about contracts, cargoes, commodity prices, and problems with the company. An exception concerned Grubb's mistress; however, she is touched upon rarely and we do not get to know much about this affair. She caused a jealous letter exchange between the two men in 1763, and Grubb mentioned her also in a letter on his return voyage to Sweden.[29]

Grill and Grubb in Canton appear to be concerned with only one thing: to get as quickly as possible as much money as possible—and go home. In spite of the many close contacts with Macao and Canton mercantile communities, and in spite of their importance on Canton-Macao markets, they do not aim to stay. They see their proper place within the mercantile elite in Sweden. The idea of homecoming appears to be present in the thinking of a majority of European merchants in Asia. Even those who built fairly large immigrant communities, such as the Scots in India, saw going home as the eventual aim of their career abroad.[30] For Swedes, the idea of homecoming had to be even more important because there were no Swedish colonies and no immigrant communities abroad in that period.

Country Gentleman and Ironworks Owner

Jean Abraham Grill's homecoming and adaptation to his next career step in Sweden was fairly carefully planned, and slow. He was at home in Sweden in 1769, but he married in December 1772 and, in 1775, six years after his return from China, he acquired the ironworks and estate Godegård and entered the proper life of a country gentleman.

A possible explanation of this slow transformation into a gentleman may be a combination of the political unrest in Sweden between 1765 and 1772 and the deteriorated conditions of trade in China. An unwelcome outcome of Swedish participation (1757–62) in the Seven Years' War was the rapid increase in Sweden's national debt and the rising disapproval of the policy of the Hats. The Stockholm uncles of Jean Abraham, Claes and Johan Abraham Grill, were leading representatives of the Hat policy and so a target of disapproval and harsh criticism by the opposition Caps.[31] And when the Caps took over the control of the Estates, Claes and Johan Abraham Grill were sentenced to heavy fines and loss of political rights.[32] Only after Gustav III's Revolution in 1772, and a new regime that replaced the protoparty system, did the situation of the Grill family improve.

Another explanation for Jean Abraham Grill's slower adjustment to gentlemanly country life was the bad business climate in China by the late 1760s. The British control of India in 1765 entailed a huge increase of credit money available in intra-Asian trade.[33] As mentioned above, on the one hand, this situation laid the ground for the profitable credit operations of Grill, Grubb, and Hahr in Canton. On the other hand, the same availability of cheap money made the trade in Chinese commodities (mainly teas) highly volatile. Tea prices in Europe collapsed and the volume of trade declined. The decline of tea trade in Europe is also reflected in the fall of the Swedish company's reexports between 1763 and 1770.[34] In fact, this crisis in the tea trade caused the British Parliament to pass the Tea Act of 1773, which in the end instigated the Boston Tea Party. These problems in tea trade and the consequent credit crisis by the late 1760s affected especially Jean Abraham Grill and Jacob Hahr, his Canton associate. By 1770, many indebted Chinese merchants went bankrupt and the correspondence between Jean Abraham Grill and Jacob Hahr began to concern Grill's claims in Canton.[35]

Just a couple of years earlier the situation was very different. Michael Grubb returned home rich in 1765, and afterward his career demonstrates how rapidly the Swedish nabobs could rise in Swedish society. Grubb married in 1766, just a year after his return to Sweden. The same year he was appointed the director in the East India Company and he acquired large ironworks in Garphyttan.[36] In 1767, he became member of the Swedish Royal Academy of Sciences and in 1768, he was ennobled Af Grubbens. All these steps might be seen as status symbols of success, marks of power, wealth, and prestige. However, just a year later Grubb/Af Grubbens made an astonishing bankruptcy that shook the Gothenburg mercantile community. The company bookkeeper commented in these words:

> Who would ever have expected such a fall as that of Director Grubb, who was reckoned very rich & has by all accts. brought home from China above 600/mille d silvrt [600.000 dollars silver money . . . luckily that neither you or I have had anything in his hands, for I am afraid his Creditors will scarcely get above 25 prc.[37]

Even Jean Abraham Grill was surprised, in spite of the fact that he was the one who should have had good insight into Grubb's affairs. It seems that Grubb did not manage to adjust to the more modest business conditions at home and continued doing business in risky ways. He made another two bankruptcies (1774 and 1799) and lost almost all his money. He died in Stockholm in 1808 as a poor man.[38]

Jean Abraham Grill's adaptation was slower but, in the long term, more successful. His copybooks from the period 1770–75 reveal a change of priorities. The letters addressed to his friends show that he still was engaged in the company trade. The lengthy and detailed letters to Jacob Hahr in Canton are full of information concerning his claims on innumerable Chinese merchants. Yet he informed his friend also about changes in the company's leadership and their possible consequences for the associates.[39]

At the same time, very different kinds of letters appeared in his copybooks. In September 1773, Grill wrote to Mrs. Elsa M. Bergius regarding the purchase of the ironworks Wahlåsen. In October and November 1773, he wrote to Mrs. B. C. Molitor and Inspector C. Wungerecht at Axberg and discussed with them the inventory of the Axberg ironworks. The letters did not concern any more bottom loans and cargoes on junks between Canton and Batvia. These letters concerned charcoal supplies for works and pig iron necessary for production of iron bars. He asked Inspector Wungerecht about details of the Axberg ironworks management, apparently seriously considering whether to buy Axberg.[40]

In 1775 the correspondence concerned the acquisition of Godegård. The purchase of this ironworks and estate took a long time, and it is evident that Jean Abraham Grill became engaged in the management of the works long before he became the owner.[41] Grill purchased Godegård for 750 thousand dollars copper money from Carl Gustaf and Alexander De Geer. Because Godegård was a noble estate, the commoner Grill could not be directly registered as the owner.

Therefore the estate was formally sold to him in a public sale first in December 1775. The public sale was a way to avoid the legal ban on sale of this kind of estate to commoners. Between 1775 and his death in 1792, Jean Abraham Grill continued to acquire land around Godegård and also rebuilt the manor house in proper style. Moreover, he invested in iron production.[42]

Even as regards the family establishment, Jean Abraham Grill followed a predictable path. His wife Ulrica Lovisa Lüning (1744–1824), was daughter of large merchant in Stockholm, Johan Christian Lüning. The pair married in 1773 in Stockholm and two years later settled at Godegård. By 1792, the family had nine children between the ages from nineteen to one year, eight boys and a girl. After 1775, family life and the management of the estates consumed a major part of Jean Abraham's time. His letters from the late 1770s and the 1780s seldom touch the company trade, and when they concern Canton, then only in connection to the old claims on the Cantonese merchants. Much more space was devoted to the management of the estates and contacts with relatives. Jean Abraham Grill was frequently acting as a trustee for close relatives in cases concerning inheritance.

Among the attributes of a successful country gentleman belonged also interest in sciences and arts. An expression of this was Jean Abraham Grills' engagement in the Swedish Royal Academy of Sciences. For example, in 1774 he delivered a speech on a typical mercantilist issue: the significance of silver trade in China and its harms and benefits for Europe.[43]

After his years in China, Jean Abraham Grill fairly easily transformed into a country gentleman. However, not all supercargoes or the company representatives in Canton were so successful in their settling home after just one voyage—even if a long one—to China. For example, Henrik Wilhelm Hahr (1724–94), brother of Jacob Hahr, spent twenty-eight years in the China trade. He made eight voyages between 1755 and 1783 as assistant and supercargo and during that time failed to accumulate enough wealth for settling down home.[44] On the other hand, the story of Michael Grubb, Grill's accomplice from Canton, shows that Asian wealth was no guarantee of a successful gentlemanly career in Sweden.

Yet investment in more stable assets appears to be a typical strategy for merchants and supercargoes who made their wealth in the China trade. Many of Jean Abraham Grill's colleagues invested in ironworks/ estates and in the company shares. Even the never-ending supercargo Henrik Wilhelm Hahr eventually invested in ironworks.[45]

Concluding Remarks

What do Jean Abraham Grill's letters say about him as a person? The letters exploited here—letters to brothers, sister, cousin, father, and other close relatives and friends—partly had a private character. In spite of their private character they say little about Jean Abraham's self-perception. The letters from his time in France come closest to answering our question. They include reflections about his career options and also about his self-perception. Nevertheless, the bulk of the letters in his copybooks show the author above all as a competent merchant. Neither marriage nor children bring much personal touch into the copybooks. For example, the only letter that I found that shows some concern about his children relates to the appointment of the Godegård estate's priest. In that letter Grill argued that he needed a priest on the estate as teacher of his children.[46] The letters give the impression of a man who solves problems, not a man who contemplates God, the world, and his own role in the world. This does not mean that he did not think about such questions; perhaps an autobiography should show another Jean Abraham Grill.

In spite of this lack of a self-reflecting perspective, Jean Abraham Grill's letters and his life story unveil much about a character of an early modern merchant in Sweden. It is obvious that he had two priorities in life: first, a successful business career, and second, to form a family and live a gentlemanly family life. It is also clear that these two priorities mark two distinct phases in his life. His time in the company service and in Canton was the business career phase. During these years he dared to carry out very risky business with the purpose of making money.

After his homecoming his behavior changed. He properly married and had nine children. He acquired a landed estate and ironworks. Without hesitation he left the atmosphere of global economy for issues of grain, charcoal, and iron supplies. After being one of the leading European merchants in Canton in the 1760s, he became an owner of fairly insignificant ironworks in the middle of Sweden. By the 1780s, his only connection with the global trade was his claims on the Cantonese debtors. In Smith's or Pareto's words, he chose being a gentleman and rentier. However, this settling down was a conscious and planned step in his life. He was prepared for it already before his voyage to Canton. The letters exchanged with his father and uncle show that "settling down" was the ultimate aim of risky and rapid wealth creation. Jean Abraham Grill simply fulfilled his family's expectations.

The perspective of social reproduction stresses the fact that human life cycle is divided into a number of distinct stages: childhood, schooling, looking for a partner, marriage, the upbringing of children, aging, and death. These stages are linked to different patterns of behavior, but also different social status and resources. Being a young and childless man means fewer resources, less responsibility, but also more openness for risky and profitable behavior. Parenthood, on the other hand, requires reliable behavior, responsibility, and sufficient economic resources.

Jean Abraham Grill's life story illustrates rather well the stages in this life cycle. From the correspondence we do not know much about his childhood, yet we can clearly distinguish a phase of schooling and making career decisions in his letters from France. The company and the Canton phase of his life is characterized by a risky, shortsighted perspective on making money. Yet the ultimate aim of this wealth creation was establishing a family in Sweden and taking up the life of a country gentleman, the phase of life that Jean Abraham Grill entered from 1772 onward with his suitable marriage and subsequent purchase of Godegård ironworks. It is also apparent that in this phase he frequently took responsibility for other members of the Grill family, for example, in the role of custodian.

The long-term behavior of Jean Abraham Grill followed this logic of social reproduction. The family, the status, the wealth, the career appear to play for him a more important role than the Weberian ideas of entrepreneurial frugality and thrift. Yet I would not hesitate to describe him also as an entrepreneur. Social reproduction is not incompatible with entrepreneurship. Even persons following the logic of social reproduction may play an entrepreneurial role.

NOTES

1. Adam Smith, *An Inquiry into the Nature and Causes of the Wealth of Nations* (London, [1784] 1838), 181.
2. I wish to thank Göran Rydén, Uppsala University, for his comments on an earlier version of this chapter.
3. See Göran Rydén and Chris Evans, *Baltic Iron and the Atlantic World in the Eighteenth Century* (Leiden: Brill Academic Publishers, 2007), 7–9.
4. Bullionism is an early version of mercantilism, though one that only perceived bullion as wealth. To increase the amount of bullion in the country, exports had to exceed imports as much as possible.
5. Anders Johan von Höpken, *Tal, om yppighets nytta* (Stockholm, 1741). For the present debate on this subject, see Leif Runefelt, "Från

yppighetens nytta till dygdens försvar. Den frihetstida debatten om lyx," *Historisk tidskrift* 2 (2004): 203–24.

6. Neil McKendrick, John Brewer, and J. H. Plumb, *The Birth of a Consumer Society: The Commercialization of Eighteenth-Century England* (London: Europa, 1982); T. H. Breen, "An Empire of Goods: The Anglicization of Colonial America, 1690–1776," *Journal of British Studies* 25 (October 1986), 467–99.
7. Vilfredo Pareto, *The Mind and Society: A Treatise on General Sociology* (New York, [1915] 1963), 1559.
8. Clé Lesger, "Over het nut van huwelijk, opportunisme en bedrog. Ondernemen en ondernemerschap tijdens de vroegmoderne tijd in theoretisch perspectief," C. A. Davids, W. Fritschy, and L. A. van der Valk, eds., *Kapitaal, ondernemerschap en beleid. Studies over economie en politiek in Nederland, Europa en Azië van 1500 tot heden* (Amsterdam: NEHA, 1996), 58.
9. On the logic of the family business, see Mark Casson, "The Economics of the Family Firm," *Scandinavian Economic History Review* 47 no. 1 (1999), 10–23. On the relationship between the family firm and social reproduction, see Leos Müller, "Familjen och släkten: sociala nätverk och borgerliga klassresor," in Martin Åberg and Tomas Nilson, eds., *Företagare som kulturbärare* (Lund, 2007), 181–93, and Müller, *The Merchant Houses of Stockholm, c. 1640–1800: A Comparative Study of Early-Modern Entrepreneurial Behavior* (Uppsala, 1998), 24–27; and A. F. Robertson, *Beyond the Family: The Social Organization of Human Reproduction* (Cambridge, 1991).
10. Jean Abraham Grill left a large volume of letters, copybooks, account books, accounts, balance sheets, and other documents. The papers were kept in the family custody until 1952, when they were donated to the Swedish National Museum (*Nordiska museet*). This collection is fairly complete. For example, the fourteen volumes of copybooks cover the period between 1756 and 1783, thus a substantial part of Jean Abraham Grill's active life. The series of the letters received is also very rich, counting more than two hundred correspondents and stretching from the nearest relatives to Grill's commercial contacts in Europe, China, and India. This material provides us with a unique opportunity to look in great detail into the worlds of an early modern merchant. The Jean Abraham Grill Papers (JAGP), Godegård samlingen, Nordiska museet, are available online; see http://www.nordiskamuseet.se/exhibs/ostindiska/ (accessed Nov. 14, 2006). The correspondence has been exploited extensively in, among others, Paul Arthur van Dyke, *Port Canton and the Pearl River Delta, 1690–1845* (PhD diss., University of Southern California, 2002).
11. The tradition is reflected in the family's coat of arms depicting a crane with grasshopper in its nib. On the Grill family, see *Svensk biografiskt lexikon* (SBL) 17, Stockholm 1967–69, 277–85; Bo Lagercrantz, "I

Ostindiska kompaniets tjänst," *Fataburen. Nordiska museets och Skansens årsbok 1956* (Stockholm, 1956); C. L. Grill, *Anteckningar om Godegårds socken och Godegårds gods* (Stockholm, 1866); Müller, *Merchant Houses*; Leos Müller, "Mellan Kanton och Göteborg. Jean Abraham Grill, en superkargörs karriär," in Janne Backlund, et al., eds., *Historiska etyder. En vänbok till Stellan Dahlgren* (Uppsala: Historiska Institutioneng 1997), 149–61; Leos Müller, "En köpmannasläkt mellan Stockholm, Göteborg och Amsterdam. Familjen Grill 1700–1800," *Släkt och hävd no. 3–4* (2002), 274–92.

12. Kurt Samuelsson, *De stora köpmanshusen i Stockholm 1730–1815. En studie i den svenska handelskapitalismens historia* (Stockholm, 1951), 232–42; Müller, *Merchant Houses*; Åsa Eklund, *Iron Production, Iron Trade, and Iron Markets: Swedish Iron on the British Market in the First Half of the Eighteenth Century* (licentiate diss., Department of Economic History, Uppsala University, 2001), 63–66.
13. For example, see Jean Abraham Grill's letter to Abraham Grill on December 17, 1756, Montpellier, F17:1, copybooks 1756–67 (JAGP).
14. Jean Abraham Grill to Abraham Grill, March 27, 1758, Marseilles, F17:1, copybooks 1756–67 (JAGP).
15. Jean Abraham Grill to Samuel Schütz, 1757, F17:1, copybooks 1756–67 (JAGP).
16. For a similar view of a career in India as a sojourn, see Andrew Mackillop, "Europeans, Britons, and Scots: Scottish Sojourning Networks and Identities in Asia, c. 1700–1815," Angela McCarthy, ed., *A Global Clan: Scottish Migrant Networks and Identities Since the Eighteenth Century* (London: I. B. Tauris, 2006), 19–47.
17. Abraham Grill's letters to Jean Abraham Grill, E1:15, 1755–61 (JAGP).
18. Jean Abraham Grill to Mademoiselle Christina Maria Grill, Nov. 22, 1756, Montpellier; see also letters dated Jan. 6, 1758, and Feb. 26, 1758, F17:1, copybooks 1756–67 (JAGP).
19. Jean Abraham Grill to Jacob Grill, Feb. 13, 1758, Marseilles, F17:1, copybooks 1756–67 (JAGP). My translation from the Swedish: "Om M K br såg mig nu skulle han aldrig säga att jag är den samma som uti Caissa Kijks tid uti Giötheborg, den tiden war jag petit maitre, och hade ey annat nöye än med flickor, nu går jag helt rätt och slätt klädder, och har mitt fönämste nöye uti comptoiret, jag har alll lägenhet i werlden att gå härstedes både i de förnämsta och uti de nöysammaste sällskaper om jag så ville, men jag finner intet nöye i de förra som jag ey spelar kort, och de sednare, som M K br förstår wäl hwad jag menar med, äro twert emot mitt humeur ock alt för farliga här o orten"
20. Instruction for Jean Abraham Grill and Jacob Hahr, Dec. 27,1764, Stockholm, F17:8, Handlingar rörande Ostindiska kompaniet 1757–70 (JAGP).
21. Van Dyke, *Port Canton and the Pearl River Delta*, 380 and app. N, 630–38.

22. On the significance of the junk trade and the Swedish (i.e., Grill and Grubb's) role in this trade, see Li Tana and Paul A. van Dyke, "Canton, Cancao, and Cochinchina: New Data and New Light on Eighteenth-Century Canton and the Nanyang," *Chinese Southern Diaspora Studies* 1 (2007), 10–28.
23. In 1768–69 there were ten hong merchants licensed to trade with foreigners, six of them were Grill's debtors, as noted by Van Dyke, *Port Canton and the Pearl River Delta*, 396.
24. Van Dyke, *Port Canton and the Pearl River Delta*, 385.
25. Müller, "Mellan Kanton och Göteborg," 156n27.
26. On the Danish remittance trade from India, see Ole Feldbæk, *India Trade under the Danish Flag 1772–1808* (Lund: Scandinavian Institute of Asian Studies, 1969).
27. Jean Abraham Grill to George Smith, Fort St George, Nov. 22, 1768, F17:2, copybooks 1766–83 (JAGP). Chambers and Hahr were the company supercargoes.
28. Lagercrantz, "I Ostindiska kompaniets tjänst," 152.
29. Jean Abraham Grill to Michel Grubb, Aug. 13, 1763, F17:9, Handlingar rörande Ostindiska kompaniet 1757–70 (JAGP).
30. Mackillop, "Europeans, Britons, and Scots."
31. On the political struggle during 1765–66 and *Växelkontoret*, see Patrik Winton, *Frihetstidens politiska praktik. Nätverk och offentlighet 1746–1766* (Uppsala, 2006), 256–63. On the Grills, see specifically Leos Müller, "Economic Policy in Eighteenth-Century Sweden and Early Modern Entrepreneurial Behavior: A Case of the Exchange Office," in Ferry De Goey and Jan Willem Veluwenkamp, eds., *Entrepreneurs and Institutions in Europe and Asia 1500–2000* (Amsterdam: Aksant, 2002), 144.
32. They were forbidden to stay in Stockholm during estate sessions (riksdag).
33. Bowen, Huw V, *Elites, Enterprise and the Making of the British Overseas Empire 1688–1775* (London: Macmillan, 1996), 38–39, 87.
34. Leos Müller, "The Swedish East India Trade and International Markets: Reexports of Teas, 1731–1813," *Scandinavian Economic History Review* 51 no. 3 (2003), 36, fig. 1.
35. Lagercrantz, "I Ostindiska kompaniets tjänst," 151; Müller, "Mellan Kanton och Göteborg," 159.
36. Hjalmar Fors, *Mutual Favours: The Social and Scientific Practice of Eighteenth-Century Swedish Chemistry* (Uppsala, 2003), 115.
37. Malm Eriksson to Charles Irwine, July 8, 1769, Gothenburg, 69–27a, Charles Irwine Papers, James Ford Bell Library, Minneapolis.
38. August Nachmanson and David Hannerberg, *Garphyttan. Ett gammalt bruks historia* (Stockholm: Bonnierg, 1945), 264–66.
39. Jean Abraham Grill to Jacob Hahr, F17:2, copybooks 1766–83 (JAGP).
40. Jean Abraham Grill to Elsa M Bergius, Mrs. B C Molitor and Inspector C Wungerecht, F 17:2, copybooks 1766–1783 (JAGP).

41. Jean Abraham Grill to Fredrick Carl Gustaf De Geer, June 2, 1775, and June 24, 1775, and to Olof Rinman, June 29, 1775, F17:2, copybooks 1766–83 (JAGP).
42. Grill, *Anteckningar om Godegårds socken.*
43. The speech was published; see Jean Abraham Grill, *Tal om silfvers årliga förande till China, huruvida är det för Europa nyttigt eller skadeligt, hållet för Kungl. Vetenskaps Academien vid Presidii nedläggande, Den 26 Octob. 1774, af Jean Abraham Grill, Abrahamsson* (Stockholm 1774).
44. Gösta Hahr, "Hinrik Wilhelm Hahr d.ä. och Ostindiska kompaniet," *Forum navale*, no. 14 (1957), 30–107.
45. On the Ärendal ironworks, see Hahr, "Hinrik Wilhelm Hahr d.ä," 89. On investment strategies of Swedish merchants engaged in China trade, see Martin Åberg, *Svensk handelskapitalism–Ett dynamiskt element i frihetstidens samhälle? En fallstudie av delägarna i Ostindiska kompaniets 3:e oktroj 1766–1786* (licentiate diss., Department of History, Gothenburg University, 1988), 2, 83.
46. Jean Abraham Grill to Herr Anders O Nordvall (Konsistoriet), Feb. 13, 1779, F17:2, copybooks 1766–83 (JAGP).

Chapter 6

Professional Ethics and Commercial Rationality at the Beginning of the Modern Era

Jochen Hoock, University of Paris, Paris 7-Denis Diderot

Preliminary Remarks

Merchant practices are, even where they contribute to social and economic change, remarkably stable. The perennial character of certain fundamental rules is such that most of the many introductions to trade and commerce present, throughout Europe, a number of common features; they create an impression of repetitiveness. One of their main aims seems to be to reduce the uncertainty that the Austrian economist Ludwig von Mises saw as one of the most important aspects of economic action. This stability of the basic rules, which corresponds to the specific relations that characterized the exchange in given networks from "one fit place to another" (Lewes Roberts, 1638), means nevertheless no real immobility or ignorance of the changing patterns of the commercial world. Change and stability are by no means incompatible. Although relying on inherited techniques, commercial discourse evolved considerably in the early modern period. Instead of defining and illustrating basic commercial rules, manuals give a progressively detailed description of admitted practices and their conditions, what we have characterized as a "discursive broadening." One of the most important aspects of this discursive broadening is the replacement of accepted rules of commercial behavior by the description and analysis of the external conditions of any commercial activity. In place of agreed conventions emerge the heavy rules and laws of economic life that impose a "mercantile science" for defining commercial and ethical conduct.[1]

Our first intention in this chapter is to describe this passage from one type of rationality to another.[2] We will underline the technical and ideological aspects of a change that owes much to political and social changes and to the subsequent development of a printed discourse addressed to merchants and, eventually, to a larger public. Instead of considering exclusively the development of techniques and methods of accountancy, we turn to the choices made by different groups of actors such as merchants, editors, directors of boarding schools, and teachers of practical arithmetic. Each responded to changing demands. The basic sources are printed textbooks explicitly intended for merchants. They have been the object of a large inquiry that Pierre Jeannin and myself undertook for the period between 1470 and 1820 and that covers the whole of Europe. At the moment, our three volumes from the end of the fifteenth century to the beginning of the eighteenth century are available. They give a bibliographic description and content analysis of 4,596 items.[3] The bibliographical principles retained are those defined by the "new bibliography" (Gaskell), giving a material description of each book, which implies that we have seen all the texts and reproduce their full titles. The content analysis is limited to an account of the main themes and questions that these texts take into consideration. The nearly eighty themes retained cover the whole field of commercial practice, from elementary arithmetical techniques and the practice of accountancy and exchange to commercial geography, the description of products and merchandise, and, last but not least, ethical considerations.

The statistical results of this inquiry for the period from 1470 to 1699 are presented in the two first volumes of *Ars Mercatoria*. The period of the eighteenth century and the beginning of the nineteenth century has been completed during the last two years and will be published at the end of 2007. As it exists at present, our volumes offer broad insights into mercantile and editorial practices in the preindustrial period. Their thematic, cartographic, and lexicographic exploitation will be the last step of the whole project. Two parallel projects of research take into account the correspondence between European countries and the flow of information thus revealed.[4]

PRACTICE AND KNOWLEDGE

The relations between mercantile practice and commercial knowledge are at the center of our inquiry. The early printed manuals are mere reproductions of the manuscripts in use in certain mercantile offices in Venice or Augsburg. They reflect a relational network that, at the end of the fourteenth and fifteenth centuries, presents linear characteristics corresponding to certain routines. The exchanges follow specific paths corresponding to operational routines such as information and transport costs, taxes, and customs. They determine the viability of each operation. The reasoning is purely commercial and normally involves simple arithmetic operations on the basis of listed information. Among the most important examples one can mention the anonymous "Due Tariffe" and "Unkost von Wien auf Venedig" (coasts from Vienna to Venice) that are closely related to the development of commercial capitalism in southern Germany and northern Italy. Ugo Tucci has given an exhaustive analysis of these texts, which circulated from one office to the other. At the beginning of the sixteenth century these manuals were taken over by printers and assumed the form of easy-to-read tables for rapid access to information. A user could put them in his belt and consult them at the marketplace. In some ways, they present the same characteristics as the modern pocket calculator with integrated routines. Printers in Venice and Antwerp, such as Plantin, for example, became specialists of this type of miniaturized manual in the sixteenth century.

The representation of the global economy that characterizes these texts bears a resemblance to the extremely simplified cartographic account of the relations between commercial places, as we can reconstruct them, and corresponds essentially to the institutional and social integration that those places procured.[5] The sphere of production and relations outside the marketplace are rarely, if at all, mentioned. Didactic reasons argued very early on for the introduction of existing persons and firms into the example books used by apprentices. Matthäus Schwarz, the chief accountant of Jacob Fugger, illustrated his exercises with great Italian names, but we are far from the realistic accounts that we find in the early seventeenth century. In these early texts, the ethical dimension of commercial conduct finds no special mention, with one notorious exception: *the prohibition of usury*, which as a practice is nevertheless fully explained.[6]

If the publications of Paxi, Pegolotti, or Uzzano, followed by those of Benedetto Cotrugli, are contemporaneous with the first treatises on the management of great estates, the commercial literature does not take them into account even when merchants are largely concerned with landed interest. Protoindustrial activities appear with their products. The notion of labor is largely ignored and often treated in the form of an association in terms of capital. In fact, the real aim of the early manuals is to offer direct and simple information on the practical conditions of circulation, as illustrated by Girolamo Quartos in *Tariffa del pagamento dei dazi . . . di Venezia*, published in 1585. Weights and measures, custom dues, and simple taxes formed the framework of these texts. Whenever they had a larger concern, it mainly included examples and techniques of commercial arithmetic as, for example, Pietro Borghi described as early as 1484 in a manual entitled *Libro de Abacho . . . opera de arithmetica nella qual se tracta tutte cosse a mercantia pertinente*. A mnemonic aspect, often complemented by some amusing games, underlines their practical ambition. The invention of a cross-table comparing the weights and measures of the provinces by the Lyons arithmetician, Jean Trenchant, at the beginning of the seventeenth century is a striking example of these techniques.[7] They give corresponding values at a glance ("d'un seul

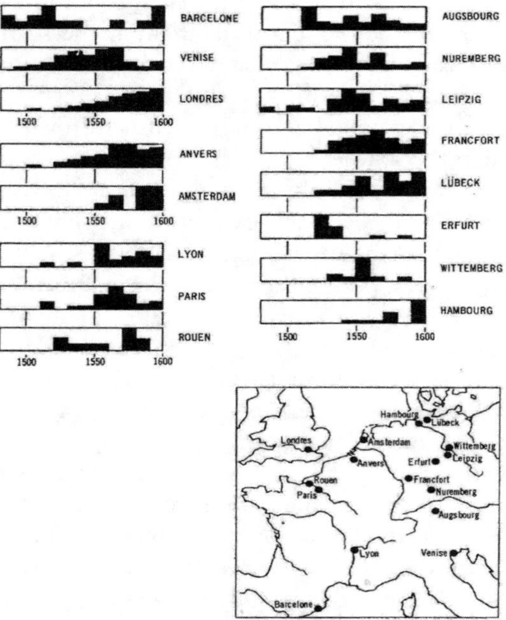

Figure 6.1 European production of commercial texts in the sixteenth century. Taken from Jochen Hoock and Bernard Lepetit, *La ville et l'innovation en Europe, 14e-19e siècles* (Paris: Editions de l'Ecole des Hautes etudes en sciences sociales, 1987).

coup d'oeil") allowing comparisons and introducing a formalized spatial dimension. But even when these tables trace the intensity of relations and the level of exchanges readable for the experienced observer, they do not correspond to a geographical description of exchanges such as we find some thirty years later. The criterion for usefulness remains in any case the *uso mercantesco.*

The diffusion of manuals reproduces, to some extent, these relations from "one fit place to another."

The general pattern of the development of European commerce in the early modern period is that of a *translatio commercii* from the South to the North as it appears in Figure 6.1. The late but exponential development of London, Amsterdam, or Hamburg contrasts strikingly with the relative decline of Venice, Nuremberg, or Augsburg. It reflects what we may call an "Atlantic Revolution" and deeply influenced the self-representation of the commercial world.

The increasing presence of merchants in the field of industrial production and their growing landed interest are components of these changes. The expansion of the Italian cities in the surrounding *contados* (the move of the Pegolotto family from the countryside to Florence is a striking element) gives the first example, followed by the development of textile industries in the Netherlands, especially around Leiden. A significant early example for this shift is Girolamo Taglientes's *Opera che insegna a fare ogni ragione de mercantia et . . . a pertegare le terre con arte giometricae*, published in 1526. The transfer of accounting techniques from ecclesiastical estates to the management of commercial fortunes is, if we consider the contributions of Flori or Luca Paccioli, an important step. But the most important development is, without doubt, the presence of merchants in the field of production, particularly outside towns. Recent research dates this protoindustrial development much earlier than Franklin Mendels suggested.[8] Production and products become a main topic of commercial literature. Garzoni's *Piazza universale*, soon translated into different European languages, is one of the first examples of this broadening perspective even where it respects the social, corporative, and institutional integration of traditional production.[9] The many translations and imitations that appeared in the following years show the importance of this break. How does this break challenge current representations of commercial activity, especially among merchants themselves?

Generally speaking, merchants were aroused by a growing sense of their leading economic role, but at the same time their profession was framed by a rigid social order. Merchants and bankers from the fourteenth century onward offer vivid accounts of this mental change toward self-representation. Some years ago Philippe Braunstein gave a fascinating account using simple notes from merchants' own accounts as well as large iconographic documentation that includes works from Vittorio Carpaccio, Marinus van Roymerswaele, or Matsy's famous "The bill-broker and his wife."[10] At the same time, we find an increasing quantity of intimate notes and autobiographical information entered into merchant notebooks, which become more and more the object of a diary held apart from the common books. The notebook of the Venetian Valori family is entitled *Questo libro non si mostri a nessuno* ("This book is not to be shown to anyone").[11] From 1494 up to 1541, Lucas Rem kept a diary that contains detailed accounts of his life and family as well as of his most important dealings. Significantly, it includes an account of his social career in Augsburg, where he aimed to regain the status of a patrician that his family had lost in the late fourteenth century.

In fact, most of these autobiographical texts are the expression and documentation of what we may call "social success." This is the case of Matthäus Schwarz's "Book of Costumes" (1538).[12] Illustrating the successive attires of Matthäus Schwarz in the course of his life from boyhood to being one of the book-holders and associates of Jacob Fugger, this text gives a real image of the career of a merchant whose behavior conforms to the sumptuary laws of that period, as well as conveys the image of the social order that we find thirty years later in the *Ständebuch* illustrated by Jost Amman. This latter work claims, in Amman's foreword, that everybody has to maintain the status in which God has placed him, this being an essential condition of human solidarity. This self-defining theme corresponds exactly to what we find in the *Facezie deli Piovano Arlotto* in the Florentine mid-fifteenth century.[13] The key to successful behavior is tied to social conventions and the rules of the profession.

The common denominator with the preceding period is what German historians have called the *Verschriftlichung* of practice (literally, the writing down of practice, putting it in black and white), which brought about a wide diffusion of such rules and conventions. The first printed manuals were contemporary with a growing degree of urban schooling.[14] Accountancy in Arabic numbers required long training. Practical arithmetical systems were regularly "authentified" by teachers, which seems to imply a face-to-face relationship. On the other hand, the diffusion of written information implied a growing market where commercial information and practical knowledge became progressively a commodity that networks of printers and editors, relying on peddlers, fairs, and local markets, exploited with increasing success.[15] This took place in the second half of the sixteenth and the first half of the seventeenth century.

The global map, which our database allows us to decompose in successive images, illustrates the spread of commercial knowledge from southern to northern Europe.[16] It does not, however, tell us *who* read the books. For any further interpretation we have to rely on the forewords, dedications, and other paratexts that the inquiry took into account, but which have yet to be exploited. A "Fonds Pierre Jeannin" has been created by the *Henri-Berr Foundation* ("Fondation pour la Science") in Paris.[17] It will be available for research. Some hypotheses allow us to formulate the present state of an inquiry that continues to be supported by the *Centre National de la Recherche Scientifique/CNRS.*

COMMERCIAL KNOWLEDGE AND MARKET INFORMATION

The generalization of market relations in the sixteenth century had more than one dimension.[18] We have to distinguish market relations *in one place* and *from place to place*, as we also have to distinguish between direct and bank money trade, which took on more and more importance with exchange, credit, and commission. At the end of the sixteenth century, these types of commercial activities determined the relations on nearly every level of commercial exchange.[19] Commercial accounts indicate a combination of very different levels of activity extending from large to quite small territories. This dimension has largely been ignored in traditional economic history—or at least until very recently.[20] Both the extension and the intensity of market relations increased.

The ideological aspects of this change became a subject of debate with the commercial crisis of the beginning seventeenth century. The controversy between Gerald Malynes and Robert Misselden marks, as Joyce Oldham Appleby has shown, only the beginning of a debate that was to last for more than a century.[21] In 1638, when Malynes's *Lex mercatoria* appeared with a largely normative presentation of commercial conduct, as a response to an international situation that historians later qualified as a "general crisis," Lewes Roberts published a manual entitled *The Merchant's Mappe of Commerce.* It takes the example of London as the "meridian of commerce" and draws up an analytical portrait of the effective conditions of commercial activity from state to state, province to province, and from place to place, dating and documenting the information. Dedicated to the Harvey brothers for "method's sake," this manual, written by an active London merchant, develops for the first time a complete typology of cities of trade. Starting with the "best known first," it offers an empirical account that broadens the traditional view of the relations from "one fit place to another." It is an empirical account of production eras where direct commerce, as, for example, the exchange of English woolen cloth for French linen cloth, still existed. The "natural and artificial commodities of all countries" (Roberts) are largely depicted, giving rise to a new science of market research that, until then, had been confined to technological procedures or products such as drugs.

At the same time, this change acquired political aspects that became more and more important over the next decades. The account of taxes and tariffs regulating the exchanges and the conditions of transport underlines the new "national dimension" that is generally associated with mercantilist options. Roberts and Malynes addressed their texts to merchants and other shareholders such as the aristocratic public, which was more and more concerned with moneyed interest.[22] This fact loosened traditional professional standards. In Italy in 1638, Giovanni Domenico Peri published a defense of credit and gains in exchange that was to provoke a wide theological debate.[23] In France, Jacques Savary pleaded, fifty years later under a similar title, for honorable commerce open to the nobility and landed interest, especially in the great companies engaged in West and East India trade.[24] This defense of trade implied a growing interest on the part of territorial and state authorities.

What in England is to some extent the expression of the Baconian impetus—furthered by technical encyclopedias such as those of Thomas Dyche, John Harris, and Ephraim Chambers—assumes in France the form of an inquiry sustained by the State and by the Academy of Sciences. Since 1690, Jacques Savary Desbruslons and his brother Philémon, both sons of Jacques Savary, were in charge of a *Dictionnaire de commerce* that aimed to cover the whole sphere of commerce, arts, and industries.[25] It was to be translated into nearly all European languages and to form the model for Malachy Postlethwayt's *Dictionary of Commerce*, the first dictionary to integrate practical information and the principles of the new political economy.[26] The merchant thus becomes an economic agent considered to be subject to, and familiar with, the laws of economic life who will conform his actions to these general conditions.

On a larger scale, private academies with a commercial slant took over what we may call general teaching in the practice and theory of private economy. At first this was largely a British phenomenon, followed by the creation of a boarding school in Hamburg in the mid-century.[27] The program of such schools included a general education in geography and ethics corresponding to traditional standards. An exception was the teaching of the Soho Academy, founded in the early eighteenth century by Martin Clare, M.A., Fellow of the Royal Society. Its intentions went far beyond an elementary education. An associate of Dr. Jean Desaguliers and also a Freemason, Clare pleaded for a program extending to morals, natural history and ancient languages that later formed the plan of a manual published in 1779 under the title *Youth's Introduction to Trade and Business.*[28]

But these developments imply no "ethical turn" that we could interpret in Weberian terms. Rather they correspond to the changing social status of merchants and to the new criteria of education. Natural history and commercial geography joined a large catalog of questions that Johann Jacob Marperger rehearses in his 1717 treatise on *The First Hundred Educated Merchants (Das erste hundert gelehrter Kaufleute).* They should be able to count, read, and write; be acquainted with all sorts of merchandise and mints; possess the fundamentals of mechanics and mathematics; speak several foreign languages; and have some notions of civil law, philosophy, geography, politics and rhetoric, exchange, navigation, and last but not least, ethics.[29] Only some kind of formal schooling could impart such a broad range of topics and concerns.

Among all these authors, the most interesting position at the end of the seventeenth century is that occupied by Daniel Defoe. Described by his contemporaries as a "dislocated hosier and bankrupt sock-seller," Defoe had quite extensive commercial experience. His insights into the changing patterns of the home markets are close to the positions defended by Nicholas Barbon and others and, as to their anthropological premises, are comparable to the Jansenist economic doctrine in France at the same period.[30] Analyzing the period since 1680 as an age where joint stock investment changed the general conditions of economic and commercial activities, Defoe reassesses the role of self-interest in social relations with a conservative outlook on the new situation of the commercial subject.[31] That Defoe interpreted the adventures of Robinson in autobiographical terms is clearly paralleled by his other stories of pirates and thieves that contrast with the autobiographical success stories of merchant writers at the beginning of our period. Society as an aggregation of self-interested producer-consumers is clearly analyzed and rejected. Defoe's manual, which appeared in 1726 under the title *The Complete English Tradesman*, tries to reestablish the "experience" of honest training in commerce, which in his eyes had largely disappeared. What Savary depicted as an honorable profession ("commerce honorable") is now confronted with a merciless world where individuals have no real choice and have to endure the general conditions of the market.

CONCLUSION

Since the beginning, the main feature of mercantile *pratiche* is the fact that they are essentially concerned with the *uso mercantesco*. Moral and ethical considerations appear in the early printed manuals almost exclusively in the examples illustrating prohibited practices such as usury. This changes with the discursive enlargement of merchant manuals, which progressively assumed in the seventeenth century the character of a handbook and even of an encyclopedia describing the economic and social conditions under which merchants exercised their profession. Commercial ethics were now intended to legitimize commercial activities, and the texts underlined their usefulness with a utilitarian dimension that corresponded to the beginning of a new economic discourse. Private academies and boarding schools with a commercial program generally included moral instructions in their courses, often associated with religious instruction. Insofar as the experience of commercial life became a main theme, as, for instance, in Defoe's *The Complete English Tradesman* (1726), Defoe could have some deep reservations, condemning the concentration on commerce by some "overgrown tradesman managing trade with some few hands," whose existence announced a new capitalist era.[32] Commercial knowledge enhances comfortable capital and an adventurous disposition. As Malachy Postlethwhayt put it in 1751:

> [T]o the ignorant in these matters commerce is but a game of chance, where the odds are against the player. But to the accomplished merchant it is a science, where skill can scarce fail: and while the one is wandering about on a pathless ocean without a compass, and depends on the winds and tides to carry him into his port, the other goes steadily forward, in a beaten track, which leads him directly, if no extraordinary accident intervenes, to wealth and honor.[33]

Notes

1. See Malachy Postlethwhayt, *The Public Counting-House* (London: Knapton, 1751), 21.
2. For the distinction between intentional and extensional forms of rationality, see Max Scheler, *Wissensformen und Gesellschaft* (Leipzig: Der Neue-Geist Verlag, 1926; repr., Bern: Francke, 1960).
3. See Jochen Hoock, Pierre Jeannin, et al., eds., *Ars Mercatoria. Eine analytische Bibliographie*, 3 vols. (Paderborn: Schöningh, 1991).
4. Resp.: Jacques Bottin (CNRS/IHMC - Paris) and Mathieu Arnoux (Université Paris 7 - Denis Diderot/EHESS-CRH - Paris). See: Action Concertée. Histoire des Savoirs, 2003–7, Recueil de Synthèses, sous la direction de Karin Chemla avec la collaboration de Mireille Delbraccio, Paris, CNRS (2007), 165–173 (169).
5. See Max Weber, *Wirtschaftsgeschichte. Abriß der universalen Sozial- und Wirtschaftsgeschichte* (Berlin: Duncker & Humblot, 1923), and Karl Polanyi, *The Great Transformation: The Political and Economic Origins of Our Time* (Boston: Beacon, 1971).
6. See, for example, Adam Riese, *Rechenbuch auff Linien und Ziphren* (Frankfurt: Egenolff, 1578), 37.
7. Jean Trenchant, *L'arithmétique . . . augmentée, tant de plusieurs règles et articles . . . que d'une Table des poids de vingt-deux prouinces, correspondans l'un à l'autre* (Lyon: Jean Pillehotte, 1602).
8. Franklin F. Mendels, *Industrialization and Population Pressure in Eighteenth-Century Flanders* (New York: Arno, 1981).
9. Thomaso Garzoni, *La piazza universale di tutte le professioni del mondo* (Venice: G. B. Somasco, 1586).
10. Philippe Braunstein, "Annäherungen an die Intimität," in *Geschichte des privaten Lebens*, ed. Philippe Ariès and Georges Duby, bd 2, Vom Feudalzeitalter zur Renaissance (Frankfurt: Samuel Fischer Verlag, 1990), 510.
11. Braunstein, "Annäherungen an die Intimität," 513.
12. This work was recently partly edited by Philippe Braunstein under the title *Un banquier mis à nu. Autobiographie de Matthäus Schwarz, Bourgeois d'Augsbourg* (Paris: Gallimard, 1992).
13. G. Folena, ed., *Motti e Facezie del Piovano Arlotto* (Florence: Riccardi, 1995).
14. See Werner Sombart, *Der moderne Kapitalismus*, vol. 1, *Die vorkapitalistische Wirtschaft* (München und Leipzig: Duncker & Humblot, 1916), 295.
15. See Pierre Jeannin, "Vertrieb und Verarbeitung der Handbücher. Funktionen und Strategien des Verlagssektors," in Hoock and Jeannin, *Ars Mercatoria*, vol. 3, 37–89.
16. See detailed maps in Jochen Hoock, Pierre Jeannin, et. al., eds., *Ars Mercatoria. Eine analytische Bibliographie*, vol. 3 (Paderborn: Schöningh, 2001).

17. Fondation "Pour la Science," ENS–Paris, 29, rue d'Ulm, F 75005 Paris CEDEX 05.
18. See Karl Polanyi, *The Great Transformation: The Political and Economic Origins of Our Time* (Boston: Beacon, 1971).
19. See for recent studies: Pierre Jeannin, *Change, crédit et circulation monétaire à Augsbourg au milieu du 16e siècle* (Paris: Armand Colin, 2001), and Jacques Bottin and Jochen Hoock, "Structures et formes d'organisation du commerce à Rouen au début du 17e siècle: le cas Michel van Damme," in ed. François M. Crouzet, *Le négoce international, XIIIe–XXe siècle* (Paris: Economica, 1989), 59–93.
20. See the case study concerning Michel van Damme by Jacques Bottin, in *Le négoce international*, which covers as well northern Europe and the lower Normandy.
21. Joyce Oldham Appleby, *Economic Thought and Ideology in Seventeenth Century England* (Princeton, NJ: Princeton University Press, 1980).
22. For the growing importance of the English aristocracy in mercantile affairs, see Lawrence Stone, *The Crisis of the Aristocracy, 1558–1641* (Oxford: Oxford University Press, 1967), 32ff.
23. Giovanni Domenico Peri, *Il negociante* (Genova: Pier Giovanni Calenzano, 1638).
24. See Jochen Hoock, "Le phénomène Savary et l'innovation en matière commerciale en France aux 17e et 18e siècles," in *Innovations et Renouveaux techniques de l'Antiquité à nos Jours. Actes du colloque international de Mulhouse (septembre 1987), réunis et publiés par Jean-Pierre Kintz* (Mulhouse: Publications de l'Association interuniversitaire de l'Est, 1989), 113–23.
25. See Jean-Claude Perrot, "Les dictionnaires de commerce au 18e siècle," *Revue d'histoire moderne et contemporaine*, 1981, no. 1, 36ff. The article gives an account of the English translations in the following years.
26. Postlethwayt was apparently in the possession of a copy of Richard Cantillon's essay.
27. See Nicholas Hans, *New Trends in Education in the Eighteenth Century* (London: Routledge & Kegan Paul, 1951), passim, and Jochen Hoock, "L'enseignement commercial anglais au 18e siècle," in ed. Franco Angiolini and Daniel Roche, *Cultures et formations négociantes dans l'Europe moderne* (Paris: Editions de l'EHESS, 1995), 159ff.
28. See Hans, *New Trends in Education in the Eighteenth Century*, 87–88.
29. See Eduard Weber, *Literaturgeschichte der Handelsbetriebslehre* (Tübingen: J.C.B. Mohr, 1914; repr., Darmstadt: Wissenschaftliche Buchgesellschaft, 1967), 37ff., and Erich Dauenhauer, *Kaufmännischer Erwachsenenbildung in Deutschland* (diss., Erlangen-Nürnberg, n.d.), 26ff.
30. See Jean-Claude Perrot, *Une histoire intellectuelle de l'économie politique, XVIIe–XVIIIe siècle* (Paris: EHESS, 1992), 333ff., and Jochen Hoock, "Der vollkommene Kaufmann. Zur Anthropologie des Händlers,"

in ed. Nils Jörn et al., *Kopet uns werk by tyden* (Schwerin: Helms Vlg, 1999), 47ff.

31. For these general aspects, see Oldham Appleby, *Economic Thought and Ideology in Seventeenth Century England*, 172ff.
32. Daniel Defoe, *The Complete English Tradesman* (London: George Ewing, 1726), vol. II, 133ff.
33. Malachy Postlethwayt, *The Merchant's Public Counting-House* (London: Knapton, 1751), 5–6.

CHAPTER 7

THE ANXIOUS MERCHANT, THE BOLD SPECULATOR, AND THE MALICIOUS BANKRUPT

DOING BUSINESS IN EIGHTEENTH-CENTURY HAMBURG

Mary Lindemann, University of Miami

It has often been asserted that eighteenth-century Europeans held an "ambivalent attitude . . . to the growth of luxury or opulence in their societies . . . they valued the advantages that the growth of commercial life brought with it . . . [yet] they were disturbed by the effects of increased material wealth upon moral well-being." How, then, "could man, as a citizen, enjoy material wealth without losing interest in the commonwealth?"[1] If this debate animated controversy in the Anglo-Saxon context, it assumed a very different character, and was certainly more muted, elsewhere. The influential Dutch polymath, Caspar van Barlaeus, was "bold in his intention to refute the common assumption that commerce stood in opposition to virtue and the pursuit of wisdom" and indeed even referred to God as "the great Factor." "Ambivalence" seems very much the wrong word for Hamburg, too, where the acquisition of wealth largely (although not solely) qualified men for civic office and underwrote their social position. In such merchant republics, and despite a recurrent moralistic hand-wringing about the evil effects of too much wealth gained too rapidly, ostentatious luxury, or the suspect business practices that made them possible, citizens took commercialism for granted. Indeed, the founding articles of the Hamburg Society for the Promotion of the Arts and Useful Crafts (better known as the Patriotic Society of 1765) recognized that "our republic is nothing more than a simple merchant-city, where . . . everyone derives his political life, his economy, and his very being from commerce."At least in Hamburg, few people considered commerce somehow antithetical to civic virtue; rather the opposite was true.[2]

The anxiety that eighteenth-century merchants felt was not so much called forth by worries about the effect of wealth on morality or from a conflict between Christian ethics and acquisitiveness, but rather about specific business practices that endangered the proper and predictable acquisition of wealth or undercut mutual understandings of honor, trust, and value.[3] Nervousness ebbed and flooded with the fluctuations in prosperity and economic ups-and-downs more generally. Early in the century, the subject perhaps most fraught with concern was speculation (in stocks or commodities, often called *Windhandel* and associated with the South Sea and Mississippi "bubbles" and the schemes of John Law); later it was *Wechselreiterei* (the exchange or sale of bills of exchange in a deceitful manner or to create credit, or even simple stockjobbing), and then bankruptcy. There were obvious links, of course, especially between *Wechselreiterei* and bankruptcy. Over the course of the eighteenth century, however, anxiety shifted from fears of the damage done by speculation to those resulting from "malicious bankruptcy." At the same time, and critically important, was a growing recognition among political economists, but also among practicing merchants, that economic disasters did not necessarily spring from personal (moral) flaws or even accidents, but originated in structural factors that individuals and even polities were badly placed to control.

By the middle of the eighteenth century, Hamburg was already large; it crossed the population threshold of one hundred thousand by the late 1780s. A self-governing free imperial city, Hamburg was also a trade entrepôt with few equals on the European continent. Its face on the north Atlantic made it a convenient transfer point for trade from western European cities, the Iberian peninsula, and the Mediterranean, and its position on the Elbe River gave it easy access to the vast hinterlands of the northern and eastern Europe. The institutional bases for economic and financial growth in Hamburg had been laid already in the sixteenth and seventeenth centuries: the Exchange

(*Börse*) was established in 1558; the Bank in 1619; and the Chamber of Commerce (*Handelskammer*) in 1663. Hamburg, however, possessed no great trading companies like the Dutch East or West India Companies and thus never could mobilize the same vast capital. Its firms were overwhelmingly family or individual firms or partnerships. Early in the century Hamburg merchants followed the pattern of most German companies, relying on their families (or those of their partners) to provide capital for investment and expansion.[4] The turn to external capital and to the acquisition of capital on slender security, however, became a hallmark of how successful Hamburg merchants did business by mid-century, if not actually earlier.

Although the city had always been sustained by commerce (and was known as early as the sixteenth century as the "florentissimum Emporium totius Germaniae"), by the 1770s Hamburg was engaging in overseas shipping on a scale unimagined for it fifty years before. At the same time, Hamburg had lost much (although by no means all) of its character as an artisanal or manufacturing center. Not the least of its commercial qualities was its position as the grain transshipping point for northern Europe and as the chief trader of textiles from farther east, and especially from Silesia. Several events—some long-term, some recent—helped propel Hamburg into economic greatness: the gradual disappearance of the Dutch as rivals, first in commerce and then (particularly after the fall of Amsterdam to the French in 1795) in finance, the favorable trade agreement concluded with the French in 1769, the ever-growing thirst for colonial products that Hamburg quenched, England's role as a major grain importer, the newly founded and eventually profitable links with the infant American Republic, and (at least at first) the turmoil the revolutionary wars unleashed.[5]

The eighteenth century was perhaps the most turbulent in Hamburg's economic history. Relatively early in the century, Hamburg had become part of a global trading network and thus subject to cycles of economic crisis and boom that typified this precocious and promising, although also unstable and unforgiving, world economy in-the-making. In response, the character of business metamorphosed dramatically. One critical indicator of these alterations was the speed with which family, firm, and individual fortunes rose and fell. One knowledgeable observer noted that "no other social group experiences shifts in economic fortune more rapidly than merchants," and another remarked that "great [and] rich houses rarely hold their positions for long."[6] Part of that volatility derived from the general unpredictability of the eighteenth-century economic world, part from specifically German and Hamburg conditions, and part from the ability of some to adapt and prosper while others floundered or foundered. Firms that thrived in one economic milieu often failed to keep pace in another. Thus the parvenu—even one with relatively limited capital—might benefit from having few or even *no* traditions (or assets or employees) over a long-standing, established firm that had "more to move" in order to change.

Another critical structural transformation in seventeenth- and eighteenth-century Hamburg was the growing dominance of commerce. While commerce was, of course, never the sole mechanism of wealth acquisition, by mid-century it assumed far greater weight than the more traditional manufacturing sectors. Johann Georg Büsch, Hamburg's (and perhaps Germany's) most important political economist, noted in 1792—near the zenith of Hamburg's economic fluorescence—that in his youth, "Hamburg was still a major manufacturing city, although it supported fewer people than today. But these fewer lived better." Büsch was particularly concerned with the plight of those perched on the bottom rungs of the occupational ladder and was the guiding spirit behind the founding of Hamburg's much-admired General Poor Relief (*Allgemeine Armenanstalt*) in 1788. His colleague in poor relief reform, Caspar Voght, himself a wealthy merchant, noted the shift as well, reminiscing that many trades (such as velvet-weaving, skilled work in gold and silver thread-drawing, and shipbuilding) "in which the common man found the most constant employment" had gone under in his lifetime. The enormous growth of commerce had, of course, generated opportunities even at the base of the labor pyramid, but these workers were especially sensitive to economic fluctuations and depended in very real ways on the crumbs that tumbled from the tables of the wealthy. In numerous publications, Büsch described the sharp structural changes in Hamburg's economy and, in particular, its growing sensitivity, even hypersensitivity, to trade imbalances, contractions, and sudden market shifts. All this combined with the increasing importance of Hamburg as a financial center, where bills of exchange passed hands almost as frequently as in Amsterdam and London.[7]

In the first half of the century, Hamburg grew if not exactly by leaps and bounds, then at least steadily. There were, to be sure, inevitable setbacks, occasioned by unfavorable economic circumstances or political constellations that disrupted trade. Hamburg was spared the "Tipper and See-Saw Time" (*Kipper- und Wipperzeit*) that so disrupted most northwestern European economies directly before the Thirty Years' War and suffered little from the great speculative ventures of the early 1700s. Indeed, Hamburg's Senat (City Council) had quickly ended attempts to engage in expansive speculative activities on the scale of the bubble trades or even to set up cooperative capital associations. In 1720, for example, a group of speculators attempted to found an insurance (*Assekuranz*) company based on stocks. The Chamber of Commerce supported the enterprise, although simultaneously expressing "heart-felt displeasure" at the "heated business in stocks" that, its members feared, would inevitably ensue. In the atmosphere of rising and bursting "bubbles," the Senat strictly forbade trade in stocks and thus stopped both *Windhandel* and stock swindles (*Aktienschwindel*). Obviously, the Senat could do little to prevent individuals from participating in the *Windhandel* that took place elsewhere, but as a whole Hamburg was not directly touched by the bubble trade, although the city suffered the (relatively brief) recession that struck northern and western Europe in 1720.[8]

There exists, of course, another form of speculation that does not necessarily have anything to do with stocks. Such speculation, defined as "engagement in any business enterprise or transaction of a venturesome or risky nature, but offering the chance of great or unusual gain,"[9] was a business practice that belonged in some form or another to the repertoire of almost all merchants. The extent to which one could engage in it—the extent to which one *should* engage in it-occasioned considerable debate and a certain amount of mercantile agonizing. "Speculative skills" could be mercantile virtues, and one knowledgeable observer of Hamburg life referred approvingly to the city's merchants as "pregnant with speculations."[10] "Imprudent speculation" was, however, a vice. When the latter was combined with mercantile ineptitude or impatience, it was blamed for fostering an economic instability of titanic proportions.

During the Seven Years' War, Hamburg profited from the war boom. By the late 1750s, however, inflation became a serious problem, as did the overextension of credit. The end of the Seven Years' War, and in particular the devaluation of Prussian currency in 1763, touched off a panic in the European money markets. It began in Amsterdam and then quickly struck Hamburg, Berlin, and Stockholm. Ninety-seven firms collapsed in Hamburg in that year alone. Not since the recession of 1720 had anything so seriously affected Hamburg's prosperity. This crisis also demonstrated (if more proof was needed) how much Hamburg's economic and commercial well-being hung on the vicissitudes of international trade and capital markets. The 1763 financial disaster gave many reason to probe the deeper background of such crashes and to identify them in structural factors and not only, or no longer principally, in ethical lapses or personal mercantile ineptitude.[11]

The post-1763 depression held on tenaciously and was not fully overcome until about 1788, although significant signs of recovery were obvious earlier. Even then, one could discern the beginnings of what would become an extremely forceful economic upswing. The growth evident in the mid-1780s became truly phenomenal in the 1790s and persisted through the end of the century. The severe winter of 1798–99, combined with unrest throughout Europe, led to a depression and, in 1799, 152 bankruptcies were recorded. Yet despite the good times—the *very good times indeed*—of the 1790s, the specter of economic malaise haunted the second half of the century. Even during the amazing economic expansion of the mid to late 1780s and 1790s, many merchants and social reformers remained uneasy about the durability of such prosperity, and astute observers sounded warnings. The directors of Hamburg's General Poor Relief pointed out that the abundance of the 1790s was not quite an unadulterated blessing. The "sudden and unexpected" proliferation of jobs had failed to nurture what they termed a "true prosperity," but rather encouraged indolence, profligacy, and immorality. Although such preachifying was never absent from the program of the General Poor Relief, nonetheless it explicitly recognized the structural factors that had made poverty such a problem in Hamburg. Büsch, for instance, perceived how the "great machine of [monetary] circulation" worked to the disadvantage of the laboring poor in Hamburg.[12]

In this atmosphere of booms and busts, speculative practices, frenzied stockjobbing, and malicious bankruptcy were the issues around which discourses about mercantile practices and the standards of proper business culture in Hamburg revolved. But moral discourses were always accompanied by structural analyses and were often overshadowed by them. Likewise, by no means did all commentators concerned broadly with "values" worry about the erosive qualities of "get rich quick" mentalities and growing materialism, as the late-century debate over "luxus" shows. Certainly much alarmist sentiment found its way into print.[13] Yet not everyone was convinced that "luxus" was all bad, or bad at all. Georg Heinrich Sieveking, a prosperous merchant about whom more will be said below, worried about the problems luxury created for the city and feared its deleterious effects on civic virtue. But he also recognized it as "a mighty driving force for useful activity" and in a very Mandevillian way argued that the same pursuit of luxury that destroyed individuals was not necessarily an evil for the polity or for the "useful citizen" who profited from the profligacy of others.[14]

* * *

Sources for a reconstruction of business practices and, especially the perception of these practices among Hamburg's merchants during the eighteenth century, are fragmentary, despite the existence of numerous family and firm papers.[15] Several older works—biographies and published collections including correspondence and diaries—often draw on rich materials that are sometimes no longer available. These materials provide additional useful information.[16] A series of bankruptcy proceedings, ranging from the 1730s through the 1790s, offers other insights into how a merchant community defined bankruptcy and judged the circumstances that led to it.

A traditional way of looking at what happened in Hamburg (and elsewhere) is to argue, as Percy Ernst Schramm did in the 1940s and 1950s that a significant alteration from a precapitalist to a capitalist mentality occurred over the course of the long eighteenth century (from about 1650 to about 1780). Schramm, for instance, portrayed the world of the late seventeenth century as one "that was still completely innocent of capitalist thinking and, as far as it knew such, rejected it entirely." For evidence, he turned to the writings of Valentin Heins (1686–1704), an erstwhile merchant but far better known as the author of a business primer.[17] Heins studded his paragraphs of down-to-earth advice with moralizing nuggets that, for instance, differentiated earthly and celestial happiness and emphasized the transience of material gain, exhorting the "proud child of fortune" to be humble.

> The wheel turns, what was yesterday on top,
> Sinks today so far as it seems it will never rise again.[18]

Heins's position apparently encapsulated a mentality that had evolved little since the Middle Ages and remained ambivalent about wealth, even while he instructed his readers on how to acquire it. But one should question whether the moral proverbs that Heins strewed throughout his otherwise quite sober, how-to-do book actually indicated a "precapitalist" mentality.

In a similar vein, the play *The Bankrupt*, published in the wake of the 1763 crisis, accepted acquisitiveness as a mercantile trait (if not exactly a merit), but expected it to be alloyed to civic and Christian virtues. Clearly a *pièce à clef* and very much a moral melodrama, it commented scathingly on the business practices that had supposedly displaced the solid mercantile values of yesteryear and landed

Hamburg in the 1763 mess.[19] The action of the play turns on the attempts of one Gerrard to bankrupt his partner and cousin, Erast. Gerrard demanded his share of the company be paid out in "Harlem currency" because he believed that "Dalem" (where Erast had his money) was going bankrupt. Rumors of bankruptcy—in Dalem or in Harlem?—drive the plot forward. Successive scenes allow each character to elaborate his own business philosophy. Erast is the honest merchant cast in traditional Christian style who would rather die than cheat his creditors: "I shall not stoop to deceitful means to recoup my losses." Moreover, "services we render our neighbors, even when we suffer thereby, nevertheless compensate us for our pains with a silent and internal satisfaction."[20] When confronted with a broker (*Makler*) who offers him a way to escape his obligations, Erast indignantly rejects his schemes. The broker refers to Erast's impending insolvency, which Erast hotly denies can be called "bankruptcy" because "others caused my losses." The broker responds that he should not be so sensitive because "bankruptcy is an inoffensive word." Indeed, "it is the most profitable business imaginable, the swiftest road to riches . . . [and] the straightest path to honor and respect." By cheating his creditors, by writing ever more bills, one could become rich, the broker crooned. "I know," responded Erast, "that crooks do so." The broker laughs: "Don't you understand our language better? One finds crooks in the pillory or [hanging from] the gallows; but no one considers the man in a fine carriage with liveried servants up behind [to be] anything other than a real toff." Erast shows him the door.[21]

The Bankrupt is obviously a morality play, although it must have resonated strongly in the climate of doom that hung over financial centers directly after the disasters of 1763. While we should not take a piece of fiction as a transparent view of what merchants thought or felt in the middle of the eighteenth century, there is also no doubt, I believe, that the images of the "good and honest merchant" and the "scheming speculator" (or "criminal broker") were stock types with which audiences were familiar. Such tropes were endlessly repeated, often in the same, often in changed but still recognizable forms. They became hardy literary perennials. Yet we encounter them not only in plays and in the spectatorial publications of the day, but also in mercantile handbooks, legal codes, and bankruptcy proceedings. Certainly, the very same speculative behaviors that Dusch so roundly condemned had become standard business practices, as the writings of merchants active in Hamburg from middle to late eighteenth century demonstrate. Even if many evince at least fleeting concern about the morality of such activities, far more suffocating is their fear of real loss.

The memoirs of Johann Michael Hudtwalcker (1747–1818)—merchant and later senator—open with a description of how his father and grandfather conducted business. His father, Jakob Hinrich, began his career working for another merchant who dealt in herring and whale oil. Hudtwalcker *père* lived a simple life, innocent of all extravagance as Hudtwalcker described it: "The whole week was devoted to ceaseless labor and Sundays he regularly went to church twice, drank his beer, and smoked a pipe."[22] After laboring for sixteen years for his employer, he set up his own business on a modest capital of five thousand Mark Banco (Mk. Bco.), which was the money of account

Figure 7.1 John Parish (1743–1829). Reproduced with the permission of Staatsarchiv Hamburg.

in Hamburg. In the 1740s and early 1750s, his wealth mounted up slowly but steadily: he married, purchased a house, then a bigger one, and acquired a garden. Until the Seven Years' War, his fortune remained quite modest. Then, like so many others, he prospered as Hamburg "raise[d] itself to the position of an important commercial state." By the end of the war, however, as paper bills and devalued currency flooded Europe, credit grew scarce and to obtain it "one had to try other methods and [he] resorted to the so-called bill-jobbing [*Wechselreiterei*]."[23] Johann Michael's own early experiences in his father's firm indicate how usual this practice had become. His first duty each morning was to remind his father's creditors when their bills fell due: "One sold almost everything on four-weeks' credit, and after six weeks one started to ask if it was now convenient [to pay up]. There were very many rich merchants who had to be 'reminded' repeatedly and their credit did not seem to suffer much thereby."[24] Obviously, either the debtor was waiting for others to pay him or was pushing the time limit to maximize profits.

The memoirs of two considerably richer contemporaries convey a greater sense of what doing business meant in these years. The first is John Parish (1743–1829) and the second, Georg Heinrich Sieveking (1751–99). The early lives of both men had much in common with that of Hudtwalcker (father and son): both began with little capital; both worked for other people; both eventually set up their own businesses; and both were exceptionably successful. Parish was a true Croesus, and his name became proverbial for wealth as the colloquialism "living parishly" conveyed.[25]

After his father died in 1761, John Parish assumed the business with a small fund of three thousand Mk. Bco.[26] Two years later, his capital only amounted to a modest four thousand Mk. Bco. He ended the century a millionaire. His initial capital, however, was too flimsy a basis from which to launch any major business ventures. Moreover, he could call on virtually no credit reserves: "[W]ith the exception of my friends the Jews, there was not a Christian in the City of Hamburgh that I could look up to for the Loan of £100. Sterling!"[27] For him, as for so many others in the city, the Seven Years' War was a profitable time and he, too, engaged in the rampant and seductive *Wechselreiterei*. Unlike many others, he escaped disaster in the crash of 1763. He thoroughly comprehended the allure of bill-jobbing, describing how one was almost inexorably drawn into the maelstrom:

> The business of accepting Bills when a Man's Credit stands high, produces an easy earned Commission, it's a business too which tends to

> give Consequence to the merchant, & his giddy Ambition is too apt to get the better of his prudence, seeing himself call'd on by the first rate Houses of Commerce, to give energy to Operations of Magnitude, flatter'd by being told that it was alone with houses such as his that matters of such a nature coul'd be transacted, & how few of us are proof against such Adulation [and] the Bait takes effect; the first part of the Work goes smoothly down; his former prudent Conduct had establish'd his Credit, & the moment he puts his foot on the ExChange, he is encercled & press'd by a Cluster of Brokers soliciting for paper—make your own Exchange, Sir! he does so, & finds that his exclusively, is readily consumed. What food for Vanity. He towers above his neighbours, & soon begins to fancy himself, the prop & pillar of the Exchange, & if this does not turn his head nothing will.[28]

Yet what a slippery slope it was. Even if one wished to halt, and if one actually possessed the nerve to "look into his Bill Book" and see how far beyond discretion he had traveled, any hope of retreat had long since disappeared: "[H]e must push forward in the Stream, even if he sees himself doom'd to founder in the Ocean; his employer then treats him with less Ceremony, they are both embarked in the same Vessel, and with her they must sink or sweam [sic]."[29] To a goodly extent, the structures of the money market determined his fate.

The emotional costs were enormous and the strain soul-eroding. He confided in his memoirs, "Such, my dear Henny, [his daughter], is the true picture of a merchant, & such a one as I have been describing, I have more than once been in a similar predicament, but happily as often weather'd the storm. The anxieties felt, & the sleepless nights which I have experienced, when under such engagements, with the Love I bear my boys, all combine, to make me pray to God, that they may not be tempted, for the sake of any Commission to the risk of similar difficulties."

But his sons were not spared and John's later quarrels with them turned on what he regarded as *their* ill-advised speculative ventures and unnecessary expenditures on, for example, "French dinners." His house, too, did not long outlive him, closing in 1847.[30]

While his late-in-life ruminations are often tinged with regret and express painfully won wisdom (if also considerable pride), it is very clear that Parish was never a "steady, cautious" merchant of the old school, if such a man ever really existed except as moral exemplar. The sage advice he distributed after his retirement from business in 1797 directed his sons to follow the "Merchant's Golden Rule" of making haste slowly. Such tempered counsel may well reflect little more than age or parental disquietude over the "rashness" of a younger generation.[31] Throughout his own career, John Parish speculated, took chances, and not just occasionally played fast and loose with his and other people's money. He embarked on new businesses with cool daring and, in the 1780s and 1790s, made a mint in exploiting the eastern European grain trade and in a complicated and dodgy operation with Liverpudlian merchants and the British government (the "Army Business"). Both short-term ventures produced windfall profits. But Parish later recalled them as dangerous and perhaps overbold, for even though "Transactions of such a Nature, are apt to give consequence to a house of Business," if offered the chance again, "'I declare upon honour,' I should not hesitate a moment to reject it."[32] There were also failures and losses, often substantial ones, of course, but by the time his sons took over the business near the end of the century, the firm had established itself among the foremost in Hamburg. According to Parish, "From 1783 [to 1789] . . . a great run of business was attach'd to my house, & at the Close of each Year I found Parish & Co. stand[ing] at the head of the annual List of Importation."[33]

If one looks at how Parish acquired and deployed capital, one sees little evidence of circumspect planning and careful hoarding of resources. Rather, his business style is characterized by bold strokes that must have required good nerves to carry through.[34] At several points in the 1770s, such as in the tight moments from 1776–79, he only saved himself by going to loan sharks (*Wücherer*). During the panic of 1783, when the bankruptcy of Peter His & Sohn—a leading firm in Hamburg—carried down several others with it, the Jewish banker, Wolf Lewin Popert, rescued him. Parish remained eternally grateful. "I could have kissed the old man," he wrote, and "while I have breath in my body, his memory will be dear to me."[35] Parish then lost some 220,000 Mk. Bco. on a West Indian expedition he helped finance, a sum that exceeded his cash reserves. In the crisis of 1793, his commitments amounted to over eight million; his own ready capital totaled only about one-half million. Such a lopsided ledger meant financial death for most businessmen, but he endured. Still, these were harrowing days for Parish, when he more than once tottered on the brink of bankruptcy, and only desperate action, credit from Popert, or sheer luck yanked him back from the edge. The earlier crisis of 1783, that left him holding huge numbers of bills of exchange having only dubious value, was, he recalled, "from the time I had been in business, . . . my hardest stand. O! Henny! what I suffer'd in that fortnight! . . . I can still recollect it, as yesterday—I shudder when I think of it . . . it shook the very marrow in my bones."[36] He narrowly escaped disaster: bankruptcy. He was saved by his connections and by that ineffable but absolutely essential mercantile asset of credit, both in its literal and figurative forms. Yet credit was inconstant and easily lost. In this crisis, and in others, chance or coincidence, encountering the right man at the right moment, for instance, preserved him or saved him at the very last minute as he readily admitted. What had he done to enjoy such "credit"? The best answer he could give was mercantile judgment and the reputation that accompanied it.[37]

The life story of Georg Heinrich Sieveking often parallels that of Parish, although he did not reflect so directly or extensively on his business practices. Sieveking's company, Voght & Sieveking, had been founded by Voght's father and, like most Hamburg firms, engaged in trade on its own account (*Eigenhandel*), took on commissions, and played the money markets. Frequently, notably in its early years, it ran short of capital. Sieveking, however, could draw on the family funds of his partner, although that solution was not without its own problems, entangling him and the firm in domestic affairs, hurt feelings, and petty jealousies.[38] By 1782, Sieveking was remarking on the changes in commerce and business into which he himself was thrust. And, he, too, engaged in bill-jobbing and bill-discounting, meticulously recording the sums, as here on February 15, 1782: "In the last few days Krogmann and Paul Lange offered me [bills worth] 4,000 Mk. Bco. at 3½% [for a term of] three months and 10,000 Mk. Bco. for six months at 4%, which I accepted." A month later, he took up bills from Dr. Schulte for 8,000 Mk. Bco., from Adolph Schmidt for 10,000 (although he was offered 20,000), and from Christian Seiler for another 8,000. Thus, Sieveking concluded, "this certainly demonstrates to you [Voght] how good our credit here is."[39]

In the heady days of the 1790s, Sieveking speculated on the exchange and discount rates and continued to take in money hand over fist; as he wrote his partner on November 4, 1794: "I have [just] made a tidy little sum on the French exchange rate." He explained how "the speculators are always eager to get bills of exchange [good] for three months, and then when they fall due they bring them to me [again] and offer me a better rate [of] ½ to ¾ shillings [more interest] for an extension over another three months, and I thus experience repeated pleasure" from this business.[40] At the end of 1794, the capital of the house reached its zenith of 130,495 Mk. Bco. Thereafter, the business began to fade and when Sieveking died suddenly in 1799, the situation was far less rosy than five years earlier, although the firm held together until 1811.[41]

The stories of Hudtwalcker, Parish, and Sieveking reveal how these successful merchants did business. Parish was more audacious than many Hamburg merchants, including Sieveking and Hudtwalcker, but most played the money markets and were to be had for enterprising ventures that far exceeded the system of slow acquisition that Pieter Poel (1760–1837) described as typical earlier. To be successful in "old style" business, one needed little more than "orderliness and punctuality." Over the course of the century, however, "the world [of business] had rearranged itself" and "new combinations facilitated far more extensive business ties, whose unplumbed lucrativeness gave the imagination much room for play." The new structures opened the door to "innovative practices" and allowed for financial and business coups of startling proportions. Into this free space, Parish and many others moved. Many firms prospered, others did not.[42] Of course, one could be both cautious *and* reckless, sometimes playing it safe and sometimes gambling. An ability to know which to do when permitted the astute man of business to triumph over his less adroit competitors.

* * *

Hudtwalcker, Parish, and Sieveking counted among the Hamburg success stories, but what about the failures? If the economic climate of the times allowed these men to prosper, what about the many others who hit the rocks and went under? Economic fortune was fickle and the sense that timing was everything pervaded business mentalities. Clearly, some merchants were just better businessmen than others, or at least they were luckier. Yet other firms of equally good reputation and apparently run by equally shrewd men—such as that of His & Son, Peter Hinrich & Nicolaus Stampeel, or Nicolaus Schuback—succumbed to bankruptcy and the stigma it imparted.[43] Hamburg's bankruptcy ordinances (the first embedded in the city's law of 1609 and the "new" one passed in 1753) distinguished between types: the accidental failure provoked by unhappy misfortune; the frivolous bankruptcy produced by negligence, inexperience, and imprudence; and the malicious bankruptcy that was planned as a way to *make* money or at least to prevent one's creditors from getting their due. Hamburg's bankruptcy laws were notoriously lax at least until the promulgation of the 1753 ordinance. By then, it was the malicious bankrupt, and his slightly less distasteful brother, the "frivolous bankrupt," who got the most attention.[44] One's opinion, and the readiness with which one judged a bankrupt an innocent victim or a villain, depended much upon point of view. While commentators and ordinances tried to preserve a distinction between the two, the practices viewed as terminating in either type of bankruptcy appeared disturbingly similar. "Frivolous bankrupts" (*leichtsinnige Falliti*) were those "who embark on risky ventures that exceed their means, engage in forbidden bill-jobbing and -discounting." Such actions were, of course, very similar to the standard business practices of John Parish, Johann Michael Hudtwalcker, Georg Heinrich Sieveking, and a host of others.[45]

Maintaining the differentiation between negligence and willful deceit was never easy, but the authors of the bankruptcy ordinances tried and defined malicious—"intentional and [therefore] wicked"—bankrupts as criminals. These men, like the frivolous, also engaged in stockjobbing, bill-discounting, and *Wechselreiterei*; but, in addition, there were those who "while still in a position to satisfy their creditors [at least in part], deliberately declare bankruptcy in order to enrich themselves, conceal their [true] assets, hide their books, and then flee [the city] taking great sums of money with them." To conceal their financial embarrassment, they played in the stocks (*Actien)* of "foreign companies," fabricated false letters of exchange, and cheated their wards. Much like the "frivolous," these men also "caused their own ruin through an opulent, indulgent life." "In a word, [they] live above their estate in life and beyond their means."[46]

Such bankruptcy proceedings are revealing. The responses the seventy-year-old Paul Hermann Trummer made to those investigating his finances in 1756 allow us to glimpse how he rationalized his actions. At times, it seems, he merely described common business practices.[47] When asked why he had declared bankruptcy, he replied: "because all his deposit-accounts were drained and his bills of exchange were protested [i.e. not accepted]." Why had he sold linen that he taken on commission and booked the money to his own account? Because he needed the money to cover his bills and an outstanding debt of some sixteen thousand Mk. Bco. owed to merchants in Cadiz. He had told his creditors in Silesia that he would pay up in three months, although he had already sold the linen so obtained and had used the money to stave off his most insistent creditors. He presented such three-month extensions of credit as usual in transactions with Silesian merchants, and there was considerable truth to that assertion.[48] The very structure of such deals virtually mandated extended credit arrangements. The magistrates, however, regarded it as "an irresponsible dissimulation." More details came to light as questioners probed the circumstances of his business in the year immediately preceding his bankruptcy. Yet here, as elsewhere in the testimony, he could give only imprecise figures, pleading that he did not know the numbers "out of his head," but that his bookkeeper would be better able to explain (he wasn't).[49]

A more important case against several business partners reached the Imperial Cameral Tribunal (*Reichskammergericht*) in 1765. It offers an excellent perspective on "deceitful schemes" and especially on the bill-jobbing of two companies: Müller & Seyler and Seyler & Tillemann. Although the voices presented here are those of their creditors, the documents nonetheless reveal how contemporaries viewed the business practices of "malicious bankrupts" and how these practices assumed particularly baleful shapes in their minds.[50] The creditors' lawyers laid out the background to the case in considerable detail. Müller and Seyler were new men; Edwin Müller had come from Hanover several years before and Abel Seyler had been born in one of the Swiss cantons. Both had, however, "learned their business" and married in Hamburg. "If one could trust their books," their actual starting capital amounted to no more than thirty-eight thousand Mk. Bco., "of which, however, well over half had been frittered away through the acquisition of furniture for two households, [for the purchase of] clothes, jewels, silver plate, and other needs for themselves, their wives, and their children, [and also for] carriages, horses, and so on." Their business was undercapitalized from the beginning. In the 1750s, this seemed a minor problem because credit was easy to obtain. When the cash flow failed, they tried to acquire money quickly through bill-jobbing. Because their ready funds could not cover their expenses and debts, theirs became "the most audacious [form of] *Windhandel*." As their business increased—as they took on ever more commissions in goods for import and export, invested in a sugar refinery, and lent money to several people—they simultaneously pursued their bill-jobbing and expanded it markedly.[51]

In 1757, they acquired a new partner, named Tillemann, who, however, contributed "not one Creutzer" to their capital, but that did not stop them from vigorously extending their business. Although their enterprises seemed to prosper in the late 1750s, they did so only "at the expense of others . . . because they always lacked adequate funds." Bill-jobbing was a dangerous game "in which even the most careful [practitioner] usually loses about 10% and sometimes even 12–14%." The partners then conjured up a fictive company under Erwin Müller's signature "and informed the world that he had thus established his own firm." Certainly, commented the lawyer drily, "that was a fine business that honored its inventor, which, however, no one who values truth and honesty could condone!"[52]

They were effectively bankrupt by August 1762, long before the "great crash" of 1763. Yet they did not stop, but plunged forward (as Parish wrote), cooking more deals as the kitchen got hotter. Seyler & Tillemann continued their trade in worthless paper and bought up large quantities of silver and coin on commission. Müller, by now separated from the firm, was up to his ears in this "windy-business" ("he had strewn into the world some one-and-a-half million Mk. Bco. in bills"). He was brought to such "despair" that Seyler & Tillemann, as well as several other local and foreign banks and businesses (principally in Braunschweig and Amsterdam), all of which were mutually involved in bill-jobbing and bill-discounting, had to come to his rescue. For their own preservation, they simply could not afford to let him fall. Still, by late 1762 they, too, were "completely insolvent."[53]

When the Amsterdam house of De Neufville collapsed, so, too, tumbled Seyler & Tillemann. The common cause of the bankruptcies, from the giant De Neufville to less-famed partnerships like Seyler & Tillemann, lay, it was argued, in "an exaggerated trade in bills of exchange, in bill-jobbing, and—particularly—in the criminal "'windy trade' that [such like] Seyler & Tillemann had engaged in." The "wind trade" of these years—and the bankruptcies that resulted—shook the major commercial centers to the core, "and many a capitalist who sought to profit from the high discount rate and who changed his money into paper, was plucked bare."[54]

Conclusions

What should we then, in the end, make of these reflections on business practices over the course of the mid to late eighteenth century? The moral tone never disappears and one would hardly have expected it to vanish. Yet, over the course of the century, it becomes a rhetorical club to beat the unsuccessful or a slur with which to stigmatize one's debtors more than a searching self-criticism or an expression of deeply seated fear or ambivalence. Obviously, some men, like Parish, from time to time felt unease—or distress—with the course they took, but there is also a sense that this was (for better or worse) the world in which they lived, and success or failure depended on what they often could not control, although their own skills could deliver them from harm or at least give them enough warning to save what they could. No one, of course, excused those who were complete frauds or built up paper money castles that the first real wind puffed away. But there was really little to choose between what successful merchants like Parish, Hudtwalcker, or Sieveking did and what Seyler and Timmermann attempted. That was precisely the problem; it was hard to tell what was or what was *not* a good business practice, let alone a moral one. Parish's survival was not solely due to luck, even if he believed quite sincerely in the "wheel of fortune." But neither was Seyler and Timmermann's fall (nor the ruin of so many others) due merely to their dubious business activities or their incompetence. And, so, despite the moral high ground that commentators and playwrights, lawyers and city fathers might take, it was hard to see that any other path was open to merchants than to follow the one that so many of them trod: whether it led to riches or poverty. They might view this arbitrariness with some trepidation, but not with enough anxiety to cancel their journey. As was so often true in the eighteenth century, the territory inhabited by scoundrels and imposters, by honest men and thieves, often seemed like common ground.

Notes

1. Prospectus for conference "The Self-Perception of Early Modern 'Capitalists,'" Conference at the Clark Library, January 19 to January 20, 2007.
2. Certainly, it has frequently been argued that commerce and wealth (especially luxury) undercut civic virtue. Much of the extensive literature on republicanism takes this line. The theme of Schama's *The Embarrassment of Riches* runs parallel. In it he explores the "anxieties of superabundance" and "the moral ambiguity of good fortune." Simon Schama, *The Embarrassment of Riches: An Interpretation of Dutch Culture in the Golden Age* (New York: Fortuna, [1987] 1991), 7. But there is another side to the story: commerce as a school of virtue, not vice, and the merchant as moral exemplar. This was especially true in merchant republics like Hamburg and Amsterdam. See, for example, Wijnand W. Mijnhardt, "The Limits of Present-Day Historiography of Republicanism," *De achttiende eeuw* 37 (2005): 75–89, and the article by Clé Lesger in this book. Quote from the founding articles of the Patriotic Society is from Franklin Kopitzsch, *Grundzüge einer Sozialgeschichte der Aufklärung in Hamburg und Altona* (Hamburg: Hans Christians Verlag, 1982), 332.
3. As Anne Goldgar persuasively argues in *Tulipmania: Money, Honor, and Knowledge in the Dutch Golden Age* (Chicago: Chicago University Press, 2007).
4. Robert Beachy, "Business Was a Family Affair: Women of Commerce in Central Europe, 1680–1880," *Histoire sociale/Social History* 34 (December 2001): 307–30; Thomas Max Safley, "Bankruptcy: Family and Finance in Early Modern Augsburg," *Journal of European Economic History* 29 (Spring 2000), 53–75. In Hamburg, there were some (albeit not terribly important) exceptions, where merchants involved

themselves in companies, such as the "Glückstadter Afrikanische Gesellschaft" founded in March 1659. It was not successful and registered a loss of over one million marks by 1672. See Heinrich Sieveking, "Die Glückstädter Guineafahrt im 17. Jahrhundert," *Vierteljahrschrift für Sozial- und Wirtschaftsgeschichte* 30 (1937): 19–71.

5. Mary Lindemann, *Patriots and Paupers: Hamburg, 1712–1830* (New York: Oxford University Press, 1990), 33–73; Johann Georg Büsch, *Geschichtliche Beurtheilung der am Ende des achtzehnten Jahrhunderts entstandenen grossen Handelverwirrung* (Hamburg and Mainz: Nestler, 1800).
6. Jonas Ludwig von Heß, *Hamburg, topographisch, politisch und historisch beschrieben*, 3 vols. (Hamburg: B. G. Hoffmann, 1787–92), 2:143.
7. Johann Georg Büsch, *Theoretisch-praktische Darstellung der Handlung in ihren mannichfaltigen Geschäften*, 2 vols. (Hamburg: Hoffmann, 1792, 1799), 1:88; idem, *Ueber die der Stadt Hamburg in jezigen Zeiten nothwendig werdende Erweiterung der Stadt Hamburg*, 2nd ed. (Hamburg: J. P. Treder, 1792), 6–8; idem, *Erfahrungen*, 4 vols. (Hamburg: Hoffmann, 1792–94), 3:11; Caspar Voght, *Gesammeltes aus der Geschichte der Hamburgischen Armen-Anstalt während ihrer fünfzigjährigen Dauer* (Hamburg: Meißner, 1838), 7–8. On Büsch's economic writings, see Jürgen Zabeck and Frank Hatje, *Johann Georg Büsch (1728–1800) - wirtschaftliches Denken und soziales Handeln* (Hamburg: Verein für Hamburgische Geschichte, 1992), 18–27.
8. Ernst Baasch, *Die Handelskammer zu Hamburg, 1665–1915*, vol. 1, *1665–1814* (Hamburg: Lucas Gräfe & Sillem, 1915), 181–84; Percy Ernst Schramm, *Kaufleute zu Haus und über See: Hamburgischer Zeugnisse des 17., 18. und 19. Jahrhunderts* (Hamburg: Hoffmann und Campe, 1949), 137–38; and Walther Vogel, "Handelskonjuncturen und Wirtschaftskrisen in ihrer Auswirkung auf den Seehandel der Hansestädte," *Hamburgische Geschichts- und Heimatsblätter* 74 (1956), Hansestädte, 63–64.
9. The *Oxford English Dictionary* dates the definition to 1774, but "speculation" in this form certainly existed *avant la lettre.*
10. Heß, *Hamburg*, 2:214.
11. Erwin Wiskemann, *Hamburg und die Welthandelspolitik von den Anfängen bis zur Gegenwart* (Hamburg: Friederichsen, de Gruyter, 1929), 122.
12. Hans Dieter Loose, ed., *Hamburg: Geschichte der Stadt und ihrer Bewohner*, vol. 1, *Von den Anfängen bis zur Reichsgründung* (Hamburg: Hoffmann und Campe, 1982), 328–34, 374–78, 442–52; Hans Mauersberg, *Wirtschafts- und Sozialgeschichte zentraleuropäischer Städte in neuerer Zeit, Hamburg, Frankfurtam Main, Basel, Hannover, München* (Göttingen: Vandenhoeck & Ruprecht, 1960), 179–217; Lindemann, *Patriots and Paupers*, 33–47; Allgemeine Armenanstalt, *Nachrichten von der Einrichtung und dem Fortgange der Hamburgischen Armen-Anstalt* (Hamburg: Benjamin Gottlob Hoffmann, 1789–1840), especially *24ste*

Nachricht (September 1798); Johann Georg Büsch, "Allgemeine Winke zur Verbesserung des Armenwesens," in *Zwei kleine Schriften die im Werk begriffene Verbesserung des Armenwesens in dieser Stadt Hamburg betreffend* (Hamburg, 1786), unpaged.

13. Katherine B. Aaslestad, "Old Visions and New Vices: Republicanism and Civic Virtue in Hamburg's Print Culture, 1790–1810," in Peter Uwe Hohendahl, *Patriotism, Cosmopolitanism, and National Culture: Public Culture in Hamburg 1700–1933* (Amsterdam and New York: Rodopi, 2003), 162–65.
14. Georg Heinrich Sieveking, "Fragmente über Luxus, Bürger-Tugend und Bürger-Wohl für hamburgische Bürger, die das Gute wollen und können . . . " *Hamburgische Gesellschaft zur Beförderung der Künste und nützlichen Gewerben, Verhandlungen und Schriften, 1793–1794* (Hamburg, 1797), 163–83, esp. p. 164.
15. Such materials are found in two major groups of *Bestände* in Staatsarchiv Hamburg (hereafter StAHbg): on firms (621–1) and families (622–1).
16. The work of Ernst Baasch is especially valuable for understanding the general history of commerce in Hamburg and, in particular, the role played by the Chamber of Commerce (*Commerz-Deputation / Handelskammer*): see *Die Handelskammer zu Hamburg*, 1665–1915, vol. 1, *1665–1814* (Hamburg: Gräfe & Sillem, 1915). Percy Ernst Schramm, scion of an important eighteenth- and nineteenth-century merchant family in Hamburg, Jencquel-Luis, combined enthusiasm for his forebearers with the training of a professional historian and wrote extensively on trade and commerce in Hamburg through the lens of family history. See his *Gewinn und Verlust, Die Geschichte der Hamburger Senatorenfamilien Jencquel und Luis (16. bis 19. Jahrhundert): Zwei Beispiele für den wirtschaftlichen und sozialen Wandel in Norddeutschland* (Hamburg: Hans Christians, 1970); *Hamburg, Deutschland und die Welt: Leistung und Grenzen hanseatischen Bürgertums in der Zeit zwischen Napoleon I. und Bismarck, ein Kapitel deutscher Geschichte* (Munich: Callwey, 1943; 2nd ed., 1952); *Neun Generationen: Dreihundert Jahre deutscher "Kulturgeschichte" im Lichte der Schicksale einer Hamburger Bürgerfamilie, 1648–1948*, 2 vols. (Göttingen: Vandenhoeck & Ruprecht, 1963–64); and Schramm, *Kaufleute*. Another descendent of a prominent eighteenth-century Hamburg merchant has also contributed much to our understanding of merchant life in the eighteenth century: Heinrich Sieveking, *Georg Heinrich Sieveking: Lebensbild eines Hamburgischen Kaufmanns aus dem Zeitalter der französischen Revolution* (Berlin: Carl Curtius, 1913) and "Das Handlungshaus Voght und Sieveking," *ZVHG* 17 (1912): 54–128. A more general treatment of Hamburg in the eighteenth century, Heß's three-volume *Hamburg* offers important observations on merchant culture and practices, especially in the section "Oeketologie von Hamburg," 2:137–378.
17. Schramm, *Kaufleute*, 126.
18. Ibid., 127.

19. See "Vorrede," in Johann Jacob Dusch, *Der Bankerot, ein Bürgerliches Trauerspiel* (Hamburg: Dieterich Anton Harmsen, 1763), xi–xvi. Dusch (1725–87) was director of the *Christianeum* (academy) in Altona.
20. Dusch, *Bankerot*, 13–14.
21. Ibid., 28, 65–70.
22. Schramm, *Kaufleute*, 193.
23. Ibid., 203–4.
24. Ibid., 216.
25. Sieveking, *Georg Heinrich Sieveking*; Richard Ehrenberg, *Das Haus Parish in Hamburg*, 2nd ed. (Jena: Gustav Fischer, 1925), 1. I have drawn on Ehrenberg's book (especially for the economic analysis of Parish's accounts) and the original memoirs Parish wrote in English. The latter are handwritten volumes, titled "Journal from 1756" and "Journal from 1797 with regard to my sons," and are found in StAHbg, 622–1/138 (Familie Parish), B1, vols. 1–2.
26. His father's business at his death had a modest capital accumulation of 18,422 Mk. Bco. But when John Parish paid off outstanding debts and split the inheritance with his siblings, only 3000 Mk. Bco. was left to him. Ehrenberg, *Haus Parish*, 6.
27. "Journal from 1756," 165.
28. Ibid., 32.
29. Ibid., 33.
30. "Journal from 1756," 33, and "Journal from 1797 with regard to my sons," passim.
31. "Journal from 1797," 33.
32. "Journal from 1756," 113.
33. Ibid., 48.
34. This description rests on Ehrenberg's analysis of Parish's capital and capital acquisition in the second half of the century. Ehrenberg, *Haus Parish*, 126–28.
35. "Journal from 1756," 42.
36. "Journal from 1797," 33.
37. Ehrenberg, *Haus Parish*, 25, 28–29, 33, 128.
38. Sieveking, *Georg Heinrich Sieveking*, 329, 332, 337–38.
39. Ibid., 349–50.
40. Ibid., 368.
41. Ibid., 391–94.
42. Piter Poel, *Bilder aus vergangener Zeit, nach Mittheilungen aus grossentheils ungedruckten Familienpapieren*, ed. Gustav Poel, 2 vols. (Hamburg: Agentur des Rauhen Hauses, 1884–87), quoted in Sieveking, *Georg Heinrich Sieveking*, 344–45.
43. Nicolaus Schuback went bankrupt in 1769 (with debts amounting to some 458,222 Mk. Bco. 5½ Sh.); Hinrich & Stampeel collapsed in 1770 (they owed creditors at least 569,354 Mk. Bco. 15 Sh.); and His & Son fell in 1783. See list of bankruptcies in StAHbg, Senat Cl. VII Lit. Ma No. 4 Vol. 1c. While there is no denying that going bankrupt was a

serious business setback that stigmatized its victims, for many it was, nonetheless, not a death knell. Many bankrupts regained their financial feet. Some went bankrupt two, three, or even more times.

44. Baasch, *Handelskammer*, 1:189–98, 203–6; on the relatively lax bankruptcy laws in Hamburg, see Ernst Baasch, "Aus einer hamburgischen Fallitenstatistik des 18. Jh," VSWG 15 (1921): 535–45; Johann Klefeker, *Sammlung der Hamburgischen Gesetze und Verfassung in Bürger- und Kirchlichen, auch Cammer- Handlungs- und übrigen Policey-Angelegenheiten und Geschäften samt historischen Einleitungen*, 12 vols. (Hamburg: Piscator, 1765–74), 3:241–360; *Neue Revidirte Falliten-Ordnung*, (Hamburg, 1648); and *Der Stadt Hamburg Neue Falliten-Ordnung, auf Befehl E. Hochedlen Raths publicirt d. 31 August 1753* [hereafter *Falliten-Ordnung 1753*] (Hamburg: Conrad König, 1753). A bankruptcy ordinance for all the Hanse cities was promulgated in 1620: *Mandat, Der Vereinigten Teutschen Hänse Städte/ wieder die muthwillige Falliten und Bancquerottirer* (Lübeck: Samuel Jachen, 1620). Deliberations in 1750–51, and again in the 1790s, on attempts to establish a commercial court (*Handels-Gericht*) can be found in StAHbg, Senat Cl. VII Lit. Ma No. 6 Vol. 3, and Senat Cl. VII Lit. Ka No. 1h. See also Johann Michael Gries, *Über die Nothwendigkeit und die Einrichtung eines Handelsgerichts für Hamburg* (Hamburg: Friedrich Herrman Nestler, 1798). Robert Beachy has documented how a similar process of defining bankruptcy law more rigorously occurred earlier in the century in Saxony: "The Eclipse of Usury: Bankruptcy and Business Morality in Eighteenth-Century Germany," in Mary Lindemann, ed., *Ways of Knowing: Ten Interdisciplinary Essays* (Boston and Leiden: Brill Academic Publishers, 2004), 171–89.
45. *Falliten-Ordnung 1753*, 77.
46. Ibid., 75–76.
47. "Arrestati Paul Hermann Trummers Examen in pto., seines Falissements," from May 14 and July 21, 1756, in StAHbg, Senat Cl. VII Lit. Me No.4b 1–15.
48. On the structure of the linen trade, see Alfred Zimmermann, *Blüthe und Verfall des Leinengewerbes in Schlesien: Gewerbe- und Handelspolitik dreier Jahrhunderte* (Breslau: Wilhlem Gottlieb Korn, 1885), and Werner Jochmann, "Hamburgisch-schlesische Handelsbeziehungen: Ein Beitrag zur abendländlichen Wirtschaftsgeschichte," in *Geschichtliche Landeskunde und Universalgeschichte* (Hamburg: "Wihag" Buch-Druckerei, 1950), 217–28.
49. "Arrestati Paul Hermann Trummers Examen in pto., seines Falissements."
50. In StAHbg, 211–2, Reichskammergericht (hereafter RKG), B58 Teil 1.
51. StAHbg, RKG, B58 Teil 1, folios 203–8.
52. StAHbg, RKG, B58 Teil 1, folios 208–9.
53. StAHbg, RKG, B58 Teil 1, folios 210–15.
54. StAHbg, RKG, B58 Teil 1, folios 216–17.

Chapter 8

Accounting for War and Revolution

Philadelphia Merchants and Commercial Risk, 1774–1811

Cathy Matson, University of Delaware

While commercial capitalism had become an adaptive way of life for trans-Atlantic merchants by the second half of the eighteenth century, individual success and even survival were never assured. The commercial lives of two North Americans illustrate the vicissitudes faced by most traders in a stormy period of war and revolution. In May 1785, Philadelphia merchant Andrew Clow received a letter from London that dashed his expectations for prosperous trade in the post-Revolutionary city. "Your partner Mr. [David] Cay was made Bankrupt," wrote a friend, and he "hath quitted the Kingdom." Clow would not "be made a Bankrupt with [Cay], unless you return to this Country," but he would be liable on his own for all debts of the partnership, the letter advised. Two weeks later another London creditor informed Clow that his goods would be sold for whatever price they might bring, since Cay had absconded, "nor have we the least Idea where he can be gone." A drawer in Cay's office held far more bills for debts due "than will discharge yr. Debt of Clow & Cay," though as "Men of Honour," and "from the very respectable Character you bear, as an honest sober industrious Man," the creditors were confident "that you may see your Partnership Debt discharged," for "it Must Be for Material Advantage to Save all we Can." Cay, however, was on the run "in outlawry." He had refused payments to London firms supplying goods sent to Philadelphia and "given out Bills [of exchange] here In the Name of Cay & Clow . . . & got money for them," then "Desapated it" in "Wanton luxury." Now, running from one Spanish or French port to another, Cay had left Clow to be hounded by creditors visiting Philadelphia from Manchester, Halifax, New York, and Bordeaux who tried to wring payments from the defunct partnership.[1]

Clow avoided commercial failure by eventually settling accounts with his foreign creditors, and he even established a modest grain trade to Cadiz, Coruna, and Vigo during 1789–90, before succumbing to the yellow fever epidemic that overwhelmed Philadelphia in 1793, leaving another set of creditors to seek satisfaction from his estate until early 1835.[2] Although his circumstances were not unusual in post-Revolutionary Philadelphia, scholars of these heady years tend to emphasize the stories of success and optimism in the Atlantic world's tangled transnational network of merchants, as well as the material signs of rapid postwar recovery. Increased shipbuilding and skilled urban work opportunities, a great influx of consumer goods, and new entrepreneurial projects all figure importantly in this optimistic view of an expansive North American republic.[3] The creation of a brilliantly negotiated federal structure of government in 1787 also was rhetorically linked to this imagined era of commercial abundance to come. As its eighteenth-century supporters argued, the Constitution helped tame the contradictory voices and legislation coming from the disconnected American states after the Revolution. More recently, historians argue that the construction of a national government marked a moment that permitted Americans to enter history in their own name, to claim their own commercial rights within the world of trading partners, and to create greater economic security under the umbrella of a centralized political authority.[4] Some even argue that prosperity actually did ensue after the Revolution, often bolstering their view by pointing to a few exceptional fortunes that were made by those Americans returning to British trade or engaging in Chinese, Latin American, northern European, and other distant markets. A seemingly unstoppable flow of credit and goods in North American ports added further support to this view.[5]

Certainly, these views of postwar commercial revival contain important truths about the anticipated results of political independence and further economic abundance. But there is much more to reveal about the early republic's commerce, which was fraught with a dizzying array of shifting transnational partnerships and insecure markets. New commercial routes, such as the one to China, emerged more slowly than optimists predicted; the China trade, for example, began with a spectacular single voyage in 1784 but did not become regular for years to come. In the Caribbean, a region indisputably linked to North American commercial maturation for generations, the foreign French, Spanish, and Dutch islands often were more important than British stopovers. Even then, wars, piracy, and revolution battered all Caribbean commerce with regularity in the 1780s and 1790s. Within North America, unpaid state and national debts, scarce capital for manufactures and internal improvements, widespread indebtedness in the countryside and cities, and dislocated populations in need of relief and employment, all eluded the majesty of the new federal government. Indeed, even the best federal structure could not have stitched together all of the swatches of America's commercial fabric in the first post-Revolutionary generation, for as good as the structure was, and as respected as many American merchants were abroad, the Atlantic world economy could not be controlled by any single national interest.[6]

A more compelling narration of North America's postwar commerce also requires a closer look at the complicated personal relationships, shifting trade patterns, and negotiated trading arrangements faced by all merchants. Their business terrain was huge and their ships carried goods and people across permeable international boundaries during periods of dramatic seasonal economic fluctuations and destroyed credit liaisons. Setbacks in foreign and coastal markets challenged every merchant's good character, and many remarked with frequency about fortunes rising and falling at an alarming rate; some vanished, while others were reconstructed, only to fall again.[7]

Philadelphia merchant Stephen Girard's long career vividly illustrates these generalizations. Unlike the forgotten Andrew Clow, Girard has been celebrated for his great investments in British banks, the War of 1812, negotiable paper instruments, land around New Orleans, and public buildings in his home port, as well as his purchase of the Second Bank of United States. But this end-of-life perspective of tremendous economic achievement, it turns out, does not account for Girard's first twenty years in city commerce. In the late 1760s, Girard left his large and economically marginal family in Bordeaux and sailed as an agent for French merchants into the Caribbean. Within three years he was accepting commissions for his brother, Jean Girard, who lived at French-controlled Cap François (Le Cap), St. Domingue; he also clerked at Port-au-Prince for friends of his father, a position that allowed him to meet arriving North American captains. When French West Indies markets grew "sluggish almost to their death" by 1768, Girard spent a short time in New York City, where he found work for the exporters Thomas Randall & Son, whose captains were well known at French and Spanish West Indies ports. Girard rose quickly in Randall's favor because he knew how to direct schooners to Le Cap, Port-au-Prince, or Mole St. Nicholas (the Mole) where he sold provisions more quickly and bought sugar more cheaply than at British islands. Randall promised to recommend Girard to other New York merchants, and his brother Jean guaranteed him plentiful cargoes at St. Domingue. Yet despite his connections to at least three important parts of the Atlantic world—France, St. Domingue, and New York—Girard did little more than lament "nests of pirates," hostile foreign vessels, deceitful crews, and, most of all, his dependence on Randall. "There is little here," the impatient Girard wrote from Le Cap to Randall in early 1776, "to attract my energies. Nothing doing."[8]

Then, just as British troops began to occupy New York, Girard's schooner, returning from St. Domingue, blew off course and went into Philadelphia, where revolutionary turmoil took him by surprise. With little start-up capital, aside from the vessel he only partly owned and its contents, and marine insurance almost impossible to secure for more voyages, Girard retreated into storekeeping in Mount Holly, New Jersey, where he supplied small quantities of local goods to patriots and loyalists alike during the first part of the war. By 1778, he reluctantly teamed up once again with Randall, who had relocated to Philadelphia, and the two of them reinitiated trade to Le Cap and Port-au-Prince. Already, Girard knew the importance of being mobile and "taking the risk" of commercial opportunities as they arose, but he continued to strive for higher profits by trading "on his own account."

Girard's wartime correspondence reveals two habits that would define his commercial decisions for years to come and set him apart from typical commercial behavior among city merchants. One was his penchant for "gambling in trade" (as a disapproving acquaintance in Philadelphia put it). While many other merchants retreated from commerce and the Atlantic basin was beset with wartime scarcities, high-priced marine insurance, and regular ship seizures, Girard set aside all expectations for security in the belief that he might reap an occasional windfall, "should just one great venture reach its mark." Second, and unlike most of his commercial peers, Girard *perceived* that commercial risks running the gamut from frustrating to frightening were *less* problematic than the unfamiliar and barely tested alternatives of investing in manufacturing, real estate, finance, or internal improvements. Until the onset of the War of 1812, Girard sank most of his capital into commerce; thereafter, banking and entrepreneurial projects absorbed more of his attention and capital.

Many Philadelphia traders who lacked credit and connections abandoned trade in the 1770s and 1780s for safer forms of investment or reduced commercial activity. But in all cases, they needed the protection of "friends," "reputation," and "prudence." Banking, brokerage, credit bureaus, limited liability, and bankruptcy protection provided only scant institutional aid in North America until the 1790s. Marine insurance covered losses of ships and goods, but rarely covered full cargoes and was notoriously difficult to collect. Philadelphia merchants had even less protection from the deceit or absconding of other traders. In response, merchants had developed intricate networks of private creditworthiness, skills in accounting and letterwriting, and formalized correspondence. Girard had little of this protection during his first years, and he also found it difficult to secure as many loans of credit and goods as he sought. Desperate to prevail against the era's odds, he engaged every available ship he could charter and demanded the fastest turnaround times his captains could muster. The risk of loss to privateers and pirates was high, and most of the vessels Girard chartered in the 1770s never made it to their destinations or were held up for months while his captains sought return cargoes. At St. Domingue, cargoes succumbed to seizures, mold, and torrential rain. But he reasoned that he could occasionally make a good profit from selling flour at rapidly rising wartime prices if he could just keep ships outfitted and launched toward the islands. Upon their return, Girard stored bags of coffee and sugar in scattered city warehouses until prices were favorable. Smuggling was also a regular feature of Girard's efforts to keep ships busy; despite periodic French decrees forbidding the entry of North American flour at island ports (because French merchants wished to corner their own imperial trade), Girard frequently instructed his agents to fill sacks "secretly with flour and put them in hogsheads of rice" from Charleston. The risk of discovery was "worth it." Despite sending word to captains that he "grew frantic with concern for news" of safe arrival and harbored "near constant fear" that privateers would seize a vessel, he reoutfitted every vessel that returned to Philadelphia as quickly as he could. When questioned by a merchant neighbor about the dangers of losses, Girard retorted, "I shall always take the gamble."[9]

Although Girard relied heavily on book credit in Philadelphia, he paid cash for goods at West Indies islands or ordered his captains to barter directly with island merchants, exchanging goods-for-goods right on the shoreline. He sent captains to Havana or New Orleans, expecting them to befriend expatriate Philadelphians who could in turn make introductions to Spanish merchants who paid for Girard's cargoes with silver. On other occasions, when captains could not directly exchange provisions for sugar or coffee at Le Cap, they set off without delay to St. Eustatius to sell their cargoes for silver. Girard's captains seldom left cargoes of flour at an island port for future sale and often they paid for coffee in advance of loading it for the return trip. Although reports reached Philadelphia in 1779 that "a swarm of men, from all parts of the world" docked at St. Eustatius, waiting for auspicious markets before selling their goods, Girard ordered his captains to "sell our flower at first contact in that place and take nothing but silver." To Girard's "mystified Chagrin," the result was "heavy losses" during 1779 to 1781, for "none but those who take a promise of payment in the future are permitted to land goodes."[10]

By 1780, St. Domingue markets were "dead" and Martinique was "a guess." Girard's captains squeezed through British blockades in the Delaware Bay, only to encounter British privateers in the Caribbean. Occasionally captains successfully landed their bags and barrels of coffee at Delaware's inlets "under cover of night," but when the Continental Army began moving south for its final campaigns, patriot officers seized the small vessels Girard and Randall used to collect flour and wheat along the Delaware coastline, producing "the most alarming agitations" in Girard. Insurance underwriters delivered a further blow in 1780 when they announced that rates would rise steeply. Unable by then to "trade on his own account," and resorting to buying shares in two other merchants' vessels, Girard was only a little better off at the close of the war than he had been at its start.

Nevertheless, in 1782, Girard announced to his brother in Le Cap that he had caught the "recovery fever." "Many houses and shops are as yet abandoned, but I see now that all my zeal of recent years was but practice for what is to come." He moved from the boarding house where he had stayed at the end of the Revolution and rented a store on Water Street, the back of which abutted the city docks; in time, he bought the building and added a counting house, where he was positioned in the vital center of Philadelphia's commerce. Behind the counting house, Girard took up residence for the next nearly forty years, at first renting and then buying the property. During the 1780s, this was a desirable location for rising men of commerce, though it was not in the fashionable part of the city where most accomplished merchants resided. Girard himself did not fashion a life of elegance in postwar Philadelphia, and most of Girard's neighbors were merchants of steady reputation and reasonable comfort, not of the "best sort."[11]

Throughout Philadelphia, perceptions of imminent commercial recovery were, by late 1783, clouded over by the problems of overcrowded neighborhoods, shortages of necessities in public markets and shops, and shortages of exportable commodities. Despite a flurry of efforts along Water Street to send out ships, no more than a handful of city merchants posted the profits they anticipated after the war. A crush of imported dry goods entered the city and soon produced gluts and tightened credit. As a depression set in, merchants in New York and Philadelphia lamented "the forlorn appearance of the shops" along streets. Girard complained in early 1785 that "business is execrable," and most goods were imported on credit lasting less than three months or "for ready money."[12] Farm recovery was certainly taking place in some quarters by the mid-1780s, but poor yields of grain kept exportable surpluses disappointingly low. Even when exporters could fill the holds of their ships with provisions, horses, and wood products, Caribbean prices for them fluxuated "to madness," and only a few of the best-placed merchants could get to new markets in the Gulf Coast, Latin America, or northern Europe at this time.[13]

Girard reluctantly pooled resources with Randall once again and repeatedly gambled on losing cargoes, ships, and crews during the next few years by relentlessly sending them to dangerous waters at St. Domingue and Martinique. But by then, British authorities, desperate for American provisions, wood products, and shipping services, had placed restrictions on American trade to the Caribbean. As Philadelphians lamented, however, the British islands alone could not produce sufficient staples exports to attract American ships, and informal hostilities by British naval and privateering ships only heightened the rancor among Americans. French merchants also tried to keep Americans away from their islands. But true to form, Girard and a few other Philadelphians disregarded warnings and sent cargoes to French (and Dutch) ports, hoping to bring back the comparatively cheaper and more plentiful exports of sugar and coffee from St. Domingue. Bribing island port officials when necessary and supplementing cargoes of Brandywine flour with Carolina rice, Girard's captains settled for "just half full" cargoes. Girard grew jubilant when France opened five Caribbean ports to "free trade" in 1784, and he redoubled efforts to race against his competitors "to make a good market" at St. Domingue. He informed captains to sail to any other ports if they must, but "at all odds, you must land my goods" and "offer them [at St. Domingue] the usual discounts of direct sales."[14]

Philadelphia's commerce was also hampered by strained relations with France during the 1780s. Despite the 1778 Congressional treaty that guaranteed rebellious Americans reciprocal and open trade with France, little bipartisan trade ensued. War and lingering Atlantic belligerence impeded some trade, but in addition, Philadelphia consumers widely believed that French merchants sent them high-priced inferior silk and brandy that had lain unsold in French markets for months already. To make matters worse, French consumers did not yet have a great sweet tooth for Caribbean sugar; nearly three-quarters of French imported sugar was reexported in foreign (mainly German) vessels to northern Europe until about 1790. A few well-placed Philadelphians and New Yorkers turned these conditions to their own advantage by carrying French West Indies goods to North America when conditions permitted, and then reexporting island sugar and coffee to France and Europe.[15]

Girard insisted that he should break into the French trade; "it seems necessary to me to run some risks or to remain always poor," for only "prudence will risk nothing." But there were still problems in the Caribbean. His captains often returned with unspectacular cargoes of coffee and sugar through the 1780s. Moreover, periodic rumors filtered through Baltimore and Philadelphia about a "plague" (perhaps a virulent strain of flu) in the French Caribbean, which forced some of Girard's vessels into quarantine at Le Cap and the Mole. As the ships sat offshore, his captains watched flour prices fall or water seep into casks of flour "render[ing] the whole lot suitable only for the [live] stock." Anxious for a quick turnaround, Girard instructed captains to write false passes for Jamaica in order to break out of the quarantine. Once released, however, his captains "missed the Jamaica markets," only to learn that the Havana markets also were glutted.[16]

Girard inherited next to nothing when his father died in 1788, but an interlude of fertile international trading from 1789 to 1791 finally lifted some of the anxiety he had nurtured for nearly fifteen years. Historians often connect the better times of these three years to the formation of a national government in America, but economic opportunities for Girard and many of his peers derived from the onset of the French Revolution and the precipitous rise in demand for provisions in the Caribbean when the lifeline to France was severed. For a short time between 1789 and 1791, Philadelphia exporters sent more vessels to St. Domingue than anywhere else in the Atlantic world. Merchants at northern American ports sent over half of their exportable cargoes of flour, beef, pork, livestock, fish, and wood products to the West Indies in 1789, mostly to French ports. Vessels entering Philadelphia from St. Domingue accounted for more than one-fifth of the city's trade during the first three years of the French Revolution.[17]

During these flush times, Girard charted more complicated voyages with stopovers at Charleston for rice, Virginia for tobacco, or Baltimore for flour, in the hope of guaranteeing higher profits with a full ship. Finally in command of his own (larger) vessels now, Girard spent hours each day overseeing the preparation of "my philosophers," the ships *Rousseau, Voltaire, Helvetius, Montesquieu*, and serving as a consignment agent for a few French correspondents. Through the spring and summer months of 1791, Girard predicted that any sugar he could get from Le Cap and the Mole would sell at a windfall profit (at least a 200 percent markup, he thought) in his home port.[18]

But by early fall 1791, the ever-gambling Girard faced reversals. The rosy conditions faded first at St. Domingue, where planters and merchants, now cut off from French goods, encouraged Americans to bring all the flour, leather, and timber goods they could, promising duty-free exportation of sugar and coffee as an incentive. Enticed by such offers, a few Philadelphians followed in Girard's earlier footsteps, happily announcing to their correspondents at St. Domingue and Martinique that they could have large vessels of high-quality flour readied quickly. But the island's revolution erupted in August, and within a couple of months widespread destruction from deepening slave unrest, outbreaks of "ship fever," rotting cargoes, and belligerent French port officials scared away most Philadelphia captains. Girard received only discouraging news in the coming weeks, first that Port-au-Prince was torched, then that civil war brought an end to almost all sugar production and planters could not pay debts to coastal merchants. Moreover, French merchants active on the island clamored for—and temporarily won—sterner regulations of international trade, including a warehousing system for imports and restrictions governing where Americans could sail to find markets. In January 1792, *Pennsylvania Gazette* readers learned that "only four merchants' houses have escaped the conflagration" of slave uprisings at Port-au-Prince.[19]

Girard held out some hope of "making a market" when he heard about opportunities to provision the French troops arriving at St. Domingue to stifle the slave rebellion. After all, they would bring silver coin with them. But within a few months it became clear that the French revolutionary government was no better at paying its commissions to suppliers than the American Congress had been ten years earlier. Depreciation of French *assignats* was about as steep in the early 1790s as Continental currency had been in the 1770s, and it drove Girard away from French government contractors into the arms of island merchants again. But he kept sailing his ships, and on every voyage to Le Cap from late 1791 to late 1792 he informed the captain to declare no more than half the goods being entered (and thereby pay only half the taxes) and to depart the island with false clearances for other islands, in order to fill the hold. Navigating all the dangers, Girard sent well over forty-five thousand barrels of flour to St. Domingue during 1792, though it is not clear how many barrels found acceptable markets, and eight vessels were captured or capsized, while seven came into Philadelphia with cargoes far too small to cover Girard's debts.[20] By September 1792, Jacob Broom of Wilmington, Delaware, wrote to his commission agent at St. Domingue that "the troubles on your Island are so great and affairs with you so Gloomy that we do not know if it will be prudent . . . to sett the Cargoe at the Cape" as they had for many previous seasons. Sending cargoes to Martinique (via St. Thomas), Guadeloupe, and St. Eustatius proved equally disappointing, and word spread quickly in Philadelphia that "the islands are but dead markets."[21]

For twenty years starting in 1793, nearly unrelenting commercial belligerency, punctuated with periods of open warfare, set the tone for North Americans' trade with the Caribbean islands and Europe. Certainly, a few spectacular fortunes were made by mid-Atlantic traders during this era, and scores of merchants rose up through the ranks of exporters to seek a measure of success in island trade. But most traders faced fluctuating markets and prices reminiscent of the first post-Revolutionary years. Complicating their efforts to trade prosperously were a dizzying array of contradictory policies and belligerent privateering, as well as the shifting declarations of neutrality by first one, and then another, nation that disrupted commercial alliances. Most of all, despite rising demand at West Indies islands for American provisions, which grew out of the earlier expansion in sugar production and slave importation, social resistance in the Caribbean challenged the best efforts of ambitious North Americans to get goods to islanders.

By the time France declared war on England in February 1793 and then expanded its war to encompass Spain and Holland, residents of St. Domingue had become desperate for food imports. Declarations of French and English conditional neutrality in March 1793 brought excitement to Philadelphia's merchants, but in the coming months neutrality became simply one more form of negotiated risk; France and England decreed that they would seize every neutral vessel carrying enemy property (in the form of exports from the islands), regardless of the ship's registration or destination. British scouts hovering near Le Cap grabbed five of Girard's vessels in just one month of 1793, on the suspicion of their carrying French goods. While his flour rotted, Girard's agents wrote that hundreds of ships from North America were also being detained at St. Eustatius, Bermuda, Basseterre, Martinique, Montserrat, St. Kitts, and other islands.[22] Philadelphia exporters responded that their only hope of protection from the seizures was to supply every captain with papers (whether official or fabricated) from every warring nation, vouching for the neutral origins of his cargo. The gamble was clear: a ship bound for the Caribbean with papers demonstrating that its goods were destined for a port controlled by the nation that stopped it might be released (or not) and the merchants "make a very handsome voyage;" but a ship that could not prove it headed toward, or came from, a port of the privateering ship's nation could summarily lose everything.[23]

North Americans' escalating illegal trade in the Caribbean was underscored by the terrible logic of revolution in St. Dominque. When internal island conditions deteriorated rapidly during 1793, Girard and a handful of other Philadelphians began to transport refugees to Baltimore and Philadelphia as part of their return cargoes. In April, revolutionaries burned Le Cap and Girard lost two ships carrying hundreds of barrels of flour; in June, Le Cap was sacked and burned, and an English decree authorized seizure of all neutral vessels going to French possessions, presenting Girard with grave prospects. Meanwhile, as the Terror began in France, Girard's agents living there were guillotined or fled from the country, so that although his ships had not carried sugar to France for some time, he feared he would never collect long overdue debts. By mid-1793, a "Malignant fever [was] raging" in Philadelphia and Wilmington, believed (but never proven) to have been introduced by Caribbean refugees, nearly halted exporting.[24] While Girard played an active role in tending to the sick and dying in Philadelphia, his letters note the "dire failures" of dozens of British, Scottish, and French agents at St. Domingue, Martinique, and St. Eustatius, and dozens of merchants in Philadelphia who could not fill export orders. Still, Girard was able to secure loans for ships and goods that he sent to Le Cap, Aux Cayes, and Jeremie—some by way of St. Eustatius and Curacao—in September and October. In November, when England tightened its commercial restrictions and ordered the detention of any ship entering or clearing a French colony, regardless of its cargo, Girard hedged his risks not by ceasing to send vessels to the French islands, but by sharing ownership in vessels and sending them by circuitous routes.[25] Still, British privateers captured Girard's chartered vessels the *Polly*, *Kitty*, and *Nancy* while on their way to French ports, "in the same manner as if they had been taken by the Algerines," while French privateers chased at least two of his captains away from St. Eustatius. When vessels returned to Philadelphia—"molested" and empty, "everything lost"—Girard meticulously noted the captain's details of the voyage while loading them up again. Finally, the *Nancy* smashed against rocks at Mogane Island, permitting Girard the luxury of declaring this a legitimate voyage and applying to his insurance underwriters for compensation.[26]

Many Philadelphia merchants gravitated toward the pro-French Democratic-Republican fervor in the city. In March 1794, a group of traders reminded newspaper readers that the hoped for "reciprocal display of impartiality" between Britain and the new states, which might have "obliterate[d] the remembrance of the wrongs" of the Revolution, had been replaced by "an ambitious and vindictive policy . . . [that] denied the rights, attacked the interests, interrupted the pursuits, and insulted the dignity, of the United States." Furthermore, they wrote, "Britain has violently seized and sequestered the vessels and property of the citizens of the U.S. to the value of several millions of dollars." Girard paced the Philadelphia wharf restlessly as news reached the city about British troops landing on St. Domingue to crush the slave uprising, then their seizure of Martinique, followed by brutal force against a large maroon uprising on Jamaica before the British reinforcements succumbed in early 1795 to a new outbreak of yellow fever. Spain handed over Santo Domingo to the French that year, too, and Toussaint L'Ouverture soon became the head of the slave and free black majority on St. Domingue, making Girard's exporting to the Caribbean "a ruinous business."[27]

Rebounding once again in early 1795 when news of abundant exportable surpluses in the Delaware Valley reached his warehouse, Girard prepared for "a gambling venture" to St. Bartholomew and St. Thomas with huge loads of flour, hoping to get them to Le Cap indirectly. Most of it, however, was captured by French privateers or spoiled sitting in harbors before it could be offloaded. Meanwhile, the French government had demonetized silver and prohibited its export, and Girard assured his French correspondent, Horquebie, that he now faced the "Calamity" of losing a great deal of money on their underinsured transatlantic ventures. And despite hearing from agents at Port-au-Prince and Le Cap that flour was selling at extraordinary prices, only one sloop got through during fall 1795. By the next March, Girard's home port was "in the greatest confusion so far as business was concerned." As fears grew that America would soon be at war with two powerful European nations, marine insurance companies closed, many ships were auctioned off, and dozens of Girard's fellow merchants in Philadelphia failed.[28]

Uncertainties continued for two more years, and then in 1798, the French government closed its West Indies possessions to American trade and the value of Philadelphia's exports to those islands fell below that of exports to Spanish and British islands for the first time in the careers of most city traders. Congress responded to exceedingly high levels of French privateering that year with an "undeclared war" and a decree allowing Americans to capture any French vessels interfering with their trade; when this action brought little relief to American shippers, Congress cut off trade with all French islands in mid-1798. Near the end of the decade, and for the first time in Girard's commercial career, it became unfeasible to trade in this part of the Atlantic world.[29]

North American merchants faced important choices at the close of the century that underscored the transnational dependencies of their enterprise more than ever. As before, some merchants withdraw from trade during the thick of warfare, and after 1800 these options were becoming more feasible. Of those who remained in commerce, the familiar patterns of trade began to shift under the weight of international war and the entry of aggressive commercial newcomers. Some tested British markets at Jamaica, Barbados, and the British Antilles in 1800, but within a few months word spread in Philadelphia that the British islands, though open, could not pay for their imports. Other Philadelphians touched at numerous islands, taking on a series of small loads of coffee and sugar, and often stopping at southern American states before returning to home port.[30]

The most significant adjustment in Caribbean commerce involved sending more ships to Cuba, where Spanish officials opened a neutral trade with Americans in early 1797 in order to attract much-needed food to the island. Long-term habits of smuggling goods into Havana were easily converted into legitimate port entries. As a result, just as the turmoil on St. Domingue shut out almost all North American importation by the late 1790s, the "sugar revolution" at Cuba stimulated absorption of that traffic. By 1802, a consortium of Philadelphia merchants took large amounts of Spanish wine to Cuba in Philadelphia-owned vessels and shipped Cuban fish and American flour to Spain. Unsurprisingly Girard joined some thirty other merchants in Philadelphia, New York, Wilmington and New Castle, Delaware, and Baltimore during 1797 to 1805 who were finally "getting the highest returns ever." Still stinging from the "derangements" of ventures to southern France and St. Domingue during 1793–97, he wrote that "the gambles upon the [French] republic will soon be put aside when we see returns from this other [Spanish] nation." A few merchants in Philadelphia began to transfer some Cuban silver into the China trade, making stops at Argentina and Peru for beef and hides sold at Havana on their return, though this route was regularized only in 1805.[31]

Trade from Philadelphia to Nante and Bordeaux revived episodically in the late 1790s, spurred by hunger in France and southern Europe. But crossing the Atlantic was still fraught was piracy and privateering, and French exports were still not in high demand in North America.[32] By 1800 Philadelphians believed Amsterdam and Hamburg markets offered better prospects, and a handful of them ventured to St. Petersburg, Copenhagen, and Riga as well. From 1801 to 1807 about one-quarter of American exports were sent to these European destinations, and well over half of Girard's now meteorically rising fortune derived from this trade. In addition, from 1805 to 1809, Girard, now over fifty years old, drew funds from his savings in Amsterdam and London to fund voyages of the *Voltaire* and *Montesquieu* to "Bengal or China."[33]

The Jeffersonian embargoes during 1807–9 cramped Girard's plans for continuous expansion, and the disruptions of Algerian pirates and Latin American revolutions set limits on where his expansion would be. But most years after 1800 were good enough for Girard to refashion himself once again from a "mariner and a merchant" into a banker and real estate investor as well. Writing in 1807 that "the alarming situation of our maritime commerce has induced me to employ a part of my funds in the banking business," he began diminishing many overseas connections and calling in overdue debts. By 1811, he had transferred large sums from Baring, Brothers Co., the great British bank, into the Bank of the United States, becoming its largest stockholder. When Congress did not recharter the Bank, Girard bought it. When the government ran out of money to finance the War of 1812, he became the country's greatest creditor by making a loan to the Treasury of more than $8 million, the fruits of land speculation around Philadelphia and New Orleans since the early 1800s. In a few years he would write a will representing a final refashioning of himself into a great city landlord and philanthropist.[34] For Girard, the American Revolution, and the chaotic juggling for commercial advantage that followed it, did not provide an unmitigated path to success. But the anxieties he expressed were less about the long-term depredations of war and revolution than they were about particular losses of ships and cargoes; the qualities of diligence and industry defined him more than those of prudence. Girard attained a degree of success that very few merchants in the Western hemisphere could emulate, largely by tolerating a very high level of risk and relentlessly pursuing his self-interest with a great deal of pluck.

NOTES

1. William Newby to Andrew Clow, London, May 31, 1785; Edward Hewitt to AC, London, June 1, Sept. 17, 1785; John Travis to AC, Sept. 2, 1785; Edward Hewitt to AC, Apr. 3, 1787, in Andrew Clow & Company, Records, 1784–1835, Hagley Museum and Library (hereafter, Hagley), Wilmington, DE. Clow is just one of many merchants in Philadelphia and New York who left records of adversity through the early 1800s, whom I trace in a larger research project. See also articles by Michelle Craig McDonald, Alec Dun, Brooke Hunter, Evelyn Jennings, and Sherry Johnson in "The Atlantic Economy in an Era of Revolutions," Special Forum, ed. and intro. Cathy Matson, *William and Mary Quarterly*, 3rd ser., 62 (July 2005), 357-526 (hereafter *WMQ*).
2. Correspondence and bankruptcy records, Andrew Clow & Company, Records, 1784–1835.
3. See, for example, D. A. Farnie, "The Commercial Empire of the Atlantic, 1607–1783," *Economic History Review*, 2nd ser. (1962), 205–18; Ralph Davis, *The Rise of the Atlantic Economies* (Cornell: Cornell University Press, 1973); Peggy Liss, *Atlantic Empires: The Network of Trade and Revolution, 1713–1826* (Baltimore: Johns Hopkins University Press, 1983); David Hancock, *Citizens of the World: London Merchants and the Integration of the British Atlantic World, 1735–1785* (Cambridge: Cambridge University Press, 1995); Thomas Doerflinger, *A Vigorous Spirit of Enterprise* (Chapel Hill: University of North Carolina Press, 1986), 77–126; Cathy Matson, *Merchants and Empire: Trading in Colonial New York* (Baltimore: Johns Hopkins University Press, 1998), chaps. 6, 8; and Jacob Price and Paul G. E. Clemens, "A Revolution of Scale in Overseas Trade: British Firms in the Chesapeake Trade, 1675–1775," *Journal of Economic History* 47 (1987), 1–43.
4. For contemporary optimism, see Robert Morris to Thomas Russell, Aug. 12, 1783, in E. James Ferguson and John Catanzariti, eds., *The Papers of Robert Morris, 1781–1784*, 9 vols. (Pittsburgh: University of Pittsburgh Press, 1973–99), 8:425–26; and Cathy Matson and Peter Onuf, *A Union of Interests: Political and Economic Thought in Revolutionary America* (Kansas City: University of Kansas Press, 1990). For historians' arguments that the political Revolution and economic growth were intertwined, see E. James Ferguson, *The Power of the Purse: A History of American Public Finance, 1776–1790* (Chapel Hill: University of North Carolina Press, 1961).

5. For rapid commercial recovery, see Joyce Appleby, *Inheriting the Revolution: The First Generation of Americans* (Cambridge, MA: Harvard University Press, 2001); Doerflinger, *A Vigorous Spirit*, ch. 5, 222–45; Stuart Bruchey, *Robert Oliver, Merchant of Baltimore, 1783–1819* (Baltimore: Johns Hopkins University Press, 1956); Douglass C. North, *The Economic Growth of the United States, 1790–1860* (New York: W. W. Norton, 1966), vi–vii, and Part I; and, for the mid-Atlantic region, Geoffrey Gilbert, "The Role of Breadstuffs in American Trade, 1770–1790," *Explorations in Economic History* 14 (1977), 378. Oddly, there is relatively little work about how, and to what extent, Americans reentered British trade after the war.
6. For qualified recovery, see Drew McCoy, *The Elusive Republic: Political Economy in Jeffersonian America* (Chapel Hill: University of North Carolina Press, 1980); John E. Crowley, *The Privileges of Independence: Neomercantilism and the American Revolution* (Baltimore: Johns Hopkins University Press, 1993); Matson and Onuf, *A Union of Interests*, chaps. 7–8; and Alan Taylor, *William Cooper's Town: Power and Persuasion on the Frontier of the Early American Republic* (New York: Vintage, 1996). For the centrality of the foreign and British islands, see Matson, *Merchants and Empire*, 135–50, 260–69; Shipping Records, 1708–1892 (mostly 1790–1820), 5 boxes, Winterthur Library, Delaware; Willing and Morris Papers, Historical Society of Pennsylvania (hereafter, HSP); William Walton Papers, New-York Historical Society (hereafter, N-YHS); John H. Coatsworth, "American Trade with European Colonies in the Caribbean and South America, 1790–1812," *WMQ*, 24 (April 1967); Liss, *Atlantic Empires*, 29–30; A. P. Whitaker, "The Commerce of Louisiana and the Floridas at the End of the Eighteenth Century," *Hispanic American Historical Review* 8 (1928), 190–203; and Franklin Knight, "The Origins of Wealth and the Sugar Revolution in Cuba, 1750–1850," *Hispanic American Historical Review*, 57 (1977), 231–53.
7. Gary Walton and James Shepherd, *The Economic Rise of Early America* (Cambridge, MA: Cambridge University Press, 1979), 186–97. The authors show effectively that in 1790–92, Philadelphia's exports levels were about where they were just before the Revolution.
8. Of the many studies about Girard, only one (unfootnoted and inaccurate) details his trade: John Bach McMaster, *The Life and Times of Stephen Girard, Mariner and Merchant*, 2 vols. (Philadelphia: Lippincott, 1918). For Girard's later years, see Donald Adams, *Finance and Enterprise in Early America: A Study of Stephen Girard's Bank, 1812–1831* (Philadelphia: University of Pennsylvania Press, 1978). This and the next paragraphs draw heavily from the Papers of Stephen Girard (GP), Series II, reels 121–23, American Philosophical Society (APS), a collection of more than six hundred reels of microfilm.
9. GP, Series II, reels 123, 127, APS; William Duer Papers, N-YHS; Willing and Morris Papers, HSP; Liss, *Atlantic Empires*, 108–91, 283–84n37; Knight, "Origins of Wealth," 242, 244; Chaloner & White

advertisements in *Pennsylvania Gazette, 1772-1774;* Ferguson, *Power of the Purse;* and Linda Salvucci, "Development and Decline: The Port of Philadelphia and Spanish Imperial Markets, 1783–1823" (PhD diss., Princeton, 1985), 85–86.

10. GP, Series II, reels 121–23; Brooke Hunter, "Rage for Grain: Flour Milling in the Mid-Atlantic, 1750–1815" (PhD diss., University of Delaware, 2001); Sherry Johnson, *The Social Transformation of Eighteenth-Century Cuba* (Gainsville: University Press of Florida, 2001), chap. 8; and Knight, "Origins of Wealth," 249.

11. GP, Series II, reel 121; Clifford Family Papers, 1722–1832, HSP; Jones & Clarke, Papers, 1784–1816, HSP; Philadelphia City Directory, 1791; and Lewden Family Papers, Delaware Historical Society (hereafter, DHS).

12. For postwar failures and ship seizures, see Stephen Girard to Jean Girard, May 28 and Nov. 28, 1783, Mar. 28, 1784, and Apr. 15, 1785, and records of the ship *Les Deux Amis*, 1785, GP, Series II, reel 121; Chaloner & White Papers, HSP; John Ball Family Papers, HSP; John Nixon Papers, 1707–1845, HSP; Willing and Morris Papers, HSP; and John Brown Account Book, 1774–1777, 1783–1787, HSP; Amos Brinton, Account Book, Hagley; and *The Delaware Gazette*, June 27, 1789. For "forlorn appearance," William Constable to Daniel McCormick, Feb. 9, 1784, Constable Papers, N-YHS; for "execrable," SG to Balthazar Ortt, Amsterdam, Mar. 31, 1785; and for "ready money," SG to Byrne & Von Dorsten, New York, Sept. 22, 1783, GP, Series II, reel 121.

13. For the 1780s downturn, see *American Museum* (Philadelphia: Carey, Stewart, and Co., 1787), 5:381; The Duke of La Rochefoucault Liancourt, *Travels Through the U. S. of N. A.* (London: R. Phillips, 1800), III:493–99, 562, 694; Levi Hollingsworth Papers and Coates & Reynell Letters, HSP; Thomas Canby Papers, Lea Ledger A, 1784–1804, and George Latimer Letters, DHS; Thomas Lea Account Book, 1775–1783, and Lea & Sons, Account Book, 1773–1787, Hagley; Arthur H. Cole, *Wholesale Commodity Prices in the U.S., 1700–1861* (Philadelphia: University of Pennsylvania Press, 1938; repr. 1969), 120, 143; Matson and Onuf, *Union of Interests*, ch. 3–4; and Lance Davis and Stanley Engerman, "The Economy of British North America: Miles Traveled and Miles Still to Go," *WMQ*, 3rd ser., 56 (1999), 21.

14. For the French West Indies, see GP, Series III, reels 44, 48, 113, APS; William Stevenson Papers, HSP; William Hemphill Papers, DHS; Robert Ralston Letters, HSP; and Lewden Papers, Joseph Shallcross Papers, and John Morton Papers, DHS. For St. Eustatius, see Jacob Clarkson Papers, HSP; and for Guadeloupe, see Hollingsworth Papers, HSP.

15. For Philadelphia and France in the 1790s, see GP, Series III, Letters, 1795–99, APS; Anne C. Clauder, *American Commerce as Affected by the Wars of the French Revolution and Napoleon, 1793–1812* (Philadelphia: University of Pennsylvania Press, 1932); Jean Meyer, "Les difficultes du commerce Franco-Americain vues de Nantes, 1776–1790,"

French Historical Studies 11 (1979), 159–83; Paul Butel, *Les negociants bordelaise* (Paris, 1974; repr. 1996); Francois Crouzet, "Wars, Blockade, and Economic Change in Europe, 1792–1815," *Journal of Economic History* 24 (1964), 131; and Silvia Marzagalli, "The Establishment of a Transatlantic Trade Network: Bordeaux and the U.S., 1783–1815" (working paper no. 03–06, Intl. Seminar on the History of the Atlantic, Harvard, 2003).

16. Stephen Girard to Jean Girard, Jan. 26, 1785, GP, Series III, reel 113; Anon., Account Book, 1781–97, Hagley; Hollingsworth Family Records, John Ashmead Papers, and Jonathan Lawrence Papers, HSP; William and Jacob Walton, Book of Insurance, Jan. 1773–Mar. 1781, New York Municipal Archives; Russell Family Papers, 1783–1823, and William Smith, Letter & Record of Vendue, 1786, 1791, Winterthur; and Joseph Waln, Jr., Letters, 1787–99, Richard Waln Collection, HSP.
17. For Girard's 1789–91 accounts of ships *Polly, Ann, Active, Virginie, Exua, Bernardo, Deux Freres*, and his "philosopher vessels," see GP, Series III, reel 113, APS; and for comments on flush times, GP, Series III, Letter book II, and Invoices for 1783–1800, reel 132. For other merchants, see papers of Dutilh & Wachsmuth, HSP; Andrew Pettit, Andrew Bayard, Henry Pratt, William Gallathea, Harvey & Daves Papers, all at Hagley; Bjork, "Weaning," 550–53; National Archives and Records Administration (Philadelphia), Record Group 36, Entry 1059B, boxes 2–15; *New American State Papers-Commerce & Navigation*, ed. Thomas Cochran, 47 vols. (Wilmington, DE, 1973) 1:72, 226, 275; *Pennsylvania.Gazette*, Feb. 10, 1790; and Alec Dun, "'What avenues of commerce, will you, Americans, not explore!' Philadelphia's Commercial Vantage on St. Domingue, 1789–1793," *WMQ* 62 (July 2005), 473–504.
18. Letter book III, GP, Series III, APS. Girard dissolved his partnership with brother Jean in 1790, leaving Stephen with two ships and thirty thousand dollars, which he used to repay creditors.
19. For 1791–92, see Warner, Stockton & Craig Papers, 1791–1804, HSP; William Hemphill, Letter book, 1792–1802; and Broom, Hendrickson & Summerl, Letter book, 1792–94 (hereafter, BHS), at DHS; and papers of Etienne Dutilh, Manuel Eyre, Charles Massey, John Brown, and John Churman, all at Hagley. For the importance of imported food at Caribbean islands, see Richard B. Sheridan, "The Crisis of Slave Subsistence and the British West Indies During and After the American Revolution," *WMQ*, 3rd ser., 33 (1976), 618–24. In 1792, flour represented about 45.5 percent of Philadelphia's exports to the West Indies and southern Europe, and 19 percent of New York's exports; *New American State Papers*, 7:148–62.
20. GP, Series III, Letter book II, reel 113; and papers of Rumford and Abijah Dawes (HSP), Peter Dorey (Hagley), Broom, Hendrickson & Summerl (DHS), and Samuel Gilford, Joseph Hallett & Co, Ebenezer Stevens, and Isaac Roosevelt (N-YHS).

21. Broom, Hendrickson & Summerl Papers, 1792–93, DHS; and Cornelis Goslinga, *The Dutch in the Caribbean and in the Guianas, 1680–1791* (Gainesville: University Press of Florida, 1985), 227–30, 582.
22. See Girard to L. Trinquart, St. Marc, June 23, 1793, GP, Series III, Letter book IV, 399. For an example of a Philadelphia ship captured by British privateers near Martinique, condemned by the British consul there, and the subsequent suit for recovery of the ship, its cargo, and the insurance premium, see the record of Brig *Betsy*, Dec. 1793, William Phillips Account Book, Hagley. For a ship taken and released, see the *Isabella and Ann*, in James Hemphill, Letter book, 1793, DHS; for ships seized and not recovered from British privateers, see the *Pratt* and the *Sally* of Isaac Hendrickson, in Hendrickson MSS, 1795, DHS.
23. *General Advertiser*, Feb. 20 and May 10, 1793; *American Daily Advertiser*, Feb. 20, 1793; *Federal Gazette*, June 6, 1793; and NARA, Record Group 36, Entries 1057 and 1059.
24. For St. Domingue in 1793, see GP, Series III, Letter book II, reel 113; Lewden Family Papers, DHS; Chaloner & White Papers, HSP; Joseph Donath & Co. Papers, HSP; BHS Papers, DHS; and Eli Mendenhall Folders, 1800–1801, DHS. For the yellow fever, see J. H. Powell, *Bring Out Your Dead: The Great Plague of Yellow Fever in Philadelphia in 1793* (Philadelphia: University of Pennsylvania Press, 1949; repr. 1993); and for the refugees, see Frances S. Childs, *French Refugee Life in the United States, 1793–1800* (Baltimore: Johns Hopkins University Press, 1940).
25. For failures, see Hendrickson & Summerl to William Stevenson of Philadelphia, Oct. 5, 1793; to Joseph Hallett of New York, Dec. 4, 1793, BHS Correspondence; William Hemphill Correspondence, DHS; Thomas Canby Papers, DHS; George Latimer Correspondence, DHS; BHS Letter book, DHS; William Hemphill Log Book, 1793, DHS; and Thomas P. Cope, Letter books, 1796–98, Hagley. For reorienting to coastal trade in 1793–94, see papers of James & Shoemaker, Offley & Paxon, Jonathan Ogden, Hayman Levy; James Willink, William Deas, Wall & Flower; and Byrnes, Sweetman & Rudolph, all at HSP.
26. GP, Journals and Letter book V, 1794, Series III, APS, esp. Girard to Capt. John Cochran, Kingston, June 18, 1794; to Edmund Randolph, Philadelphia, June 6, 1794; to Jean Girard, New London, Apr. 20, 1795; to Jean Girard, New London, May 21, 1795; and to Paul Bentalou, Baltimore, Jan. 6, 1796. The quote is in the letter to Randolph.
27. *Pennsylvania Gazette*, Mar. 26, 1794; and for the Democratic-Republican circle, Andrew Shankman, *Crucible of American Democracy* (Lawrence: University Press of Kansas, 2004), 99, 143.
28. Girard to Paul Bentalou, Baltimore, Dec. 14, 1796, GP, Series III, Letter book VI, 135, APS; records of Girard's vessels the *Good Friends, Polly, Kitty, Nancy, Liberty*, and *Sally*, GP, Series III, APS; and for the merchant protest, *Pennsylvania Gazette*, Nov. 19, 1794, and July 29, 1795. For failures in Philadelphia, 1795–97, see papers of Robert Ralston,

Samuel Hopkins, and Henry Bell, HSP; GP, Series III, APS; and Thomas Shallcross Correspondence, DHS.

29. Coatsworth, "American Trade with European Colonies"; and for comparative prices at French and Spanish islands, *New American State Papers, Vol.* I.

30. On turning to the British West Indies, see Masters & Markoe Accounts, box 9, 1800–1806, Hagley.

31. Girard to Sebastian de Lasa, Havana, Mar. 31, 1798, Letter book VII, 75; to Paul Bentalou, Baltimore, Dec. 29, 1798, Letter book VI, 447; to William Douglas, Petersburg, Jan. 22, 1798, Letter book VII, 22; Captain's Reports on the ships *Liberty, Modesty*, and *Sally*, GP, Series III, 1797–99, APS; Robert Morris Papers, and John and George Morton Letter book, both at HSP; Liss, *Atlantic Empires*, 200, 210; Salvucci, "Development and Decline"; Javier Cuenca Esteban, "Trends and Cycles in U.S. Trade with Spain and the Spanish Empire, 1790–1819," *Journal of Economic History* 44 (June 1984), 521–43, esp. 541–43; Knight, "Origins of Wealth," 241.

32. For trade to Bordeaux and Nantes during the 1790s, see Girard's voyages of the *Liberty, Good Friends, Sally*, and correspondence with French merchants Bonnaffe, Fenwick & Mason, and Horquebie, as well as Hamburg merchants Berenger, Gossler & Co. in GP, Series III, Letters, 1796–99, APS; and records of Jonathan Jones, John Bernard, John Gernon, Justin Foussat, John Bousquet, and Bousquet & Odier, all at HSP.

33. For Amsterdam and Hamburg, see Warner, Stockton & Craig Papers, HSP; William Hemphill Letters, 1794, DHS; and GP, Journal, 1786–90, reel 113, APS. There is little evidence that mid-Atlantic American exporters *preferred* Europe *over* the West Indies until 1798; for evidence of reticence about Europe, see Thomas P. Cope, Letter books, 1792–98, Hagley. For redirecting cargoes from the West Indies to Europe *after* 1797, see Manuel Eyre Papers, 1777–1845, and Masters & Markoe Papers, 1788–1814, both at Hagley; the papers of Savage & Murgatoyd, Francis Breuil, Abraham Piesch, Augustin Bousquet, Louis Crousillat, and John W. Foussat, all at HSP; and Sam Mustafa, *Merchants and Migrations: Germans and Americans in Connection, 1776–1835* (Burlington, VT: Ashgate, 2001). For China, see GP, Series III, reel 125, #335; and Coatsworth, "American Trade," 254–55.

34. For Girard's foreign banking dealings, see Adams, *Finance and Enterprise*; Ralph Hidy, *The House of Baring in American Trade and Finance: English Merchant Bankers, 1763–1861* (Cambridge, MA: Harvard University Press, 1970); for his American banking and real estate dealings, see GP, Series II, reels 127, 184, 477.

Part IV

Individuals and Striving

Chapter 9

Accounting for Science

How a Merchant Kept His Books in Elizabethan London

Deborah E. Harkness,
*University of Southern California **

In the summer of 1608 the jurist and philosopher Francis Bacon began to keep a notebook. Entitled the "Loose Commentary" ("*Commentarius solutus*"), in it he recorded his debts, aspirations, and health complaints, as well as rough jottings on patronage and science that would later find their way into more polished works. Bacon intended his private notebook to function "like a merchant's waste book, where to enter all manner of *remembrancia* of matter, service, business, study, touching myself, service, others, either sparsim [scattered] or in schedules, without any manner of restraint."[1] Two centuries later, the German polymath and professor Georg Lichtenberg borrowed the genre of the waste book from English merchants and tradesmen and filled his with a range of notes so unrestrained they would have done Bacon proud: scientific observations, aphorisms, enthusiastic reviews of the work of Shakespeare and Hogarth, and thorough analyses of his

* I would like to thank Ann Blair, Bill Sherman, and Peter Stallybrass for their assistance with the issues discussed in this chapter. I would also like to thank Margaret Jacob and Catherine Secretan for inviting me to present my research, and the other conference participants for their questions and advice.

own vivid dreams.[2] Just a few decades before Lichtenberg, the natural philosopher Isaac Newton recycled an old commonplace book of his father's, renamed it the "Wastebook," and used it to set out his notes and queries on a set of mathematical and mechanical problems.[3]

This chapter began with a book historian's interest in knowing just what a waste book was, and a science historian's curiosity about why (out of all the genres in all the world) these three intellectuals found that a form of writing developed in sixteenth-century England by and for merchants was ideal for recording their scientific and intellectual work. Here, I examine the reasons why they chose this particular form of note-booking and examine what they can tell historians about capitalist habits of mind, merchant self-perception, and the emerging culture of experimentation and close observation that we call the Scientific Revolution. In particular, I argue that the system of merchant note-booking established in the sixteenth century promoted habits of observation and analysis in merchants and their household members that could be easily adapted to the new science. Before the establishment of gentlemanly scientific academies in the seventeenth and eighteenth centuries, merchants saw themselves—and were seen by others—as a bookish group with a set of important analytical and record-keeping skills. As such, many English merchants of the time became valuable members of European-wide networks of intellectual exchange in which natural objects, accounts of natural occurrences, and reported observations circulated.

The early modern belief that merchants were acute observers of their world and could be relied upon for later accurate accounts of those observations hinged, I contend, on the well-known note-booking practices that they employed. It was this tradition that made it possible for Bacon, Lichtenberg, and Newton to so readily embrace this genre when casting about for exemplars and templates to shape their own note-booking practices. Here, I will first explore the sixteenth century development of the waste book and situate those notebooks within broader merchant reading and writing practices. Waste books and their companion volumes reveal mercantile habits of mind and set standards of detailed observation and analysis that are important when considering why Bacon or Newton were drawn to this genre. From a survey of merchant bookkeeping I move on to consider how merchants saw themselves as a learned and bookish group, a perception that was sharpened through urban education, published accounting manuals, and contact with other capitalists and scholars at home and abroad. Finally, I will present three sixteenth-century case studies of Elizabethan merchants whose notebooks shed light on how an appreciation of merchant bookkeeping practices can help us to better contextualize the ways in which merchants saw themselves as producers of knowledge and valuable contributors to the emerging vernacular science of the time. When some Elizabethan merchants became interested in pursuing natural knowledge, their note-booking techniques proved instrumental in establishing a vernacular natural science in the city of London that was distinct from the learned natural philosophy studied at the universities.

My objects of study here are not confined to the merchant ledgers that my title might seem to indicate. Instead, in my definition, merchant books include not only business records, but notebooks devoted to household affairs, medicine, technology, and other forms of natural knowledge. Indeed, one of the larger points I am trying to make is that merchant books were not merely business ledgers, and that merchant bookkeeping practices were not always applied to capitalist affairs and consumer goods. How merchants kept *all* their books in Elizabethan London—their waste books, their ledgers, their library books, and other notebooks—can help us to account for the development of the new science and also shed light on how capitalists saw themselves and their world.

Merchant Bookkeeping and Habits of Mind

When Bacon explained that the form, content, and intentions underlying his "Loose Commentary" notebook were closely aligned with those of the merchant waste book, he referred to one of the most common books to be found in early modern London. In houses, workshops, and counting houses all over the City there would have been thousands of these waste books sitting open on tables, shelved over desks in the family's lodgings, or lying neatly closed awaiting the next day's business. Mere mention of the waste book during Bacon's lifetime would have quickly conjured up concrete images of not only one's own waste book but also the related bookish artifacts of merchant life. Today, the merchant's waste book is a far murkier object of study and represents an overlooked genre of middle-class writing. As in the case of the early modern humanist commonplace book, the merchant's waste book had specific conventions; manuals were penned to guide merchants in the proper making and use of the books, and they fit within a broad set of reading and writing practices.[4]

The waste book was but a single volume in a multivolume reading and writing process that merchants used to keep themselves on top of the people, places, and things central to their capitalist business activities. Mathematical authors and accounting teachers in England (both of which had good reason to make the systems as complicated as possible) urged merchants to consider the most basic accounting practices as grounded in no less than three regularly kept books: the waste book or memorial; the journal or daybook; and a properly indexed ledger. Some merchants kept other records as well, including correspondence registers, copybooks of letters sent and received, cashbooks, books that listed prices for merchandise, invoice books, receipt books, *remembrancia*, to-do lists, and household expense books.[5]

Merchant bookkeeping practices differed throughout Europe and were identifiable by particular national features. Double-entry bookkeeping was known as bookkeeping in "the Italian manner" well into the seventeenth century. Though Luca Pacioli is credited with first putting information about double-entry bookkeeping into print in 1494 in his *Summa de arithmetica*, the techniques had been in use in merchant centers like Genoa and Florence for at least a century by the time his book was printed. Most countries, including the Netherlands, followed in the footsteps of the Italian examples and emphasized the use of only two books in merchant bookkeeping, the journal and the ledger. Dutch bookkeepers also tended to keep two books, but their journal was divided into transactional categories. And while other European nations embraced the greater simplicity of the two-book system of journal and ledger, the English were known for their use of the waste book. Richard Dafforne noted that "in Holland . . . the buying people affirm not the waste book," and in the eighteenth century Georg Lichtenberg was clear that he was making a cosmopolitan decision to use the English custom of waste booking in spite of his German antecedents.[6]

Detailed merchant record-keeping in England began with the waste book. Also known as a memorial, the waste book got its name from the fact that it was always superseded by subsequent, more polished volumes of accounts and then discarded. "When the matter [in the waste book] is written into the journal," the accounting author Richard Dafforne explained, "then is this book void, and of no esteem."[7] The recognized eventual obsolescence of the waste book may account for why so few early modern waste books have survived. Despite their slim rate of survival, the waste book had several distinctive features that set it apart from other books kept by merchants. First, it was a public book that was to be freely accessible in a merchant's household. Anyone conducting business on behalf of the merchant, including women, apprentices, and servants, was supposed to record the details of their transactions in a running commentary written in the plainest fashion to ensure it could be comprehended later. Second, everything should be "expressed at large" in the waste book "as it is truly acted," with the result that waste books were the most complete record of what happened in a merchant's business "in plain sincerity" and "without omission of any thing."[8] Merchants were told to instruct their servants to record the "day, name, and surname of the Merchant, the place of his dwelling, and of what faculty he is; the kind, quantity, and quality of the wares bought, or received, sold, shipped, or delivered; the price, weight, measure, and color; the number, and mark; the contract in buying and selling, be it for ready money or time, or in barter."[9] Third, the waste book was the only book kept by merchants that should contain evidence of multiple authorship and use. It was a compiled text or miscellany, rather than a text with a single author or point of view.

The waste book was the foundation for all subsequent accounting efforts. From the waste book a merchant extracted the most important information from all the detailed jottings and transferred them into the second merchant accounting book: the journal. No more than a week after business occurrences were richly described and recorded in the waste book, the merchant or his bookkeeper was expected to sift through the contents, extracting the nuggets of mercantile significance from the dross of superfluous information and record them in the journal "in a good order . . . daily as they happen." What stood for good order in this case were grammatical correctness, concision, and a formality of style that stood in marked contrast to the casual chattiness of the waste book.[10] There was an excellent reason for merchants and their accountants to take particular care with the wording and the form that journals took: the journal could be entered into evidence should a merchant be embroiled in a controversy or dispute. Judges did not need to be confused by the rich details contained in the waste book; instead, they were content to see the expertly abridged and edited account of business dealings drawn out of the waste book. Because of its legal standing, "blotching or [e]rasing out" passages in a merchant journal was both "unbeseeming" and could lead to later questions about the falsification of records.[11] For the journal to be considered "authentic" and reliable, it was imperative that the person transferring the waste book entries into the journal be highly skilled, analytical, and exacting. In most cases, journals were written out either by professional bookkeepers or by merchants themselves. This was not a book to be left on the dining table for any servant or woman to scribble in their notes.

Finally, an early modern merchant drew from his journal to compile the best-known volume of his accounts, and the one we see today as emblematic of mercantile culture: the ledger. Ledgers, whether drawn up in the relatively new Italian, double-entry style or in more traditional paragraph formats, were the books of accounts that provided an overview of where a merchant's finances stood. Often described as a "mirror of man's estate," the ledger was the most authoritative wide-angle perspective of a merchant's business affairs.[12] Richard Dafforne reported that the "end of book-writing is to give contentment unto the book-owner, and to show him . . . at all times . . . how his estate stands," and this certainly depended upon an accurate and comprehensive ledger.[13]

But the ledger was also the book that was most removed from the daily life of a merchant. Our emphasis on this one type of account book, and on the data that social and economic historians often extract from it, has overshadowed the other books that preceded it as well as the scribal processes and habits of mind that fashioned it.[14]

The scribal processes and merchant habits of mind that emerge from early modern bookkeeping practices emphasized three important ways of being and knowing that helped to shape merchant self-perception and the increasingly self-conscious attitudes of the capitalist. These included placing value on consistency, underscoring the importance of accuracy and precision, and managing multiple sources and types of information. Consistent record-keeping practices were of utmost importance, both legally and financially. Haphazardly made entries, and long gaps between entries, were to be avoided at all cost by successful and ambitious merchants.[15]

Given the laborious and exacting work required to make exact, reliable business journals and ledgers, it is perhaps not surprising that English merchants were reluctant to give up the casual waste books as the *urtexts* of their bookkeeping practices. Educating all members of the household—women, children, apprentices, and servants—so that they could contribute to the keeping of consistent accounts by writing in the household waste book was ultimately both a time- and labor-saving device. The popularity of the waste book helped to fuel the market for mathematics education in Elizabethan England, and can be linked to funeral monuments like that for Elizabeth Withypool Lucar (d. 1537). Carved into the stone that fashioned the monument was praise for her feminine talents with the needle, her modesty, her devotion to Holy Scripture, and her ability to "speak of algorism, or accounts, in every fashion."[16] These may not all have been conventional wifely talents, but they were highly desirable in a merchant household where the family's business dealings required a firm grasp of basic arithmetic and even algebra.[17]

Advocates of consistent record-keeping also promoted the value of accuracy and precision in business records. "I will counsel and advise you to number the leaves of all your books," Elizabethan accounting teacher John Mellis warned his readers, to ensure that fraudulent entries were not made or pages were not torn away.[18] Despite these high standards, merchants' trustworthiness remained open to question since they were assumed to be acting in their own financial interest.[19] Mellis, who could be hired in the City to reconcile a merchant's account books when they were in dispute or chaotic, knew that a merchant's public image was based on his honor and credibility. Accurate, precise records were a marker of professional competency among merchants, much like a finely carved cabinet was evidence of a craftsman's skill. The waste book played an important role in establishing the accuracy and precision of a merchant's records, for it depended upon an expansive treatment of detail. In the waste book, everything was to be remarked upon, "for merchants can in no wise make too large a declaration in writing" of their business affairs.[20] It was this casual, seemingly open-ended feature of merchant bookkeeping, and especially the waste book, that drew men like Bacon, Newton, and Lichtenberg to it as a writing genre.

What all this lush, unregulated detail led to, of course, was a need for merchants to be able to successfully manage multiplicities: multiple books, multiple sources of information, multiple (sometimes conflicting) accounts of business affairs, multiple business partners, and multiple objects. Merchant account books helped to ensure that their owners could categorize different mercantile items, distinguish among different types of debts, and over time evaluate the success and failure of different kinds of financial arrangements.[21] This skill set made the merchant ideally suited to making, recording, and evaluating the empirical observations on which not only business life, but also the new science, depended.

Accounting, Science, and Self-Perception: How Merchants Saw Themselves as Producers and Consumers of Knowledge

A merchant's account books helped to situate him in a network of texts, obligations, debts, people, places, and things. While a great deal of scholarship has investigated the scribal habits and note-booking practices of humanists in an effort to understand scholarly culture and how they saw themselves and their world, very little has been done with respect to merchant notebooks and the men and women who produced them. Both merchants and humanists were bookish people in early modern Europe, however, possessing distinctive technical and language skills. In the case of merchants, their bookkeeping practices and related habits of mind would have helped to promote a sense of self and a corresponding public image that was intimately tied to issues of literacy. Merchants were among the most literate groups in early modern England, and they eagerly participated in educational initiatives in London. Moreover, by exchanging information with businessmen, scholars, and political figures, merchants would have come to see themselves as not only consumers, but also producers, of knowledge.

Relatively high levels of literacy among merchants in Elizabethan London were instrumental in fostering this belief. Studies by David Cressy indicate that Londoners were the most literate group in Elizabethan England, and that 59 percent of London tradesmen and craftsmen were literate in the 1580s. By 1610, the percentage of literate citizens in the City had swelled to 80 percent.[22] The increasingly complicated world of trade, travel, and manufacturing made an ability to both read and write desirable among ambitious merchants and tradesmen.[23] The City's most literate citizens were scriveners, merchants, vintners, grocers, saddlers, and apothecaries, while those least likely to read and write were watermen, gardeners, shoemakers, brewers, tailors, and (surprisingly) innkeepers.[24] With the exception of the saddlers, the most literate occupational groups were associated with businesses or trades that were linked to social mobility.

London's public and private schools played a crucial role in raising literacy rates in the City. Grammar schools, academies, and the suburban presence of the Inns of Court—gentry "finishing schools" that catered to educated young men training for careers in the law—were all available to students, though they often charged a fee.[25] Though few of London's schools were as integrated as Richard Mulcaster's idealistic vision of classrooms filled with the children of gentlemen and guildsmen sharing their teachers and building common knowledge, during the first few years of instruction, students likely encountered classmates from a range of socioeconomic backgrounds.[26] Several of these schools were heavily subsidized by donations from London guilds, like St. Paul's School, which was supported by the Mercers, and the Merchant-Taylors' school in the parish of St. Lawrence Pountney. Individual parishes, like St. Saviour and St. Olave

Southwark, also constructed schools funded by charitable donations to serve a local clientele.

The curriculum of London's schools and academies was surprisingly wide-ranging and included basic instruction as well as guidance in more specialized subjects. In guild and parish schools, students were taught the rules of grammar, given religious instruction, provided with an introduction to Latin (and in some cases Greek and Hebrew) to facilitate their study of Scripture, and schooled in French; they also performed amateur theatricals drawn from classical as well as contemporary plays.[27] In addition to the guild-based training of apprentices, London also boasted a variety of more specialized academies, including foreign-language schools, mathematics schools, and schools that taught the art of navigation.[28] The curriculum was entirely in French at the St. Anthony's Hospital School run by the French Church, for example, while the language of instruction was Dutch at the Dutch Church's school in Austin Friars. Humphrey Baker, a well-known mathematical writer, took boarders into his house on the north side of the Royal Exchange to facilitate their immersion in his mathematical curriculum. Pupils in Southwark could take writing, drawing, and accounting courses from author and teacher John Mellis, while courses in the natural sciences were taught in both the Leadenhall Chapel and in the old Blackfriars monastery.[29]

With a literate and increasingly well-educated populace, printing shops and bookstores multiplied in the City at a rapid rate. The book trade employed hundreds of men as typefounders, typesetters, printers, compilers, editors, and illustrators. It is impossible to establish an exact figure regarding how many Londoners were involved in making and selling books during the early modern period, and firm statistics regarding how many books were printed are equally elusive.[30] For bookish groups like the merchants, however, living in London provided them with ready access to all the latest titles, whether they were cheap broadsides and pamphlets or more expensive folio-size illustrated travel books. London merchants and apprentices with less expansive wallets but avaricious reading tastes could often gain access to books from the libraries associated with many guild and company halls. In 1565, the Bishop of London attempted to resurrect an ambitious scheme for a public library. Edmund Grindal wrote to the City's aldermen urging the foundation of a "common library within this city."[31] The Aldermen sent the City's chamberlain out to scour London for a suitable site. Though a site was quickly found and carpenters were sent out the next day to begin the work of transforming an unused house into a library (an unusually efficient turnaround for sixteenth-century London), the plan never came to fruition.

Given the potential number of interested readers, it is hardly surprising that accounting teachers and bookkeeping experts were quick to offer merchants and their apprentices manuals that promised to teach them how to properly compile and use merchant books.[32] Authors of accounting how-to books were typically members of prominent London guilds like the Salters, or merchant groups such as the Merchant Adventurers, and they often took in mathematical and accounting pupils in addition to engaging in a wide range of business affairs. John Weddington, a writer on accounting practices whose *A breffe instruction and manner, howe to kepe marchantes bokes* was printed in Antwerp in 1567, was a Merchant Adventurer, a cloth exporter, and one of Sir Thomas Gresham's chief business representatives, for example.[33] The first English accounting manual was published by Hugh Oldcastle in 1543, and like many much-used early books, not a single copy now survives. Accounting manuals typically went through several editions in the early modern period before they passed out of print, and some were such perennial best-sellers that they continued to be issued long after the author was dead. In addition to narrative pedagogical sections that were often modeled on a Socratic dialogue, these printed accounting manuals typically contained model waste books, journals, and ledgers that illustrated each book's different form and function.

With their bookishness, relatively high levels of literacy, and enthusiasm for education, it is less surprising that merchants saw themselves as qualified producers and consumers of knowledge. Merchant knowledge was not restricted to the business of buying and selling, or to familiarity with foreign currencies and customs. Instead, merchants saw themselves as producers of a wide range of knowledge that derived from a combination of observation and analysis. Whether it was knowledge of trade routes, how business partnerships could be established that were legal and profitable, or New World flora and fauna, sixteenth-century English merchants proved to be founts of information and expertise. Once again, merchant facility with observation and analysis came not just from their education or the books that they read, but from their accounting practices. When Richard Dafforne set out to train students how to think like a merchant and keep reliable account books, he produced mock waste books full of information that he then expected them to abridge, edit, and analyze into journals and ledgers.[34] Merchants were seen as analysts capable of sitting down with a bewildering assortment of information and then sifting through it, establishing categories of information, assessing value to that information, and assessing the credibility of customers, investors, and informers.

Accounting for Science: How Three Elizabethan Merchants Kept Their Books

By turning to the surviving notebooks of an apothecary, a long-distance merchant and mining speculator, and the Cambridge-educated son of a London brewer, we can see how three Elizabethan businessmen kept a full range of notebooks and employed analytical and observational skills rooted in merchant accounting practices when they turned to investigate the natural world. Despite their apparent differences, Edward Barlow, Clement Draper, and Hugh Plat were all well-to-do Elizabethan merchants with an interest in the new science. All three of them left behind a wealth of bookish remains—business journals, medical formularies, manuscript miscellanies, notebooks, printed books, and library lists—that reveal how a merchant's sense of self could develop. And while none of them show the concern with religiosity and matters of faith that we see in the case of Joseph Ryder, discussed in this book in the chapter by Matthew Kadane, they are concerned with matters related to the natural world.

Edward Barlow (fl. 1581–94) was a London grocer and apothecary who loved books and was deeply interested in astronomy, medicine, and chemistry.[35] In the winter of 1589–90, at his house in the parish of St. Mary Magdalene Old Fish Street (near St. Paul's Cathedral), Barlow compiled a catalog of his extensive collection of over 190 volumes including printed works, manuscripts, and pamphlets.[36] He added this booklist to a volume that already included daily receipts regarding medicines made in his shop, and a textual miscellany of scientific works copied out by hand. These included works by Paracelsus, Ripley, and Thomas Aquinas and were mainly concerned with alchemy. Part waste book, part inventory, and part compilation, Barlow's notebook provides us with a snapshot of his interests and they ways in which they bled into each other.

The wide range of titles Barlow collected in his library demonstrates how bookish a merchant could be and confirms that the apothecary was right to think of himself both as a consumer—and a producer—of knowledge. Edward Barlow's library catalog also reveals how mercantile accounting methods were applied to Elizabethan London's largest documented scientific library. The list suggests that Barlow was able to read several languages, as he owned books in Latin, French, Italian, and English as well as foreign language grammars and dictionaries to help him through the more difficult passages. While the library's holdings included books on a number of scientific and nonscientific subjects, including travel guides, books on astrology and physics, an Italian translation of the *Koran*, and political pamphlets, the library's greatest strength was its medical holdings. This was the working library of an apothecary, after all, and Barlow owned several plant guides and herbals including expensive, lavishly illustrated foreign imprints from the Plantin printshop by authors like Rembart Dodoens and Matthew de L'Obel and important new titles like Frampton's English translation of Monardes's book on New World medicines. Practical handbooks on distillation, including works by Gesner and Ulstadius, sat on his shelves alongside the official pharmaceutical formulary for the city of Cologne and Giovanni Ventura Roseta's book on the secrets of perfume making. Barlow also collected popular compendia of medical case notes, especially those coming out of Italy by authors like Giovanni Baccanelli, Girolamo Capivaccio, Leonelli Faventini, and Girolamo Cardano.

Evidence from Barlow's library list, when combined with his other surviving papers, suggests that he saw himself as both a learned medical man and a merchant. He recopied arcane medieval alchemical manuscripts that were circulating around the City, and in one case he even sketched out an illustration for one of the treatises. Some of the manuscripts were in verse, others were translated from the Latin, and one was a copy of a text on magic written by the German autodidact, chemist, and physician Paracelsus. The treatise had never been published in England, and how it came into Barlow's hands remains a mystery. He was clearly on the lookout not only for printed books that addressed subjects of interest to him, but manuscript works as well. In all probability Barlow actively participated in informal networks of manuscript exchange that enabled Londoners to add rare items to their collections that were not available in the bookshops. Barlow also applied his accounting skills to compiling lists of all the churches in England, catalogs of all the nobles in England, and other features of his contemporary world.

Like any good merchant, Barlow was concerned with assessing the true value of objects or information, and this was especially true of his library. Barlow carefully valued each title that he owned, and the whole library's worth he estimated at £25 12 shillings and 9 pence—a capital investment equal to two years of wages for a London craftsman. The books ranged from expensive folios valued at £1, to humble pamphlets estimated to be worth a mere penny each. Most valuable of all, Barlow thought, were his own translation of Apian's *Cosmographia* and his other original contributions to natural knowledge: a treatise on the passions of women, several compendia of medical receipts, and a treatise on medicinal simples. Producing knowledge, in Barlow's estimation, had more value attached to it than merely consuming it.

Barlow not only produced knowledge on the page, he also produced knowledge in his apothecary shop. Until the Apothecaries formed their own guild in 1617 (and even for some time afterward), men like Barlow belonged to the Grocers' guild and could be general merchants as well as dispensers of medicines. There is also evidence to suggest that apothecary shops, like London's later coffeehouses, were places where people congregated, swapped news and gossip, and conversed about political and cultural affairs.[37] By keeping accurate patient records, Barlow established his credibility as a businessman and made his learning and expertise evident to others in his shop. With detailed remarks about the patient, the prescribing doctor, the date, and the ingredients that went into every prescription that he filled, Barlow kept a consistent paper trail that could be used to defend him in disputes he might have with medical authorities in the City. In 1581, 1585, and 1586, for example, Barlow tangled with London's College of Physicians who accused him of practicing medicine without a license. When the physicians charged him with improper practice on June, 2 1586, Barlow defended himself by responding that "with Mr. Pett of Limehouse he had merely prepared medicines according to the instructions of the physician, Mr. Edwardes of Oxford."[38] This was precisely the kind of proof his medical formula could be relied upon to provide.

Like Edward Barlow, merchant Clement Draper found himself at odds with the authorities, but in his case careful record-keeping was not enough to keep his opponent, the powerful Earl of Huntington, at bay. Fortunately for Draper, he loved books so passionately that he spent much of the 1580s transcribing them in his cell in the King's Bench prison in Southwark, where he was incarcerated for failing to pay debts owed to Huntington. Writing in a tiny, meticulous hand Draper copied treatises on distillation and alchemy and gathered together anecdotes, medical receipts, and ideas for chemical processes from fellow prisoners and friends. While there is no record of Draper ever attending school or university, sixteen volumes of Draper's notebooks have survived, all preserved in the British Library, and a single item in Draper's hand is in the Ashmole collection at the Bodleian Library. The notebooks span over two decades and are a testament to Draper's interest in the natural world.[39]

One of Draper's notebooks contains the records of his trading company and the business that it did with merchants in Hamburg, Lubeck, and other Baltic cities between 1579 and 1580. Draper specialized in trading flax, leather, paper, wine, and wax and had business associates throughout Europe and even as far away as Moscow. The accounts show that Draper had a weakness for speculation and at times owed staggering sums of money that ran into thousands of pounds (the equivalent of hundreds of thousands of pounds in today's money). One page from a business journal of October 11–13, 1578, for example, shows debts his firm owed to William Romney, a London merchant and exchange agent active in Hamburg. The handwriting in the business journal does not belong to Draper, indicating that he employed a professional bookkeeper to draw items from a waste book that no longer survives into the journal.[40]

Draper's journal, compiled by a professional bookkeeper, does not give any sense of the merchant's priorities, interests, or preoccupations. While it paints a clearer picture of the money he received and owed, we are missing the merchant waste book that would have allowed us to flesh out the data in the journal and learn more about how Draper saw himself and his world. Fortunately, Draper's sixteen remaining notebooks provide further evidence regarding the note-taking techniques of the merchant, even though the subject matter is scientific, rather than mercantile. Draper's other notebooks are striking examples of the rich tradition of vernacular textual miscellanies in Elizabethan London. Note-taking skills and methods for organizing insights from one's readings and life experiences were taught to students in the grammar schools, and hundreds of receipt books, experimental notebooks, and compilations of texts survive from the period and testify to their teachers' effectiveness.[41] Though many surviving examples are anonymous, each was composed by a man or woman like Draper who was trying, in Ann Blair's words, to bring "order and coherence to ever-increasing quantities of knowledge."[42]

Draper's note-taking skills contrasted sharply with those that would be employed by an educated humanist taught to keep a commonplace book. While humanists were trained to organize and classify their notes by author and subject, Draper's notes resemble the "unrestrained" methods of the merchant waste book, even as they show a merchant's concern for precision and accuracy. In his notebooks he wanted to capture every detail of place and time, the identity of his informant, and the particulars of every medical receipt, alchemical text, or metallurgical experiment that he performed. In this notebook page, for example, Draper records a medical receipt for treating green wounds from a fellow prisoner, William George. Crammed into this one entry are the visible botanical features that distinguished ribwort leaves from plantain leaves, how long a salve made from May butter and ribwort leaves can be preserved in a box, how to apply the salve, how to supplement the salve with applications of egg whites, substitute ingredients used for wounds in men over the age of fifty, and how old, scarred wounds could be treated with honey and lint.[43] The next receipt for sore eyes has no relationship medically or anatomically to the receipt for treating green wounds. Instead, Draper was just recording the receipts as he gathered them, using thick black lines to separate entries.

Draper used his bookkeeping skills to establish himself within the prison's knowledge economy. New insights into nature cropped up everywhere in Elizabethan London, even within the walls of the King's Bench prison, and Draper was able to copy a fifteenth-century alchemical text into one of his notebooks, describe a medical procedure performed on his own knee, and record insights into the Great Red Work of alchemy given to him by a Jewish metallurgist Joachim Gans, who was also in prison for debating the divinity of the Trinity at a public house. In prison Draper established himself as a knowledgeable and learned man, and his fellow inmates came to him with contributions for his scribal work. Like everything else he read, saw, and heard, these accounts were all recorded in his notebooks, just like a merchant recording the details of business life in a waste book. And so Draper recorded the alchemical dream of prisoner Thomas Seafold, whose long-dead tenant Robert Jeckler appeared one night in 1581 and told him how to make a medicinal elixir with mercury, pork, and human excrement that promised to restore health to all who consumed it.[44] Later, he copied Francis Archer's method for fixing arsenic out of "an old, worn, written book [in] a ragged hand, which I had much ado to read."[45] In exchange for books and other pieces of information, Draper may have treated his fellow prisoners' medical complaints.[46]

While Draper was participating within an economy of knowledge within prison walls, his contemporary Hugh Plat was roaming the streets of London with a notebook in one hand and a pen in the other. An acute observer of the natural world and an avid recorder of the efforts ordinary Londoners made in an attempt to understand nature and put its powers to good use, Hugh Plat was a peripatetic enthusiast who would go to any lengths to gather information about his passions and pursuits. Thanks to the careful planning and investments made by his brewer father, Plat was educated in the law at

Cambridge University and his notebooks provide us with an example of how merchant note-booking practices and humanist commonplacing practices taught at the university could be combined. Unlike Barlow or Draper, Plat's rough, intellectual waste books survive, as do the more polished commonplace books that he drew from them. Like the relationship between the merchant waste book and journal, the relationship between Plat's rough notebooks and his scientific commonplace books reveals how he analyzed, sifted, and edited the natural knowledge that he gathered and recorded.[47] Plat also published books of experimental knowledge, including *The Jewell House of Art and Nature* (1594) and early modern England's most popular cookbook, *Delightes for Ladies* (1602). Plat's printed works occupy the same place in his intellectual work as a merchant's ledgers did for business affairs: they provide the most formal evidence of his interest in nature, but stand at the farthest remove from his daily experiences in the City.[48]

Within both his notebooks and printed treatises, Plat shows a merchant's knack for juggling multiplicities of subject matter. Chemistry and natural history, both broadly conceived, frequently appear on the pages, but so do other subjects such as brewing, viticulture, agriculture, husbandry, and textile manufacture. In the rough notebooks, designs for new distillation equipment and new methods for preserving food often are recorded side by side with remedies for snake bites and tricks for keeping bees. Plat gleaned these valuable bits of natural knowledge from an array of informants as well as his own experimental practices, which added to the challenges he faced analyzing and coming to terms with such disparate information.

Plat's eclectic collecting and recording habits required that he exercise a merchant's ability to critically judge, analyze, and evaluate his sources of information as well as the insights into nature that they reported to him. High status was not always sufficient to convince Plat that you were a person with credible knowledge. Instead, he preferred to assess each piece of information on its own merits. Always on the lookout for fresh ideas and approaches to the natural world, Plat enthusiastically supported the physician William Gilbert's theories of magnetism, but only after Gilbert taught him to construct a magnetic needle using household items such as a bowl of water, a piece of cork, a wire, and a chimney piece. With his homemade magnetic needle, Plat noted with satisfaction, "[Y]ou shall see the sharp end always pointing to ye north [and] this proves the earth to be of the nature of a loadstone according to D. Gilbert."[49] While famous men of science like Gilbert do appear on the pages of Plat's notebooks, most entries involve more ordinary Londoners, both native-born English and immigrant strangers. An Irish saltmaker taught him how to cultivate thin-shelled walnuts and stop a chimney from smoking.[50] The queen's physician and her surgeon showed him how to construct distillation apparatus and make inexpensive medicines.[51] Chemical knowledge, such as how to attenuate mercury in water and the properties of antimony, were imparted to him by the Bishop of Bristol and Plat's muskmelon vendor.[52] Foreign physicians demonstrated how to make artificial coral.[53] As we see, Plat's mercantile background had taught him that even unlikely sources could produce items of value.

In the City, Plat was prone to jotting down whatever struck his fancy in the unrestrained manner that Bacon so admired in merchant waste books, content to sort out the most valuable insights into the natural world later. He immediately "wrote the receipt" in one of his notebooks for a Dutch immigrant's method of stirring molten lead with a finger after seeing the feat performed in a Southwark beer garden.[54] Plat's urgent sense that he had to record the details of something he had eyewitnessed quickly and clearly is also apparent in other notebook entries. Based on these recorded accounts he was able to go back later and use them to pose questions about the information he received, adapt the practices, and suggest ways to further modify the experiences and experiments. Plat frankly admitted his preference for concrete information about nature that could only be based, like Dutch Hans's method for stirring lead, on "the infallible grounds of practice" since insights gleaned merely from "speculative kinds of contemplation" would "when they come to be tried . . . in the glowing forge of Vulcan . . . . vanish into smoke."[55] Plat's plans to draw his intellectual waste books into more polished journals and printed works did not always come to fruition, however, as his fully categorized and outlined but largely blank commonplace book makes clear.[56] Despite the considerable time and energy required for Plat to record and analyze the information he gathered in London, he was also a busy inventor and active experimenter in his own right. Even with his own inventions—such as designing new agricultural implements or making medicines—Plat employed the same mercantile record-keeping practices and analytical skills. These are evident in his accounts of the proprietary medicines he devised and dispensed in and around London, including his "characteristic cure" for tertian fevers, his use of embalmed human bodies or *mumia* for quotidian or quartian fevers, his red powder for burning fevers, and the large lozenges of herbs and chemicals called "plague cakes."[57] Plat delighted in recording when his medicines had cured patients when other physicians had failed. Mr. Pennington, a vintner in Cheapside, was cured of a fever after taking Plat's red powder, even though "he had taken much physic of Dr. Barrow, [and] Dr. Bredwell," and taken another proprietary medicine, "Anthony's Pill," without result.[58] Plat was such a careful and consistent keeper of records that he included a list of the fifty-one patients he had cured with his medicines between 1593 and 1605. The patients included members of his household, his family, his neighbors, his friends, and others in London. According to these records, he was entirely successful at curing all his patients—though that may strain our credulity.

Plat's confidence in his medical knowledge and his sense of himself as a producer of valuable medical knowledge both swelled after the success that he had with his plague cakes during London's 1593 outbreak of the disease. Not until after the Great Fire of London in the late seventeenth century did the bubonic plague cease being a regular and deadly visitor to the City.[59] Plat's plague cakes contained an expensive combination of plants, herbs, chemicals, and ground bezoar stones, the reputably medicinal gallstones of Peruvian goats. Though some of the cakes were given away to "persons whose names are not here recorded," Plat was still able to account for how nearly 500 were dispensed during the summer of 1593. Sixty of the plague cakes went to the Queen's Privy Council, two apothecaries purchased fifty of the cakes to sell in their shops, and Plat gave forty-five to Charles Howard, the Lord High Admiral of England. The Bishop of Worcester purchased fifty of the lozenges to preserve his diocese from the infection. And in the London parish of St. Marie Abchurch, a Justice of the Peace for Middlesex "made one special trial" of the medicine by administering it to thirty-three people. Every person who took Plat's remedy "were preserved from the plague, to the great contentment of the Lords of the Council who sent . . . to be fully informed of the report."[60]

CONCLUSION

The history of merchant capitalism has important points of intersection with the history of science, and these points need to be explored more fully and completely than they are at present. Joel Kaye has made compelling arguments that the monetization of medieval society led to major conceptual shifts in fourteenth-century natural philosophy, for example, which took the study of nature in increasingly quantifiable, geometric, and mechanistic directions. Edward Barlow, Clement Draper, and Hugh Plat provide clear evidence that merchant bookkeeping practices, skills, and priorities could prove enormously beneficial to students of nature. Careful, consistent records of experiments and the administration of drugs to patients marked important steps along the way toward the development of verifiable and replicable experiments. So, too, the evaluative and analytical skills required to keep a set of business books made merchants like these ideally suited to the work of sifting and sorting through an increasingly large and daunting body of information about the natural world. By the seventeenth century, scientific figures such as Galileo Galilei were using mercantile concepts of trust and creditworthiness to gain patrons and operating as entrepreneurs to open up new markets for their intellectual goods and services. At the same time, a new class of gentlemen interested in science began to question whether any merchant was capable of a disinterested study of nature, and to call up old caricatures of the shifty merchant to help bolster their own position in the intellectual culture of the time.[61]

Despite these points of overlap, however, the role of capitalism and the interest that merchants like Barlow, Draper, and Plat took in the natural world have been largely overlooked by historians of science, just as the full range of merchants' books have been overlooked by social and economic historians. Though my research into the links between merchant bookkeeping specifically, and merchant bookishness more broadly, is still in its early stages and much more needs to be done to situate merchant reading and writing practices within a broader framework of humanist and scientific efforts, understanding how merchants kept *all* of their books in Elizabethan London promises to reveal new interconnections between capitalism, urban life, and the new science.

NOTES

1. Bacon's notebook is British Library MS Add. 27278, and the quote here is from folio 13v.For an analysis of the manuscript, see Michael Kiernan, "Introduction: Bacon's Programme for Reform," in Bacon, *Advancement of Learning*, xxxiv–xxxvi.
2. Georg Christoph Lichtenberg, *The Waste Books* (New York: NYRB Classics, 2000); Linda Katritzky, "Georg Christoph Lichtenberg, F. R. S.," *Notes and Records of the Royal Society* 39 (1984): 41–49.
3. See J. Herivel, *Background to Newton's* Principia*: A Study of Newton's Dynamical Researches in the Years 1665–1685* (Cambridge: Cambridge University Press, 1965), 128–82; I. B. Cohen, *The Newtonian Revolution* (Cambridge: Cambridge University Press, 1980), 56–62; Rob Iliffe, "Abstract Considerations: Disciplines and the Incoherence of Newton's

Natural Philosophy," *Studies in History and Philosophy of Science* 35 (2004): 427–54.

4. On the better-known genre of commonplace books, see Ann Moss, *Printed Commonplace Books and the Structuring of Renaissance Thought* (Oxford: Clarendon, 1996); Ann Blair, "Humanist Methods in Natural Philosophy: the Commonplace Book," *Journal of the History of Ideas* 53 (1992): 541–51.
5. Hugh Oldcastle, *A Briefe instruction and maner how to keepe bookes of accompts*, ed. John Mellis (London, 1588), sig. [F6v]; John Carpenter, *A Most Excellent Instruction for the Exact and perfect keeping of Merchant Bookes of Accounts, by way of Debitor and Creditor* (London, 1632), sig. [A3v].
6. Richard Dafforne, *The Merchants Mirrour: or, Directions for the perfect Ordering and Keeping of his Accounts: Framed by way of Debitor and Creditor, after the (so-tearmed) Italian Manner* (London, 1684), 6. On the development of accounting practices from Pacioli through the early modern period, see M. F. Bywater and B. S. Yamey, *Historic Accounting Literature: A Companion Guide* (London: Scolar Press, 1982). For the features of the Dutch tradition, see Terry Cooke and Kees Camfferman, "Dutch Accounting in Japan 1609–1850: Isolation or Observation?" *Accounting Business and Financial History* 11 (2001): 369–82.
7. Dafforne, *Merchants Mirrour*, 6.
8. Oldcastle, *Briefe instruction*, sig. B8r; Carpenter, *Most Excellent Instruction*, 5; and Dafforne, *Merchants Mirrour*, 6. There is a relationship here between the waste book's running commentary, the structure and content of the personal diary, and the study of nature, see Lotte Mulligan, "Self Scrutiny and the Study of Nature: Robert Hook's Diary as Natural History," *Journal of British Studies* 35 (1996): 311–42.
9. Carpenter, *Most Excellent Instruction*, 5.
10. Oldcastle, *Briefe instruction*, sig. B8r.
11. Dafforne, *Merchants Mirrour*, 6.
12. Ibid., 5. Also, Mary Poovey sees double-entry ledgers as a tool of control and surveillance, in *A History of the Modern Fact: Problems of Knowledge in the Sciences of Wealth and Society* (Chicago: University of Chicago Press, 1998), 35.
13. Dafforne, *Merchants Mirrour*, 4.
14. A recent exception to this trend is Anke te Heesen's study of how double-entry bookkeeping practices in the ledger helped eighteenth century naturalists order and index their information, see "Accounting for the Natural World: Double-Entry Bookkeeping in the Field," in Londa Schiebinger and Claudia Swan, *Colonial Botany: Science, Commerce, and Politics in the Early Modern World* (Philadelphia: University of Pennsylvania Press, 2005), 237–51.
15. Runs of merchant account books were carefully labeled to indicate the order of entries and to whom they belonged. John Carpenter instructed

his readers to write the names of each account book "on their backsides or covers, with this note No. A, or No. 1," and to place the merchant's ownership mark in the same location. The following year, new books were to be marked with a letter B, then a C, and so forth; see Carpenter, *Most Excellent Instruction*, 2. See also Oldcastle, *Briefe instruction*, sig. B6r. For a discussion of these important characteristics of merchant accounting practices, see Poovey, *History of the Modern Fact*, 29–91.

16. Inscription on the funeral monument of Elizabeth Withypool Lucar (d. 1537), St. Laurence Poultry Church, London, courtesy of Judith Bennett. The monument was probably constructed in the Elizabethan period based on its stylistic elements.
17. For mathematics education in Elizabethan London, see Deborah E. Harkness, *The Jewel House: Elizabethan London and the Scientific Revolution* (New Haven, CT: Yale University Press, 2007), 97–141. For England more broadly, see Mordechai Feingold, *The Mathematicians' Apprenticeship: Science, Universities, and Society in England, 1560–1640* (Cambridge: Cambridge University Press, 1984).
18. Oldcastle, *Briefe instruction*, sig. B6v.
19. Steven Shapin, *A Social History of Truth: Civility and Science in Seventeenth-Century England* (Chicago: University of Chicago Press, 1994), 93–95.
20. Oldcastle, *Briefe instruction*, sig. B7r. For the importance of descriptive detail in the natural sciences during the early modern period, see, for example, Pamela Smith, *The Body of the Artisan* (Chicago: University of Chicago Press, 2004); Brian W. Ogilvie, *The Science of Describing: Natural History in Renaissance Europe* (Chicago: University of Chicago Press, 2006), esp. pp. 174–206.
21. See, for example, Oldcastle, model inventory, *Briefe instruction*, sig. B1r-v.
22. David Cressy, *Literacy and the Social Order: Reading and Writing in Tudor-Stuart England* (Cambridge: Cambridge University Press, 1980), 124, 146. While the study of literacy is fraught with complicating factors such as gender and class, and scholars regularly interrogate Cressy's data and approach to see if there are ways of removing biases against women and the nonpropertied, most agree that Londoners were among the most literate of all early modern English men and women. For a more recent interpretation of this evidence, see Margaret W. Ferguson, *Dido's Daughters: Literacy, Gender, and Empire in Early Modern England and France* (Chicago: University of Chicago Press, 2003), passim.
23. Cressy, *Literacy and the Social Order*, 11.
24. Ibid., 134–35.
25. Joan Simon, *Education and Society in Tudor England* (Cambridge: Cambridge University Press, 1966), 292.
26. Simon, *Education and Society*, 353.
27. Ibid., 316–32.

28. Ibid., 386–90.
29. Ibid., pp. 302–16; also Humfrey Baker, *Such as are desirous, eyther themselves to learne, or to have their children or servants instructed* (London, ca. 1590); John Mellis, "To the Reader," in Oldcastle, *Briefe instruction*.
30. Cyprian Blagden, *The Stationers' Company: A History, 1403–1959* (Stanford: Stanford University Press, 1960); Mark Bland, "The London Book-Trade in 1600," in David Scott Kastan, ed., *A Companion to Shakespeare* (London: Blackwell, 1999), 450–63; Peter W. M. Blayney, *The Bookshops in Paul's Cross Churchyard* (London: Bibliographical Society, 1990); Adrian Johns, *The Nature of the Book: Print and Knowledge in the Making* (Chicago: University of Chicago Press, 1998).
31. Corporation of London Record Office (London), Rep. 15, f. 400r (December 5–14, 1565).
32. See Harkness, *Jewel House*, 115–24.
33. Bywater and Yamey, *Historic Accounting Literature*, 58.
34. Dafforne, *Merchants Mirrour*, sig. Ar.
35. Documentary evidence about Barlow survives in the following records: London College of Physicians, *Annals* 2: 5b, 6b, 43b, 59a-b; Margaret Pelling and Charles Webster, "Medical Practitioners," in Charles Webster, ed., *Health Medicine and Mortality in Early Modern England* (Cambridge: Cambridge University Press, 1979), 178–79; Bodleian Library MS Ashmole 1375, f. 39r; Prerogative Court of Canterbury 47 Dixy (will of Edward Barlow); Bodleian Library, Oxford, MS Ashmole 1487 (notebook, formulary, and miscellany of Edward Barlow, c. 1588–89).
36. The library catalog is contained in Bodleian Library MS Ashmole 1487, folios 215v–218r. Notice of the catalog was included in Sears Jayne, *Library Catalogues of the English Renaissance* (Berkeley: University of California Press, 1956), 129.
37. See David Boyd Haycock and Patrick Wallis, eds., *Quackery and Commerce in Seventeenth-Century London: The Proprietary Medicine Business of Anthony Daffy*, *Medical History Supplements*, no. 25 (2005); Patrick Wallis, "Consumption, Medicine, and Retailing in Early Modern London," *Economic History Review* (forthcoming).
38. London College of Physicians, MS *Annals*, 2: 59a-b.
39. For a more detailed treatment of Draper, see Harkness, *Jewel House*, 181–210.
40. British Library MS Sloane 320, folios 1–32, folio 4r.
41. Blair, "Humanist Methods," 66.
42. Ibid., 7. On the tradition of commonplace books and miscellanies in English Renaissance literature, see Arthur F. Marotti, *Manuscript, Print, and the English Renaissance Lyric* (Ithaca, NY: Cornell University Press, 1995), 19. John Dee, for example, kept both a daily alchemical notebook to record his progress, as well as an elaborately organized (and largely blank) commonplace book. See William Sherman, *John Dee: The Politics of Reading and Writing in the Renaissance* (Boston and Amherst:

University of Massachusetts Press, 1995); Bodleian Library MS Rawlinson D241. For an English example of a printed commonplace book, see Hugh Plat, *The Floures of Philosophie* (London, 1572).

43. Medical receipt book of Clement Draper, British Library MS Sloane 3690, f. 111v.
44. Alchemical notebook of Clement Draper, British Library MS Sloane 3686, f. 71r.
45. Ibid., f. 78v.
46. See Draper's medical receipt book, British Library MS Sloane 3690, f. 27r. The prevalence of migraine remedies, methods for ridding the body of worms, and tooth preparations suggests that Draper was called on to provide remedies for these prevalent conditions.
47. British Library MS Sloane 2209, f. 7r and British Library MS Sloane 2216, f. 32r.
48. For more information and a full bibliography on Hugh Plat, see Harkness, *Jewel House*, 211–53. A surprisingly large number of Plat notebooks (nearly two dozen) survive in manuscript form and are now in the Sloane collections at the British Library.
49. British Library (hereafter BL) MS Sloane 2189, f. 23v.
50. BL, MS Sloane 2210, f. 139v.
51. BL MS Sloane 2210, f. 118v and MS Sloane 2216, f. 18r.
52. BL MS Sloane 2245, ff. 30v-31r, MS Sloane 2189, f. 29v, MS Sloane 2210, f. 166v.
53. BL MS Sloane 2216, f. 142r and 37r.
54. Plat, *Jewell House*, 30. Plat's notebook account in BL MS Sloane 2210, f. 68v, does not include the detail that he immediately recorded the experiment.
55. Ibid., sig. B3v-[B4r].
56. BL MS Sloane 2249, f. 12v.
57. For his medicines, see BL, MS Sloane 2209 f. 15r. For the medicinal uses of mumia, see Karl H. Dannenfeldt, "Egyptian Mumia: The Sixteenth-Century Experience and Debate," *Sixteenth Century Journal* 16 (1985): 163–80; Harold J. Cook, "Time's Bodies: Crafting the Preparation and Preservation of Naturalia," in Pamela Smith and Paula Findlen, eds., *Merchants and Marvels: Commerce, Science, and Art in Early Modern Europe* (New York: Routledge, 2002) 230–32. Plat discusses the corpses most suitable for mumia in BL MS Sloane 2249, f. 5r. His oath to preserve the secrets surrounding mumia is in BL MS Sloane 2246, f. 60v.
58. BL MS Sloane 2209, f. 19r. "Anthony's Pill" may relate to Francis Anthony's sensational cure-all, potable gold; see Anthony, *The apologie, or defence of a verity heretofore published concerning a medicine called aurum potabile* (London, 1616).
59. For the Elizabethan period, Paul Slack's classic work, *The Impact of Plague in Tudor and Stuart England* (London: Routledge, 1985), is indispensable.

60. BL MS Sloane 2209, f. 22r-25v.
61. Joel Kaye, *Economy and Nature in the Fourteenth Century* (Cambridge: Cambridge University Press, 1998); Mario Biagioli, *Galileo's Instruments of Credit: Telescopes, Images, Secrecy* (Chicago: University of Chicago Press, 2006); Steven Shapin, *A Social History of Truth: Civility and Science in Seventeenth-Century England* (Chicago: University of Chicago Press, 1994).

Chapter 10

Coming of Age in Trade

Masculinity and Commerce in Eighteenth-Century England

John Smail, University of North Carolina, Charlotte

In June 1719, as Caleb Dickinson lay dying, he wrote a letter to his children. Since they were quite young at the time—the oldest was eight—this letter-from-the-grave was a classic in the genre of parental advice, missing no opportunity to play on the pathos of the situation in order to drive home the lessons being offered. (The pathos was somewhat undermined by the fact that Caleb survived the illness and lived into his children's adulthood.) However, while it is addressed to "My Dear Tender Children," the letter largely ignores his daughters, who are simply admonished to marry well with the consent of their guardians. Instead, it focuses its attention on his two sons whose transition from youth to manhood was clearly more problematic. To guide his son's development, Dickinson named four trustees (whose qualities he enumerated at length) and enjoined the boys to "take these my friends to be your best friends and follow their direction

* The author would like to thank Marilyn Morris, Karen Harvey, and Anna Clark for helpful comments on an earlier draft. Thanks are also due to Margaret Jacob and Catherine Secretan for their invitation to the Clark Library conference on Bourgeois Self-Perception and to the participants for their comments.

and advice as you g[row] to be men." Dickinson expected his sons to be bound apprentice "to a suitable trade and to honest friends," clearly intending them to pursue a trade in their adult lives, and he also enjoined them to fear God in terms appropriate for the family's Dissenting background. The pitfalls Dickinson wanted his sons to avoid were the classic bugbears of middling existence—idleness, profligacy, dishonesty, and licentiousness—vices to be countered by virtues such as industry, sincerity, honesty, and sobriety (extending far beyond drink per se). He was particularly insistent that his sons be on the lookout for the corrupting influence of company that might seek to take advantage of them, singling out "those bred perfect gentlemen as we call it in England, but Dutchman calls it idleman, [who] are often very unhappy . . . [for] not being bred to industry and business and are not useful to themselves or their families."[1]

Though wealthier than most, Caleb Dickinson was thus quite typical of middling parents whose anxieties about the uncertain futures their sons faced led them to see youth as something of a gauntlet to be run; a short period in which they could make their boys "grow to be men" by hammering home the lessons about the impermanence of wealth, the need for industry, virtue, and thrift (and marriage to a woman of good reputation). Such lessons were crucial because, as Margaret Hunt has ably and thoroughly shown, life in trade in the eighteenth century was fraught with uncertainty. In the absence of limited liability laws, credit bureaus, and anything but the most basic insurance, merchants and manufacturers were highly exposed. Anything from a shift in markets to the failure of a business associate might lead them to lose not only their trading capital and livelihood, but also their home and other assets. In such an imperfect and uncertain world, it was thus imperative that young men be brought up with both the skills—literacy, bookkeeping, and commercial knowledge—and the values—diligence, frugality, and honesty—needed to survive.[2]

If, thanks to Margaret Hunt, we have a good idea of what middling parents expected of their sons and why, historians have not so closely examined the ways in which young men themselves experienced this difficult transition to manhood, nor what that experience suggests about their perception of themselves as commercial men.[3] The sons of Caleb Dickinson left no record of their response to their father's letter (beyond preserving it in the family papers), but in other sources we can explore this transition from the perspective of youth. Consider, as an introduction, the following passage written by William Pollard, an import merchant in Philadelphia, to a boyhood companion still living in Halifax who was working as a clerk on the Calder and Hebble Navigation, a letter from one young man to another. Pollard agreed with his correspondent's sentiments "that very few if any are free from trouble and anxiety during their journey through this life, rich or poor," adding that indeed, the rich often seemed more troubled than their poorer neighbors despite their means. Nonetheless, Pollard noted,

> [T]he greater part of mankind are anxiously industrious to obtain the rich man's situation and I must confess myself one of that party, but I think it is by no means clear that we are not pursuing a shadow (that is if we expect greater happiness therefrom). However in my attempt if I am so happy as to conduct my affairs with satisfaction and approbation to those I am or may be connected with and with satisfaction in my own breast, I shall hold myself excusable to mankind as to the merits of my pursuit.

These musings, crucially, were embedded in a letter in which Pollard was apportioning blame for the parlous state of his business, accepting some responsibility himself but also implicating the Halifax merchant who had sponsored his emigration and who had promised to extend him credit.[4]

Pollard's reflections suggest that for young men in trade, coming of age was indeed an anxious time, a period of tension between an idealized and sought-after independence and the reality of continued dependence upon the assistance, and capital, of others. It was a period, moreover, in which one's motives (and thus prospects) were open to complex and contradictory interpretation, with the desire for gain held in check both by a realistic assessment of one's chances and moral and ethical considerations. Given the inherently uncertain and interdependent nature of eighteenth-century commerce, no one in trade could ever really outgrow these tensions and contradictions, and, as I have argued elsewhere, these issues remained important in the self-representations of commercial folk well into adulthood.[5] Such concerns, however, were particularly acute in the passage from youth to adulthood and were central to the way in which young men understood and developed their masculinity. For Pollard, and others like him, coming to manhood in the commercial world of the eighteenth century presented a series of challenges, challenges that inflected their masculinity in particular ways.

As recent work has made clear, this analysis of middling masculinity cannot be understood as a quest for a single, coherent, masculine identity, for there were multiple masculinities circulating in eighteenth-century society whose inflections were shaped by factors such as class, marital status, and age, not to mention personal predilections. This more complex reality has emerged as scholars such as Michele Cohen, Karen Harvey, Tim Hitchcock, and Alexandra Shepard have questioned the simple progression from an early modern masculinity rooted in a man's patriarchal control over his household to an eighteenth-century masculinity built around politeness, civility, and reason.[6] I will argue, however, that there are patterns to the ways in which individuals, in this case young men growing up in trade, interpreted and negotiated masculinity as they matured into manhood. The social position these young men sought to give their masculinity is complex, for boundaries were fluid and shifting, but it does appear that masculinity and capitalism were linked in the way these individuals saw themselves.

This chapter explores these questions about masculinity and capitalism using letters from or to young men in trade written during the eighteenth century, most from the 1770s and 1780s. All came from families that were relatively well founded, possessing a gentility that was secure rather than precarious. Two collections predominate. One consists of the letters received by Richard Tolson during his late teens and early twenties, mostly from his father but also from acquaintances. During this time, Richard was first at a merchant academy in Holland and then traveled through northern Europe seeking orders for the family firm.[7] The second is a collection of letters written to and by George Wansey of Warminster in Wiltshire, again probably during his late teens and early twenties. His correspondents were acquaintances from his youth who had left town and, in one case, a friend he had made while at school. George was from a family of West Country clothiers and set up trading on his own account during this period, but some of his correspondents had more varied experiences.[8]

Their Father's Sons

While we don't know what Caleb Dickinson's sons made of the not-quite-posthumous admonitions he left in his letter, the sources consulted for this study suggest that young men, as a rule, internalized such rhetoric and sought to follow the paths their parents had set as they grew to manhood.

Like their parents, young men saw the transition from childhood to adulthood as a perilous phase of life, beset with possible temptations and particularly prone to error. Thus Henry Wansey wrote to his brother George in the 1770s noting that it was uncommon for such a large family to have not a single prodigal in their ranks and expressing his hope that "we have escaped from the evils of pride, vanity and youthful lusts. I mean the pursuit of such pleasure as youth are too apt to run into and which generally ends in shame disappointment and unhappiness. Happy are those youth who foreseeing these evils prudently avoid them by devoting that time which the unthinking spend in gratifying their pleasures in laying up a fund of useful knowledge in improving their minds in true wisdom and studying to be well grounded in the knowledge of the Xtian religion."[9]

William Curtis, also writing to George Wansey, berated himself for idleness, a "motive by which youth are very much actuated."[10] Curtis's letters also express a closely related, if less dangerous, concern that youth was a period characterized by a lack of seriousness: "I wish I had a little more of the sedateness which sets off the man, but I know my high spirits . . . expose me by leading me into childish actions."[11] Wansey echoed such sentiments, wishing he could trade the "turbulent pleasures and wild ungovernable spirits of youth for the calm composure of declining age."[12] (He was only twenty at the time, a young fogy if there ever was one.)

Young men were also anxious about the transition to manhood, particularly about their ability to successfully establish themselves in trade or a professional career. The uncertainty William Pollard expressed in the passage quoted in the introduction was equally evident in the poem that Richard Tolson copied into his travel journal from the window at the lodgings of one of his companions in Frankfort:

> And *this* is Frankfort on the river Main
> Where many goods are sold for little gain
> Oh! We poor merchants that we thus must ramble
> For orders small and for which we scramble.[13]

Moreover, he communicated the same in his letters home, prompting repeated assurances in his father's letters such as the following: "I *beg and request* that if you have not the success at Frankfort you wish for after the fair that you will not be uneasy or grieve yourself about it."[14] Finally confronting the implications of the large stock of unsold cloth he had on hand, George Wansey was forced to conclude in 1784 that he would have to reduce trade and thus "forgoe the expectation of rising in the world and forsake the agreeable and honourable connexions and acquaintances which I have lately formed." It would, he reflected, allow him more time for his books, but he could not "with calmness behold my honor and reputation sink in the world my good name blasted or bear with patience poverty shame and derision."[15]

Finally, as these young men saw it, a successful passage to manhood required them to eschew the many vices that might lead them astray. Back in Leeds after finishing his schooling in Delft, Richard Tolson received a letter from Thomas Stevens, who was working as a clerk for a Dutch merchant in Amsterdam, expressing his concerns about his ability to do just that: "I hope you'll follow the rules you give me in yours of which I make no doubt of as you have not so much opportunity of being ruined as I have, being in foreign country and having as much liberty as I myself think proper as having no father or brothers to tell me whether I do right or wrong."[16] We can get some idea of the "rules" Richard had enjoined his friend to follow from another poem copied into his travel journal, also taken from a window pane. Entitled "On a Watch," it reads:

> Could but our temper move like this machine
> Not urged by passion nor delayed by spleen
> And true to natures regulating power
> By virtuous acts distinguish every hour
> Then health and joy would follow as they ought
> The laws of motion and the laws of thought
> Sweet health to pass the present moments o'er
> And everlasting joy when time shall be no more.[17]

Individually enumerated, the list of vices that could disturb one's watch-like equilibrium was quite long, including licentiousness, vanity, drunkenness, dishonesty, and frivolity, but the two most prominent (and perhaps the ones that enabled the others) were extravagance and idleness. The former is clearly at the root of the predicament in which Walter Long found himself. Long, in London training to be a lawyer, drafted a letter to his father describing himself as the only "gall" in his father's otherwise happy life and announcing that he was £120 in debt, a state which he found "worse than death." He begged his father to pay off the encumbrance and count it as his patrimony, and he assured him that doing so would help him learn "by experience (the best mistress) the vanity and emptiness of everything." Thomas Long's reaction was predictably apoplectic, not least because he had been warning his son to beware the vices and temptations of the town. He pressed his son for details, wanting to know whether it was "clothes, wine, women, or gameing or all of them" that had led to the debt and expressing doubt that his son would be able to "restrain [his] extravagant and vicious courses." Walter insisted that he was fully sensible of the trouble that he, as an "undutiful son," had given to his father through "folly and extravagance" and tried to reassure him that he had withdrawn from company "to avoid the temptations to destruction." Evidence from the remaining letters in the correspondence suggest that the crisis passed, though two years later Walter was questioned rather closely about the cost of a suit of clothes he wanted.[18]

Richard Tolson was also worried about extravagance, though he was, for the most part, able to keep his impulses in check. Indeed, his father even had to press him to take something for supper each night, since it appears Richard had been skipping this meal out of concern for the expenses attendant on his traveling.[19] The one occasion on which he slipped up was, to his credit, an extravagant act of charity rather than of dissipation—an expense of £15 to buy the discharge of an English soldier he met in a Flemish border town. It nonetheless taught him a very sharp lesson about the dangers of living beyond his means and occasioned an extended admonition from both his brother and his father.[20]

Idleness was also perceived to be a particularly serious problem. William Curtis, already quoted, thought idleness to be a vice to which youth were particularly susceptible, one that would lead to "depravity," and in a later letter he berated himself as "a most intolerable lazy cur," bemoaning that the temptations of Christmas gambols had distracted him from sitting down to write and thus from "retriev[ing] my lost character."[21] His sentiments are echoed by Thomas Stevens, a correspondent of Richard Tolson's who wrote in 1781 to complain of the "idle state" he had entered into upon returning to London when the Dutch war broke out.[22] Such anxieties were familiar to Richard, whose doubts in his letters about his own ability to fight idleness with industry prompted constant reassurances from his father that he was being as industrious as possible.[23] George Wansey, hardly grown himself, took on a parental role in his correspondence with a Sam F., though not without some rather obvious comments on his own situation. Sam, a native of Warminster whose father Wansey knew, was already in trouble for getting into debt while living in London, but he made matters much worse by considering a career in acting, a profession that the good people of Warminster thought tantamount to being a highwayman. That fancy seems to have passed, and while young Sam was considering a move to Edinburgh to study medicine, Wansey advised him of the advantages of living in a city, remarking that the "boasted tranquility of a country life is too near akin to indolence and tends to rust and diminish the active powers of the soul." He went on to bemoan the pattern of life "in a certain town that you know," a town "inhabited by a most ignorant and insipid race of young men and who are at the same time profligate to the utmost extent of their abilities [and] whose summum bonum is to spend the morning in hunting and the evening in drinking strong beer."[24]

The point is perhaps obvious, but it is nonetheless worth noting that these vices were all seen in a feminine light. Evidence to this effect is subtle but ubiquitous. Walter Long ascribed his downfall to "folly and extravagance," the first in this pair of vices giving a particularly feminine flavor to what was readily acknowledged as the feminine vice of unnecessary spending, and he iced the cake by referring in another letter to his "vanity." If he saw the vices that had brought him down as feminine, he was equally clear that the virtues that would lead to his resurrection were masculine: "[I] will arm myself with courage and resolution against all the attacks of pleasure and indolence and by my utmost diligence and industry rather cut my way through flints and steal."[25] The Christmas gambols that fed William Curtis's self-proclaimed tendency to idleness were clearly feminine in relation to the manly discipline of writing a serious letter, and a similar contrast emergences in George Wansey's pointed comparison of the "sharp treble" of the female tongue heard in Bath and the "manly voices" of Oxford.[26]

What Kind of Man?

George Wansey's preference for virtue over vice, for masculine Oxford over feminine Bath, is clear, and the same could be said of Long and Curtis, perhaps all the more so since, unlike Wansey, they actually had some experience with vice. The clarity of their choice, however, was more negative than positive. These young men knew what kind of man they *did not* want to become, rejecting the vices they identified as feminine. However, when it came to knowing what kind of men they *did* want to become, what masculine virtues they sought to adopt, they were not as certain, for they were confronted by a range of virtues and masculine traits and thus multiple masculinities.

There were, to be sure, some universals. The most obvious, and quite clearly the most fundamental, was independence, for these young men were certain that coming of age meant becoming one's own master in the world. This imperative is succinctly represented in the congratulations that George Wansey offered to Richard Lawrence on hearing that his plans to set up a small school had come to fruition. It was a modest start, but a school would provide a maintenance sufficient for a sober single man, and as he put it, "better is a handful of one's own than a bushel of another's." Wansey went on to assure Lawrence that he would find "great satisfaction in being no longer burdensome to your relations. You may now join the rest of the world with a greater degree of confidence and hold up your head among the rest and say 'I am a Man.'"[27] Wansey himself was clearly very proud of his independence; his spiritual autobiography, for example, mentions in several places the date on which he set up in trade on his own account independently of his father.[28] For his part, Thomas Stevens, a correspondent of Richard Tolson's, chafed because of his *inability* to establish himself on an independent footing. We first encounter him in the letters working as a clerk to a Dutch merchant in Amsterdam, a "miserable place where I have not prospect of advancing myself." The outbreak of war in 1781 forced him to return to London where he accepted a position working for his brothers, that being "preferable to remaining clerk all my life." In the end, being clerk is what Stevens may have had to accept, for his brothers released him after only a few months and he took a situation as clerk for a corn factor in London who needed someone familiar with the Dutch.[29] Richard Tolson's family was much more supportive than Stevens's, but the desire to be independent may well have prompted his hasty and ill-advised leap into a partnership with a Mr. Merac of Ostend in 1781.[30]

Three other virtues—vigor, fraternity, and politeness—also run throughout this material, but more as commonplaces than deeply held elements of masculine identity. With respect to the first, these young men clearly understood their manhood as involving a commitment to a physically active life. Both Richard Tolson and George Wansey walked regularly, largely for reasons of health (both physical and mental).[31] However, as Richard Tolson's journal entry recording a walk over a frozen river to get to Dort suggests, there was an element of audacity involved as well, and the natural connection his father made in assuring his son that "your weakness will naturally go off when you come to Eat Roast Beef and use exercise" is similarly tinged with a masculine air.[32] For his part, George Wansey clearly took pride in relating his more heroic jaunts to his friends. These included a "fishing excursion of fourteen miles on foot" and an expedition to see Stonehenge, which, at something like forty miles round trip, he acknowledged as an act of bravado that he would not soon repeat.[33]

These young men also understood their masculinity as involving a particular kind of relationship with other young men—"fraternity," for lack of a better term. This relationship was restricted to other men, for the handful of letters in these collections to and from women were quite different in tone. Even the letter from George Wansey's sister, where propriety might have permitted some hints of intimacy, was more formal in tone, more superficial in subject matter, than the letters between men.[34] It was not, however, differentiated by familial relationship, for both George Wansey's and Richard Tolson's correspondence with their respective brothers shares the same earnest engagement with ideas and feelings as their letters to friends. There was also a commitment to honesty and directness most obvious in the mutual exchange of admonitions to good behavior and a tone of open self-reflection: "you will smile at the alteration in me," wrote William Curtis, commenting on his newly adopted air of gravity and seriousness.[35] With one exception, none of these relationships gives any hint of being anything more than a robust masculine friendship. The exception, George Wansey's fairly extensive correspondence with Richard Lawrence, was heavily inflected with a language of sensibility most evident in the poems the two exchanged on a regular basis.[36]

The third of these commonplace virtues, politeness, is perhaps the most intriguing. That it was universal is hardly surprising given what we know of eighteenth-century society. George Wansey's sister Anne described the fiancée of Miss Jeffries (from a family with close ties to the Wanseys) as "a polite well bred young gentleman," and his brother advised him to study Lord Chesterfield's letters for their good advice on such subjects as dress, conversation, manners, and the like.[37] William Barrell was "sensible to [the] politeness" of the tactful request of his London suppliers to be allowed to draw on the balance due to them and apologized in another letter for a long and "disagreeable" string of complaints.[38] Richard Tolson noted in his travel journals a visit to Mr. J. C. Augstell in Frankfort "who behaved uncommonly politely to me," and his father's advice that he behave "like a stoic philosopher" when confronting a recalcitrant payer suggests he would have sought such a mien himself.[39] However, nothing in the surviving letters suggests that politeness was particularly meaningful to these young men, confirming Karen Harvey's suggestive observation about the relative unimportance of politeness to the middling folks studied by Margaret Hunt.[40] These young men lived in a society in which the ethos of politeness was ubiquitous, and they did not reject it in the least, but it does not seem to have been central to the self-image they had of themselves.

While some values were fairly universally held, other virtues we find in this correspondence suggest the potential for contradictions and ambiguities in what it meant to grow up to be a man. As an illustration of the potential for contradiction consider again Walter Long's vision of the way out of his predicament: "[I] will arm myself with courage and resolution against all the attacks of pleasure and indolence and by my utmost diligence and industry rather cut my way through flints and steal."[41] Which was it to be? Was he to defeat extravagance by girding his loins for a vigorous armed assault or by making a bookish retreat to study his law books? As an example of the potential for ambiguity, consider the passage in the letter that Richard Lawrence wrote to George Wansey just after graduating from Oxford and setting up his penurious existence as a schoolteacher. Referring to his uncle's laughter at the state of his housekeeping, Lawrence explained: "While I live I am determined as far as in my power be to keep always out of debt." This classic rejection of luxury and extravagance, however, was followed by something verging on its antithesis: "I hope and believe I shall never grow stingy. No vice at present appears to me more miserable and unchristian like than avarice." Which was it to be? Prudent but therefore stingy? Generous but therefore in debt? Lawrence's quandary lay in the fact that the virtue that protected against one vice might well lead straight into the maw of an equally pernicious failing. I am not suggesting that Lawrence or Long, *as individuals*, were in serious doubt about how they wanted to behave. Their statements, however, suggest the outlines of what we might identify for simplicity's sake as two alternative constructions of masculinity from which these young men drew. Without suggesting that these two masculinities were the only masculinities circulating in eighteenth-century society, or (b) that they existed independently of the individuals who lived them, or (c) that they were stable and coherent, each is consistent enough to be worthy of analysis.[42]

On the one hand, evident in Richard Lawrence's aversion to debt and Walter Long's invocation of his diligence and industry, there is what one could call a prudential masculinity that glorified diligence, prudence, and thrift and defined masculine honor in terms of integrity, honesty, and quiet achievement.[43] In his advice to young Sam F., George Wansey elaborated on the need for hard work—"I think that with diligence you cannot fail of doing well in any part of the world"—and reminded him that "God has attached almost every advantage of this world to labour and prudence and without these we may in vain expect that our virtue or natural abilities will make us rich."[44] Another of George's correspondents, William Green, wrote to thank him for a gift of money and assured Wansey that "it has always been my endeavour to manage my little affairs with the strictest oeconomy I am capable of and I hope by observing the prudence you have prescribed to me I shall always preserve the esteem of my friends."[45] Richard Tolson expressed similar aspirations, and his father assured him that "[I] have *Entire Confidence in* your prudence and oeconomy and industry in everything."[46]

The close relationship between prudence and economy was particularly important because in the commercial environment in which these young men operated it was often necessary to spend money in order to make money. Thrift in and of itself, therefore, was less important than the discretion of knowing when and how to spend money. Thus we find William Barrell, a young colonial merchant who was just setting up trade in Philadelphia, writing to the London firm whose credit was underwriting his trade in 1771 to inform them that he had rented premises on one of the city's major thoroughfares. The rent was considerable, and there were going to be costs in outfitting the shop, but he was at pains to assure his correspondents that the expense was worth it because he would do more trade and save money by living in a room over the shop for no additional charge.[47] Prudence, moreover, was not limited to matters economic, for it encompassed good judgment generally. To give but one example, Richard Tolson's concerns about declining an invitation to travel to Russia with the head of a well-established Leeds firm were judged by his father, and by the family's confidant and mentor Mr. Tottie (another prominent Leeds merchant), as "prudent and manly"—heady praise indeed for a boy who was just sixteen.[48]

On the other hand, evident in Lawrence's impulse to generosity and Long's arming himself there is what one could call a chivalric masculinity that glorified nobility, magnanimity, and the classics and defined honor in terms of bravery and prowess.[49] Richard Tolson was congratulated on his "proper and manly" response to a Catholic religious procession he encountered in Dusseldorf.[50] Walter Long resisted his father's demand that he return to Wiltshire, arguing that to run away from his troubles would make him virtuous simply "by want of opportunity to be vicious." Instead, he wanted to stay in town to "gain the noble victory of conquering ones self."[51] George Wansey wished to have the resources needed to travel the world so that he could join in with the "noble pursuits" of Captain Cook, and elsewhere he allowed that he was not deaf to the call of glory and honor, qualifying the latter by adding: "honor, true honor such as a rational and religious man might consistently aspire to."[52] There is, hardly surprising, a strong militaristic element in this strand of masculinity. Wansey, for example, joined one of the many volunteer militias that sprang up in the latter part of the eighteenth century. He relished the prospect of marching in "files, divisions, and columns," and looked forward to the "martial appearance" his company would have once supplied with uniforms and the thirty-two guns ordered from Birmingham. In his opinion, such organizations would help to reestablish a military spirit that would speed the reformation of both morals and the constitution, for "almost all the vices that are predominant in the present age spring from the same pernicious source: Effeminacy of Manners."[53] Tolson and his companions never seem to have been tempted themselves, but the numerous references to "brave" admirals, generals, and garrisons in the news items indicate that they were not immune from this sentiment.[54]

Each of these masculinities, however, had its problematic side. Prudential masculinity was undermined by its potential to lead one into a superficial pursuit of ill-gotten gain, a money-grubbing existence full of compromise and uncertainty, a downside of which William Pollard was acutely aware. Wansey was equally ambivalent as to the merits of his calling, particularly as related to a higher calling in the professions: "Think how glorious will hereafter be the reflection that you have raised yourself and family to a more honourable rank that you have redeemed them from the paltry tricks of little peddling trades to fairer and nobler pursuits or at least that you have been able to place them in those higher walks of trade where integrity and justice are still esteemed and where a man may earn his sixpences without damning his soul."[55] Another correspondent, William Curtis, was of much the same opinion, declaring that he was not suited "to act the part of a mere man of trade," for "man was formed for nobler purposes than to scrape away the best part of his life in pursuit of trash which, when obtained, yields perhaps so much care and anxiety that the pleasure are not adequate to the pain."[56]

The potential pitfalls of following the path of prudential masculinity were, ironically, somewhat contradictory. On the one hand, Wansey was convinced that getting rich almost inevitably required a degree of dissimulation if not outright dishonesty, thus earning any successful tradesman the "just hatred" of his neighbors and leading him to wonder "what riches compensate for the breaches of humanity?"[57] Richard Tolson was caught out in just such a breach, resorting to some rather underhanded stratagems in order to get out of his partnership with Mr. Merac.[58] However, all too many examples showed that following the path laid out by prudential masculinity was no guarantee of success. "After all his labor and pain," wrote William Curtis about a family friend who lay dying, "he has hardly acquired enough to live comfortably, a case that is . . . too common with people of his generous and . . . way of thinking. A shocking but a natural consideration."[59]

Chivalric masculinity, on the other hand, was undermined by its association with the superficial and wasteful enjoyment of unearned wealth, an idle existence where the pursuit of (usually false) prowess overcame right reason. In a letter to Sam F., George Wansey passed on news of a mutual acquaintance who had joined the Second Dragoons as a coronet and "launched forth with full sails and a prosperous wind into the stream of dissipation, visits, masquerades, operas . . . the whole routine of a modern voluptuary." His behavior was, as Wansey wrote in a letter to Lawrence, "[a] folly which is so unbecoming a tradesman."[60] And it was precisely because of such tendencies that William Curtis, having in the previous sentence pronounced that man was formed for "nobler purposes" than trade, acknowledged that "the proneness of our nature to vice lays us under the necessity of having something in view in order to avoid depravity."[61] Several of George Wansey's letters indicate that the young men in his neighborhood defined their masculinity in terms of hunting, horse racing, and drinking bouts. Accused of lacking "spirit" for refusing to join them, Wansey deemed it better to suffer their reproaches rather "than, by engaging in their foolish pursuits, to sink . . . own opinion or diminish that veneration which is at once the enjoyment and the surest safeguard of virtue."[62] Wansey, however, was most critical of excesses to which chivalric masculinity could lead, excesses epitomized in the duel fought between "two Bath heroes" over a "trifling dispute." In a long passage that was prompted by the widely publicized news of the event, Wansey identified those who followed the "laws of honor" as "votaries" serving a "merciless deity" against the "dictates of reason."[63] Lawrence shared his opinion of dueling and expanded his critique of the ideals of chivalric of masculinity to comment derisively on the actions of Bath's volunteer association whose members had avenged an unflattering caricature by an "impudent painter" "not with the sword or pistol but with the plain rustic fist. One would really think that they attempted to make themselves as ridiculously consequential as possible."[64]

At this last step, however, Wansey balked. A member of the Warminster Volunteers himself, he believed, as already noted, that England was suffering from a lack of military spirit, and after defending the manly way in which the Bath Volunteers had sought to settle their quarrel, he went on to gently chastise his friend as one "who is destined to wear the unwarlike toga and is determined of consequence to make his ideas correspondent with his profession."[65] Of course, part of what was going on here is the verbal and intellectual play of two friends, but their different takes on the behavior of the Bath Volunteers is also indicative of the complex masculinity that these young men negotiated as they were growing up in trade. In addition to the fact that the masculine identities on which they riffed were ambiguous in and of themselves, we have here evidence that they were not consistently held, for we can quite easily imagine Wansey agreeing with Lawrence on this particular point. While, in his mind, the flaws and folly of chivalric masculinity were all too clear when illuminated by the prudential virtues of industry, prudence, and reason, the same was true in reverse. The young men examined here thus seem to have been tugged in two directions, defining, with some ambiguity and contradiction, their masculinity both in terms of prudential and chivalric virtues.

This observation raises a number of further questions—about what happened when these young men reached adulthood, about youth from other social backgrounds, and about the degree to which this pattern was specific to the last third of the eighteenth century—that I will not answer here.[66] One question I do want to take up concerns the relationship between these variant masculinities and individuals' experiences. In key respects, the findings advanced here are in agreement with most of the recent work on identity in suggesting that identity is not fixed (by social class, sex, or race) but is rather something that is adopted and adapted by individuals. That formulation, however, raises the question of why individuals adopt particular identities at particular times. Why does Wansey embrace militarism in the fall of 1779 and then castigate "red coated slaves" whose ignorance allows them to become the "tools of knaves or detestable ambition" in 1780?[67] I would argue in general terms that the answer lies in particular experiences: in individuals' interactions with friends and family; in their successes or failures; or in political or cultural events. In the particular case just cited, for example, there are hints that Wansey's reactions to the political fallout from the worsening situation in the North American colonies were behind this apparent change of heart, just as it is possible that a discouraging bottom line after doing the annual accounting might have prompted sour reflections on the ultimate value of a life spent in trade.

It is, however, possible to go a step further. Wansey's sense of his own masculinity may well have shifted both in the medium term as he matured and the short term as he reacted to specific experiences and interactions. However, his appropriations from the lexicon took place within a circumscribed cultural space defined by Wansey's perceptions of his place in society. How he understood that place is suggested in his sister's response to his gentle chiding on her refusal to accept invitations from the family of a Miss Cam, for she acknowledged her error and agreed with him "that to *covet* acquaintance with our superiors in rank [and] fortune is wrong but to avoid all indiscriminately on that account is equally so and may be construed as proceeding from a kind of p[ride] that cannot bear a consciousness of inferiority."[68] Thus there were masculinities, elite *and* plebian, from which Wansey was unlikely to borrow, a fact that gives significance to the ambiguities and contradictions that lay within and between the prudential and chivalric masculinities of these young capitalists. It is worth noting, too, that while the prudential and chivalric masculinities appear to be the antitheses of one another, the mapping is not balanced. As these young men clearly acknowledged, the danger inherent in too assiduous a pursuit of the prudential virtues was that one might pursue gain for its own sake, riches at the expense of honor. This was, however, a fairly traditional critique of the merchant's mindset, widely held in early modern society. The same is not true of the obverse. These young men clearly felt that the danger inherent in too assiduous a pursuit of the chivalric virtues was that one would be tempted into idleness and irrational behavior. This was a newer formulation of limited—though arguably growing—circulation in eighteenth-century society, and it was, moreover, a formulation that validated the experiences of those engaged in commerce.

WOMEN

In a recent polemical review of the relatively new field that is the history of masculinity, Toby Ditz has rebuked practitioners for straying from the insights and the agenda of a feminist history that created the field in the first place. She is particularly critical of the tendency in some histories of masculinity to focus exclusively on relations between men without considering the ways in which masculinities differ with respect to the relations with and domination of women. She goes on to show, using examples drawn from recent historical work on the colonial era in U.S. history, how an approach to the history of masculinity that forefronts relations between the sexes can offer insights into the history of masculinity, particularly the ways in which masculinity is connected to the exercise of social and political power.[69]

Ditz's call to reintroduce patriarchy into the history of masculinity is a challenge given the sources available for this project, but a preliminary attempt does provide some suggestive insights that can serve as a conclusion to this essay. Only one of the sources offers any direct information as to how young men from commercial backgrounds related to women in sexual terms, though I suspect this is an underreporting. The instance is a letter from Richard Tolson's friend Law Atkinson, also in Holland learning languages and accounting, describing the pornographic print he had received for his collection from a mutual acquaintance, a print he had taken to show one of the household's maids in the hopes of getting her into bed.[70] Rendered in Dutch, either because letters might be read by parents and friends or to add an extra frisson to the crude language used, the passage hints that sexual license played an important, if somewhat suppressed, role in these young men's masculinity.

Marriage, however, was a more serious business. To George Wansey, marriage was a mistake, a sentiment summed up in his advice to "shun matrimony as the gates of hell." His antipathy to marriage was in part pure misogyny. Confident that he could distinguish a generous man from a base man, he did not think the same was true for women "in this age of dissimulation."[71] He also saw marriage as a significant drain on resources, leading to nothing less than "poverty and distress." Above all, he thought that marriage while young would give admittance to a "soft yet troublesome intruder [while] in the heyday of your age when the passions are in full force and not otherwise eagerly engaged," an attempt to "gratify inclinations that are inconsistent with prudence."[72] Although he didn't seriously contemplate marriage until he was about thirty (and did not get married until he was thirty-five) Wansey was, to judge by the frequency with which he offered his advice, clearly swimming against the tide, for most of these young men seem to have been looking for a wife in their twenties—though usually in the period after they had established a modicum of independence.[73] We know from his autobiographical memoir, for example, that Richard Tolson pursued a string of women from as early as about twenty. The first few were temporary infatuations, while those mentioned later were more serious, though none of the courtships recorded in the memoir were successful.[74] Tolson was drawn to the women he courted by considerations of romantic love, but practical qualities are also in evidence. Although he was not so crass as to estimate the value of the dowry each of these women would have brought, it is clear that he confined his matrimonial attentions to women from polite society. In considering marriage as a practical matter, Tolson would have found support from George Wansey, who warned Sam F. that his second "apprenticeship" in the field of medicine might not bring the "dowry and fortune" that it had in former times.[75]

Wansey's metaphor and Tolson's choice of partners acknowledge the crucial importance that marriage played in shaping the fortunes of young men. That observation is nothing new, but in light of Ditz's admonition, it does suggest one potentially crucial feature specific to the masculinity of men in trade—men who were at once dependant on their wives' capital and their wives' willing partnership in running a frugal yet genteel household. This aspect of commercial masculinity would have had little resonance in plebian life where a woman's labor power might often equal the earning capacity of her mate.[76] Nor did it have much resonance in landed society where control over women's land—and the income it produced—was crucial, but where the wife's role in managing a prudent household was not as relevant. As I have noted, marriage typically came after manhood, but if subsequent analysis supports this tentative argument, it would be one more element indicating the existence of a distinctive commercial masculinity that young men in trade sought to assume as they came of age.

Therefore, while I would not wish to return to a model in which identity is fixed by social class, I do think we need a model that recognizes patterns in the ways in which individuals from similar backgrounds constructed identity within the fluidity of eighteenth-century culture. In this light, what I am arguing here is that young men growing up in trade shared certain values, in particular a repertoire of masculinity that emerged out of their experiences in that economic and social environment. Attracted to and influenced by chivalric ideals that enjoyed wide currency in this society, their sense of what it meant to grow to be a man was more profoundly shaped by the virtues of reason and prudence that made sense in a commercial setting. This commercial masculinity, with its ambiguities and complexities, was not monolithic. Wansey, from a relatively wealthy family of clothiers whose education included a solid grounding in Latin and Greek and who had the leisure to meet his friend for a day of fishing, was by no means in the same position as young Richard Tolson, who was sent to Holland to learn Dutch, German, and accounting before traveling through Europe to drum up orders to keep the family firm afloat. But they, and young men like them, seem to have shared a fundamentally similar sense of their manhood and how that positioned them within eighteenth-century society.

NOTES

1. Somerset Record Office, Taunton, UK, DN/485 Caleb Dickinson's letter to his children, June 14, 1719. Dickinson's concern with the temptations of an idle life and the consequences of living beyond one's means were a particular emphasis in his case because the family's estate, which included plantations in Jamaica, an estate in Somerset, and portions of £5000 for each daughter, was sufficient to make a choice between idleness and industry possible.
2. Margaret Hunt, *The Middling Sort: Commerce, Gender, and the Family in England, 1680–1780* (Berkeley and Los Angeles: University of California Press, 1996), esp. chap. 2.
3. Other works on youth in the early modern period are similarly top-down or sociological in their approach: John R. Gillis, *Youth and History: Tradition and Change in European Age Relations, 1770–Present* (New York: Academic Press, 1981); Ilana Ben Amos, *Adolescence and Youth in Early Modern England* (New Haven, CT: Yale University Press, 1994).
4. Historical Society of Pennsylvania, Philadelphia, USA, William Pollard letterbook, to Thomas Simpson, July 1, 1772.
5. John Smail, "Credit, Risk, and Honor in Eighteenth-Century Commerce," *Journal of British Studies*, 44 (July 2005): 439–56.
6. The case studies in Hitchcock and Cohen's valuable collection, *English Masculinities*, for example, reveal that different markers of masculinity were employed by different individuals in different ways, particularly when considering individuals of different social groups: Tim Hitchcock and Michele Cohen, eds., *English Masculinities, 1660–1800* (London: Longman, 1999). The work of Shepard and Harvey in a special issue of the *Journal of British Studies* makes much the same point, and also undermines an image of a unitary masculinity by pointing out that many of the aspects of an eighteenth-century masculinity defined by politeness existed in both previous and subsequent periods and that these differences may simply be an artifact of the dependence upon cultural rather than social analysis in studies of the eighteenth century: Karen Harvey and Alexandra Shepard, "What Have Historians Done with Masculinity? Reflections on Five Centuries of British History, circa 1500–1950," *Journal of British Studies*, 44 (2005): 274–80; Alexandra Shepard, "From Anxious Patriarchs to Refined Gentlemen? Manhood in Britain, circa 1500–1750," *Journal of British Studies*, 44 (2005): 281–95; Karen Harvey, "The History of Masculinity, circa 1650–1800," *Journal of British Studies*, 44 (2005): 296–311; and Michele Cohen, "'Manners' Make the Man: Politeness, Chivalry, and the Construction of Masculinity, 1750–1830," *Journal of British Studies*, 44 (2005): 312–29. See also Alexandra Shepard, "Manhood, Credit, and Patriarchy in Early Modern England, c. 1580–1640," *Past and Present*, 162 (2000): 75–106; Toby Ditz, "The New Men's History and the Peculiar Absence of Gendered

Power: Some Remedies from Early American Gender History," *Gender and History*, 16 (2004): 1–35; and Lawrence Klein, "Politeness and the Interpretation of the British Eighteenth Century," *Historical Journal*, 45 (2002): 69–98.

7. The Tolson collection is held by the West Yorkshire Archives, Kirkless branch, Huddersfield, UK, DD/TO/various (hereafter cited as DD/TO/__). The collection also includes travel journals kept by Richard Tolson and a memoir of his life. In the context of this article, the letters of the Tolson family require special handling for it is the letters *to* Richard Tolson, most from his father, that have survived.
8. One, the son of a watchmaker from Bath, was at Oxford and went on to become a bishop; another began an apprenticeship as an upholsterer and then opted to train for a career in medicine. The Wansey collection is held by the Wiltshire Record Office, Trowbridge, UK, 314/4/various (hereafter cited as 314/4/__). The collection also includes one of George Wansey's memorandum books.
9. 314/4/1, Wansey letters, from Henry Wansey, Salisbury, no date (hereafter n.d.).
10. 314/4/1, Wansey letters, from William Curtis, Clapham, July 16. 1773.
11. 314/4/1, Wansey letters, from William Curtis, Clapham, n.d.; word obscured in binding. In a later (undated) letter, Curtis expanded on this theme, announcing to George that their friendship needed to move past its basis in "some trifling incidents in our boyish days" and expressed his desire "to be introduced a bit more into life, not from any foolish puerile motives but because I thought I might be more usefully employed."
12. 314/4/2, draft letters of George Wansey, to Richard Lawrence, Sept. 1778.
13. DD/TO/4, Richard Tolson journal, 1779–80, fol. 31. It is worth reflecting that the existence of this passage in Tolson's journal required some English merchant to have written it, and Tolson's companion to have noticed it and brought Tolson along to see it.
14. DD/TO/11, Peter Tolson Sr., Aug. 19, 1780, emphasis in the original.
15. 314/4/3, Wansey journal, Oct. 10, 1784. Wansey was about twenty-five at the time. The "connexions" refer to his trade, specifically those to whom he sold cloth; "acquaintances" might have been commercial or social.
16. DD/TO/8, Richard Stevens, Jan. 18, 1777. Stevens did not even have the benefit of the watchful eye of his master, as the custom in Dutch counting houses was to have clerks live on their own.
17. DD/TO/4, Richard Tolson journal, 1779–80, fols. 46–47.
18. Wiltshire Record Office, Trowbridge, UK, 947/1874 (hereafter cited as 947/1847) Long letters, to Walter Long with draft replies, n.d., and March 22, 1730/31, March 28, 1731, and November 11, 1732. The

undated reply is attached to an undated letter that clearly precedes the letter of March 22.

19. DD/TO/11, Peter Tolson Sr., October 4, 1780.
20. DD/TO/2, Richard Tolson memoir, 1776–84, fols. 12–25. Tolson also gave the soldier some money for traveling expenses. These entries detail at length the problems Richard encountered upon having expended his ready money to help this soldier out. See also DD/TO/11, Peter Tolson Jr., August 12, 1780 and Peter Tolson Sr., August 19, 1780. Richard initially hoped to keep knowledge of the affair from his father.
21. 314/4/1, Wansey letters, from William Curtis, Clapham, Jan. 24, 1774, and Aug. 17, n.d., ca. 1773.
22. DD/TO/12, Thomas Stevens, Mar. 26, 1781. Richard had met Thomas while both were attending an academy for merchants in Holland.
23. DD/TO/7, Peter Tolson Sr., July 31, 1776; DD/TO/11, Peter Tolson Sr., Aug. 19, 1780.
24. 314/4/2, draft letters of George Wansey, to S.F., n.d. and Oct. 9, 1780.
25. 947/1874, Long letters, to Walter Long with draft replies, n.d. and Mar. 22, 1730. The reading of "flints and steal" is conjectural as the orthography is very poor. Other possible readings for "flints," are "thickets" or "sticks"; the word *steal* is clearer. No matter, the vigorous, active, and thus manly nature of the promised response is clear.
26. 314/4/2, draft letters of George Wansey, to Richard Lawrence, n.d., ca. 1778 or 1779. Lawrence was in Oxford training for a career in the church but his family lived in Bath. The two probably met at school.
27. 314/4/2, draft letters of George Wansey, to Richard Lawrence, July 1778.
28. 314/4/3, Wansey journal, June 18 and June 29, 1783.
29. DD/TO/11, Thomas Stevens, Nov. 8, 1780; DD/TO/12, Tho[ma]s Stevens, July 30, 1781, Dec. 22, 1781
30. DD/TO/11 and DD/TO/12, letters dating from Dec. 25, 1780 onward.
31. DD/TO/4, Richard Tolson journal, 1779–80, fol. 68; and 314/4/1, Wansey letters, from Henry Wansey, Apr. 22, 1772. I am grateful to Marilyn Morris for bringing the issue of manly vigor to my attention.
32. DD/TO/4, Richard Tolson journal, 1779–80, fol. 48; DD/TO/8, Peter Tolson Sr., Apr. 2, 1777.
33. 314/4/2, draft letters of George Wansey, to Richard Lawrence, July 1778, and n.d., ca. March 1780.
34. 314/4/1, Wansey letters, from Anne Wansey, July 29, 1783.
35. 314/4/1, Wansey letters, from W. Curtis, n.d., ca. 1773.
36. See both 314/1/1 and 314/1/2, letters to and from George Wansey. Whether these two had an unrequited homosexual attraction or were simply taking the language of sensibility to its extremes is difficult to tell.

37. 314/4/1, Wansey letters, from Anne Wansey (sister) at Clapham, July 29, 1783. The young man was employed in a banking house, but to Anne, as to most of her contemporaries, a man's employment and the source of his family's wealth was not the fundamental test of gentility. Also from Henry Wansey, July 24, 1778.
38. Massachusetts Historical Society, Boston, USA, MS N 2030, William Barrell letterbook, 1771–76, letters to Amory, Taylor and Rogers, June 19, 1773 and Hayley and Hopkins, May 16, 1774.
39. DD/TO/4, Richard Tolson journal, 1779–80, fol. 28; DD/TO/11, Peter Tolson Sr., Oct. 4, 1780.
40. Harvey, "The History of Masculinity," 307.
41. WRO, 947/1874, Long letters, to Walter Long with draft replies, n.d. and March 22, 1730/31.
42. Philip Carter's analysis of Boswell's journals and letters is suggestive in this regard in identifying alternative masculinities that Boswell adopted: "man of dignity," "pretty man," and "blackguard." While there are some areas of overlap, Boswell's "choices" clearly do not correspond to the alternatives of the individuals studied here, not surprising given his landed background: "James Boswell's Manliness" in Hitchcock and Cohen, eds., *English Masculinities*, 111–30.
43. This label borrows from Margaret Hunt's discussion of the "prudential virtues" of middling families: *The Middling Sort*, 46.
44. 314/4/2, draft letters of George Wansey, to S.F., Oct. 9, 1780.
45. 314/4/1, Wansey letters, from William Green, Basingstoke, Mar. 23, 1786.
46. DD/TO/11, Peter Tolson Sr., Oct. 4, 1780.
47. Massachusetts Historical Society, MS N 2030, William Barrell letterbook, 1771–76, letter to Armory and Taylor, Nov. 30, 1771.
48. DD/TO/7, Peter Tolson Sr., Nov. 16, 1776.
49. This label borrows from Michele Cohen's analysis of the ways in which masculine identity was shifting in the last decades of the eighteenth century: "'Manners' Make the Man."
50. DD/TO/11, Peter Tolson Sr., Aug. 12, 1780.
51. WRO, 947/1874, Long letters, draft replies, Mar. 22, 1730/31.
52. 314/4/2, draft letters of George Wansey, to Richard Lawrence, July 1778; to S.F., n.d.
53. 314/4/2, draft letters of George Wansey, to Richard Lawrence, August n.d., ca. 1779, and Oct. 1, 1779.
54. DD/TO/11, Peter Tolson Sr., Aug. 12, 1780 and Thomas Stevens, May 19, 1780.
55. 314/4/2, draft letters of George Wansey, to S.F., n.d. He went on to warn about the pursuit of riches for its own sake: "All this and much more is the reward of industry but let us take care that we do not mistake riches which are but the means for the end itself and by a too earnest

pursuit after them involve ourselves in those aims the temptations to which it is the chief advantage of riches to exempt us from."

56. 314/4/1, Wansey letters, from William Curtis, Wandsworth, Aug. 17, n.d.
57. 314/4/2, draft letters of George Wansey, to S.F., Sept. 1778.
58. DD/TO/12, Thomas Stevens, Oct. 29, 1781 to Nov. 13, 1782.
59. 314/4/1, Wansey letters, from William Curtis, Clapham, Jan. 24, 1774; two words missing because of torn margins.
60. 314/4/2, draft letters of George Wansey, to Richard Lawrence, n.d., ca. early 1780.
61. 314/4/1, Wansey letters, from William Curtis, Wandsworth, August 17, n.d.
62. 314/4/2, draft letters of George Wansey, to S.F., Oct. 9, 1780; one word missing at the margin.
63. 314/4/2, draft letters of George Wansey, to Richard Lawrence, Dec. 1778.
64. 314/4/1, Wansey letters, from Richard Lawrence at Bath, Sept. 21, n.d., ca. 1779; /314/4/2, draft letters of George Wansey to Richard Lawrence, Oct. 1, 1779. Lawrence was the first to mention the incident; Wansey replied in defense of the Bath Volunteers and provides additional detail.
65. 314/4/2, draft letters of George Wansey, to Richard Lawrence, Oct. 1, 1779.
66. Saving Walter Long who fell from grace in 1731, all of the examples here come from the 1770s and 1780s.
67. 314/4/2, draft letters of George Wansey, to S.F., n.d., ca. late 1780 or early 1781.
68. 314/4/1, Anne Wansey, July 29, 1783, original torn; the reconstruction of the word *pride* fits both the sense and the space in the letter, but it is only a supposition.
69. Toby Ditz, "The New Men's History and the Peculiar Absence of Gendered Power: Some Remedies from Early American Gender History," *Gender and History* 16 (2004): 1–35.
70. DD/TO/8, Law Atkinson, Aug. 4, 1777. The original text reads: "he [a mutual friend] has sent me in his letter a nice print for my *Horologie*, it depicts a *Lady* with her skirts pulled up halfway, and in truth the cunt is exceptionally natural. As soon as I received it I went upstairs were Mietje the ironing maid was alone; I showed it to her, and while she was holding it away from herself, I thoroughly felt her up, not having the time to do something different, but she promised me that coming Friday I can fuck her because she will be alone." I am grateful for Dr. Oscar Lansen's assistance with the translation from Dutch.
71. 314/1/2, draft letters of George Wansey, to S.F., Sept. 1778.
72. 314/1/2, draft letters of George Wansey, to Sam (probably the same as S.F.), n.d., and to Richard Lawrence, Jan. 27, 1780.

73. 314/1/3, Wansey memoir, see entries from 1788 onward.
74. DD/TO/2, Tolson memoir, fol. 10, 31–32, and 42-54.
75. 314/1/2, draft letters of George Wansey, to S.F., n.d. This observation is embedded in a longer passage that compares S.F.'s servitude in pursuit of his medical training to Joseph's second period of service in pursuit of Rachel.
76. Margaret Hunt delivered a suggestive paper on this topic at the North American Conference on British Studies meeting in Boston, November 2006, exploring how the Admiralty handled women's claims on sailor's pay. See also the discussions of plebian marriage in Anna Clark, *Struggle for the Breeches* (Berkeley and Los Angeles: University of California Press, 1994).

Chapter 11

Success and Self-Loathing in the Life of an Eighteenth-Century Entrepreneur

Matthew Kadane, Hobart and William Smith Colleges

Amid all the "self-love," "self-approbation," and "self-applause," not once did Adam Smith follow "self" with "perception" in any of his six editions of *The Theory of Moral Sentiments.* The two words were apparently hardly ever joined until the age of modern psychology.[1] But Smith, if anyone, should have beaten psychologists to the punch: in conceiving of the self as a reflection of a "mirror" in which we search for social approval, Smith made what we mean today by self-perception the linchpin of social and economic success.[2] Smith also recognized that mirror gazing could run the risk of vanity. But in his heavily revised final edition of the work, vanity ceased being a problem and instead became "almost always a sprightly and a gay, and very often a good-natured passion." It is the "great secret of education," he explained in an era whose luminaries routinely linked education to enlightenment, "to direct vanity to proper objects."[3] Preeminent among those objects was the free market, and in the final act of what was effectively a century long de-morality play on the subject of self-interest and the new economy, Smith made vanity and self-love acceptable outcomes of self-perception.[4]

But well into Britain's eighteenth century, and even among some entrepreneurs busy augmenting the wealth of the nation, staring in the social mirror still led resolutely to a spiritual crime. This should go without saying. If no one in the eighteenth century carried around the traditional moral meaning of what were becoming keywords of the psychology of capitalism—self-approbation, vanity, acquisitiveness, and so on—then Smith and others would have wasted less ink trying to demoralize and redefine those terms. Or at least so runs the logical implication. The detailed and visceral evidence of the self-perception of ordinary people who gave their time equally to God and commerce has been thin.[5] In light of a recently rediscovered spiritual diary written in an environment thick with commercial meaning, this chapter seeks to put a face on the view a deeply pious British capitalist had of himself at the end of the early modern period.

JOSEPH RYDER

The Leeds clothier, religious Dissenter, and spiritual diarist Joseph Ryder (1695–1768) lived the "story of textiles" that Maxine Berg has called "the epitome of the whole story from protoindustry to Industrial Revolution."[6] By 1700, and the beginning of his life, four-fifths of Leeds's workers were occupied in the wool industry, which along with worsted cloth-making would come to make up half of the value of all national exports at the time of his death.[7] Daniel Defoe rolled into town in 1725, right around the time Ryder could claim financial independence, and marveled that "the whole Country is infinitely populous . . . [a] noble Scene of Industry and Application Growth."[8] By the mid-1750s, a new cloth hall could hold twenty thousand people in its yard, and with other smaller markets it brought business to the region on an unprecedented scale: Yorkshire would see its share of the national total of woolen exports increase from one-fifth to three-fifths over the century, while Leeds, the region's most urbanized, specialized, and capitalized area, would see output in textiles production swell by a staggering 800 percent.[9] None of this is to deny stagnation and decline in other parts of the country, the important exceptions to the older image of Britain's economy as ubiquitously growing on the eve of industrialization, but Ryder's protoindustrialized Leeds, with its market links to overseas and domestic demands, with its plentiful supplies of capital, labor, raw materials, and entrepreneurs, and with a population that nearly trebled, from six thousand in 1700 to sixteen thousand by the year of his death, is a striking exception to the exceptions.[10]

The precise details of Ryder's economic life are limited by the spiritual focus of his diary.[11] We can still infer from his surviving book of dye recipes that he, his wife Elizabeth, and their family of adopted orphans dyed and scribbled yarn, and countless diary references to regional travels suggest he then commissioned people in the villages surrounding Leeds to spin and, possibly, to weave.[12] Ryder was, in other words, a manifestation of the sort of putting out clothier who Max Weber saw as the quintessential early modern capitalist employer on the verge of becoming modern.[13] Like Weber's archetype, Ryder also placed himself in the very middle of the middling sort. In his final will, written after a decade of, at best, sporadic work, Joseph was still able to earmark £250 for his beneficiaries (Elizabeth died, leaving the couple childless, in 1754) and funeral expenses.[14] In better times he seems to have had greater assets. In early middle age, for example, he recorded a friend's description of his house as commodious (which worryingly led to a "rising of pride").[15] Three years later he recorded the purchase of a "small estate" and by the next year conceded when a friend noted that he should be "fixt" financially (a statement—and more generally a state—that led Ryder to meditate on life's great uncertainties).[16] Throughout his most successful years in the 1740s and 1750s, the diary often references a housekeeper, a manservant, and other tenants and alludes to more abundant material goods (which demand greater spiritual "watchfulness"[17]). The diary's impressionistic images of material life can be given focus with advertisements in the *Leeds Mercury* for homes "very convenient for a clothier" that detail a few acres of land surrounding double-storied houses with over a half dozen rooms, a loom-shop, farm buildings, yards, gardens, tenters, and domestic quarters.[18] Ryder was never possessed of the kind of wealth associated with town's major textiles manufacturers like the Denison family, whose family estate was worth £500,000 by the early 1780s, or even with the bigger Leeds cloth merchants who sold to foreign markets, employed dozens of workers, and regularly traveled to London, where Ryder went only once.[19] But as a man of smaller capital Ryder had just enough wealth to occasion constant worry about the threat it posed to his soul.

It was religious life that Ryder would have spoken of first when introducing himself. He was a deeply committed member of Leeds's Dissenter community and shuttled back and forth throughout the week between the town's two largest Dissenter chapels: the Independent Call Lane and the Presbyterian Mill Hill, where he was baptized.[20] The latter gave Ryder some exposure to Enlightenment religiosity. By the 1740s Mill Hill, like many Presbyterian churches, had moved toward Unitarianism, and in sermons there Ryder, mostly disapprovingly, heard radical ministers deny the Trinity and even at times promote a gentle version of deism (after hearing a Mill Hill sermon "exalt reason and plead for the liberty of judging for themselves," Ryder countered in his diary that "if, in the substantial of religion, I differ from my neighbour, one of us must think amiss").[21] It is revealing of Ryder's moderateness and irenicism that in spite of its heterodoxy he went to Mill Hill weekly, but it was in any case Call Lane where he felt more at home. Call Lane's uncontroversial minister, Thomas Whitaker, who presided over the chapel from 1727 to 1778, was Ryder's spiritual mentor, and the ethos of the congregation also resonated with the general outlook of the authors prominent on Ryder's bookshelves: Richard Baxter, Isaac Ambrose, John Bunyan, Isaac Watts, Matthew Henry, and Philip Doddridge. Whitaker made the case in sermon after sermon that salvation rested on sincere piety, watchfulness, diligent worship, and moderation in theology, and Ryder mostly affirmed that message in some two thousand verses, all rhymed in the style of Dissenter hymns, that he wrote in his diary after his summaries of Sunday sermons.

Ryder's immersion in religious life was, at the risk of understatement, thorough. He attended church service twice on Sundays and throughout the week found himself at various other services—public lectures, funerals, days of thanksgiving and fasting, ordination services held throughout the West Riding, evening meetings—that altogether gave him occasion to write commentaries on roughly five thousand formalized religious events.[22] Outside of the chapel he filled a role between ordinary parishioner and minister as an elder; he was entrusted with his church's charities, which suggests the high esteem in which he was held by his coreligionists; on occasion he led his fellow parishioners through informal services; he visited criminals, the insane, and the poor in the workhouses; he served as a coroner's juror; and he was sought out for spiritual and financial advice and mediation between aggrieved coreligionist business partners.

The diary Ryder kept was also an outgrowth of his religious commitment and diligence. Diary keeping was a common practice among Dissenters and their Puritan forebears, in no small part because works of practical divinity and pastoral advice regularly recommended written self-accounts as aids to spiritual watchfulness. But between

1733 and 1768 Ryder took the practice to extraordinary lengths in creating an artifact of his spirituality that amounted at his death of "old age," a mere five days after his last entry, to nearly two and a half million words in forty filled and bound octavo volumes and the opening pages of a forty-first.[23] In content the diary reflects what on first reading seems to be the outlook of a seventeenth-century Puritan trapped in a time warp: his views on politics, the weather, and the news were deeply providential; his view of family life was predictably patriarchal; and his sullen outlook satisfied the biblical injunction, which he quoted dozens of times throughout the diary, that it is better to go to the house of mourning than the house of mirth. On closer inspection, though, the diary constantly reveals the agony that arose when a hotter sort of Protestant piety more commonly associated with the seventeenth century met the capitalist economy of the eighteenth.[24] One of the most striking consequences of that encounter is the length of the diary itself. What Ryder called his "active frame in courts below"—namely, his constant buying, producing, and selling—demanded especially attentive "watching," as he and other diarists often put it.[25] The diary encouraged watching in the first place, but the potential sins he saw in commercial life gave him even more reason to watch daily, and that need in turn goes much of the way toward explaining the massiveness of his self-account.

It should be stressed that Ryder directed his watchful eyes toward multiple spheres of activity and various strange, noteworthy, and frightening events: the natural world, elections, the movements of armies during the Jacobite rebellion of the mid-1740s, the deaths of friends, the harvest, the birth of a neighbor's live triplets, overseas conflict, a late-April blizzard, even the very act of watching, which a guidebook of spiritual diary-keeping warned might fall prey to the devil's power to deceive the senses.[26] But to the extent that personal salvation was the ultimate goal of the godly, watching was preeminently a form of self-perception. One had to watch oneself for the smallest signs of deviation from the godly course, and Ryder saw those signs everywhere: in conversation with coreligionists and business associates that veered for too long into secular subjects; in his melancholy outlook; in an admiration of the town's elites that could turn to envy; in his immersion in his own business or, alternatively, in any lapse of diligence; and, not least, in any success that crossed the line—a line that no amount of watching ever clearly situated—between success and excess. As Ryder explained in one of his verses, "Of Watchfullness and Prayer":

> The Dangers numerous are, Which Every Saint Surround
> Each Worldly pleasure has its snare if riches do abound.[27]

This is what is so extraordinary about Ryder with respect to Smith. Like Smith's impartial spectator, Ryder too saw society as a mirror, but when that mirror reflected his material successes too brightly, the watchful clothier felt not the warm approbation that led to self-love but the glaring evidence of his vanity.

THE VANITY OF SELF-PERCEPTION

"Vain" and "vanity" are keywords in Ryder's diary—one or the other appears hundreds of times throughout his forty-one volumes—and both words always carry a negative valence. Jean Calvin once called the Psalms an anatomy of the soul, and for Ryder few biblical passages captured his mood quite like the first line of Psalm 119:113: "I hate vain thoughts."[28] At least since the fourteenth century "vain" had, in English, suggested something worthless, unprofitable, unavailing, or devoid of real value. By the seventeenth century it had also come to characterize someone with an excessively high regard for his attainments, appearance, or social approval.[29] Ryder's uses of the word indicate that he hated the kinds of thoughts that conformed to either definition—to him, high self-regard *was* spiritually worthless. "Vain thoughts," as he once put it with reference to a biblical episode that drew together the commercial and spiritual, embraced "all admiring Thoughts of our Selves & Despising of Others as ye Pharisee Who when He came to ye Temple to Pray Began to Bless God for his own attainments above ye Publicans."[30] At the same time, vain thoughts were not simply those of a rich man overflowing with pride; riches, if not put to spiritual use, were themselves also "vain" in the sense of being worthless. As he explained in a verse titled "A Contempt of ye World":

> What Sweet refreshment might ye Rich man find
> Was he but unto Piety Inclin'd
> But if his Wealth proves fuell to his Lust
> Or if on Riches he for Safety Trust
> Vain is ye product he from them does find
> And poor Contentment will they Give ye mind.[31]

What is striking here is that vanity was a keyword for both Ryder and Smith, but with inverted meanings. Smith, again from *The Theory of Moral Sentiments*, wrote:

> To be observed . . . to be taken notice of with sympathy, complacency, and approbation, are all the advantages which we can propose to derive from [bettering our condition]. It is the vanity, not the ease, or the pleasure, which interests us.[32]

Ryder, in one of his most successful years:

> Swarms of Vain Thoughts do greatly me Infest
> By approbation Guilt is much Increast.[33]

For Smith, "vanity" augmented national wealth; for Ryder it augured spiritual impoverishment. The beginning of the explanation of the disjunction between Ryder and Smith is that Ryder possessed a godly state of mind in an increasingly secular and commercialized town. In a mood celebratory of the secular, Defoe called Leeds's textiles industry "a Prodigy of its kind . . . not to be equalled in the World."[34] Ryder—who apparently never read Defoe, Smith, or any of the other paragons of the British Enlightenment—instead echoed John Bunyan's warning about Vanity Fair: "he that lives in such a place has need of an item to caution him to take heed, every moment of the day." On the day the Mixed Cloth Hall opened in Leeds in August 1758, replacing the smaller cloth market at Briggate that had so struck Defoe, Ryder reported:

> This day there was the first Publick markett in the new cloth hall, and a procession of persons Occupied in Serverall branches of the trade bearing Severall Flaggs, and a Considerable Sum of money given to the persons, but this transaction as well as others mett with a different approbation. Some commended the Contrivance, Others sett light by it, as a piece of Vanity. Spectators were very numerous, but we may Say of it, and very truly, All here below is Vanity.[35]

And yet for all these contrasts, Ryder's story is not simply that of an individual standing against the tide of economic change. For one thing, "*Others* sett light by it, as a piece of Vanity" suggests Ryder's outlook was not solitary; for another, "this transaction as well as others" reveals that the vast cloth hall was not the only feature of commercial Leeds that aroused spiritual worry. More to the point, Ryder had had an economic interest in places like the Cloth Hall for most of his life. If he worried about the surplus wealth that afforded him social approval, as an employer of a handful of cloth workers and a diligent clothier himself he also worried about the alternatives of idleness and apathy, which both suggested spiritual impoverishment. Had he actually read Smith, Ryder surely would have dissented on the grounds that acquisitiveness fed by vanity was hateable, yet he nevertheless issued sentiment after sentiment like that capsulized in the title of one of his sermonic poems, "Poverty the Product of Sloth."[36] Ryder and Smith may have used language that suggested they lived in radically inverted parallel universes, but Ryder was no simple critic of capitalism. He had commitments to business life that worryingly seemed to run as deep as his commitments to God.

Ryder thus disavowed and resisted wealth even as he persisted in acquiring it. And it is here where his hatred of vain thoughts exposes the predicament at the heart of his self-perception. If vanity is excessive self-admiration, then to hate one's self-admiring thoughts, as the Psalm recommends, is to hate oneself for loving oneself; self-admiration can lead nowhere by such logic but back to self-hatred. Put more concretely, Ryder's fear of vanity came regularly from his worldly achievements, which were in turn driven by a religious impulse to honor God by doing well in this world. "This morning," he once wrote, "I was desirous that I might not henceforward be slothfull in Business, But fervent in Spirit serving the Lord."[37] But Ryder did not possess a foolproof means to draw the line between success and idolatrous excess. "If I'm concerned too much in things below/it makes my progress heavenwards but slow," ran one of his couplets, where the operative words were *if* and *too much.* By daily striving for worldly achievements undertaken to honor God, Ryder risked transforming his successes into excesses and his achievements into vanity. His worldly behavior could both temper and reinforce the spiritual anxieties it was meant to allay.

Self-Perception and Creditworthiness

Much as Ryder did not want to dwell on his image in the social mirror, he did not want to reflect too brightly the images of others. Doing so could in one sense lead to failure to recognize the spiritual meaning of his material attainments. On a Sunday in the summer of 1734, possibly after an encounter at chapel with one of the town's wealthy Dissenters, he writes of "beholding a man with Superior accommodations for ye World to my Self." He continues, "At first, "[I] was ready rather to admire them, But by ye blessing of God I hope this thought was Quasht, Lest it should raise me Unthankfullness for what I did comfortably Enjoy."[38] Thinking too highly of others could also lead to envy, which Ryder relied on his watchfulness to mitigate. While waiting one evening for "Guests of a Superiour Rank" to arrive at his house as he and his family prepared "Suitable preparations for their Entertainment," he was, by a quiet moment, "led a little to meditate upon that preparation which was Daily made for ye Rich and Great, and for my Self was brought to this Conclusion in my own mind, to Chose Rather, with Jacob to be a Plain man Dwelling in Fonts, with plain & Comfortable accommodations, rather than Enjoy all that Grandure which ye World with all its fullness was Capable of Affording."[39]

If Ryder did not want to reflect his or anyone else's image too brightly, the alternative was not to retreat from business society. The self's perception by others was the basis of reputation and creditworthiness, without which the acquisition of capital was all but hopeless.[40] The cash poor eighteenth-century wool economy depended on an extensive web of credit that enabled clothiers to buy their raw materials and pay for various postmanufacturing procedures. Reputation and trust were crucial for securing loans with drawn-out repayment periods, and there can be no doubt that the pressures to maintain good standing contributed to the self-regulation of behavior. Moreover, given the nature of the economy and the fact that his business was growing, it is extremely unlikely that Ryder completely restrained from pushing the limits of his capital and credit resources or managed to operate without accruing at least temporary debts.

It is striking, then, that the thousands of pages in Ryder's diary evince none of the intense anxiety over holding debt or trying to acquire resources that Craig Muldrew and others have taken as evidence of credit's totalizing effect on early modern English social life.[41] Quoting Max Weber on Benjamin Franklin's famous "time is money" passage, Muldrew contends that, contra Weber, Franklin's advice "was not about the creation of a 'capitalist spirit': all the advice about diligence and frugality was concerned with reputation. Its aim was outward into the community, not inwards, concerning belief."[42] On the contrary, in the few passages in the diary where Ryder shows some concern about debt—typically the debt of someone else—his mind and pen in fact *always* turn inward and toward belief. Consider a late-life entry from 1766:

> This day has been a fine pleasant day, but many unpleasant accounts have I heard of one and another, great extravagancies which have been found too apparent both among professors and prophane, whereby they are become unable to pay their honest debts, which ought to be warnings to us all that think we stand, to take heed lest we fall. But what is further distressing is that I find my self so cold in religion, and

so prone to wander, and to turn with the dog to his vomitt, and with the sow that was washed to her wallowing in the mire . . . the wages of sin are death.[43]

Ryder was tuned in here to the problems of debt (and may incidentally be saying something as well about a slowdown in the wool trade in Leeds in the late 1760s, amid the ascendancy of cotton), but the situation commanded little attention as he moved on in the entry to his own spiritual shortcomings.

The point, in any case, is not that Ryder was unconcerned about his image in the eyes of his neighbors and business partners, but rather that the social implications of failure to meet credit obligations were subordinate to his worry about God's perception of him. In one of the few entries that actually mention credit, the prospect of losing his good financial standing is simply one item in Ryder's long list of earthly activities and occurrences with serious spiritual consequences:

> This Day I have somewhat of a hurry of business and sadly am I afraid lest anything here below should ever have any unhappy tendency to prevent my warmest pursuits after a better world. Now I am in health, my earnest desire is to be preparing for sickness. Now I am in prosperity, I desire to be well prepared for adversity in whatever shape it may be sent, whether by providentiall losses, persecution or whatever God ye ruler & righteous Judge may see meet to send it. Now I am in credit, I desire to be prepared for disgrace, if it may not be brought upon me for sin, I desire in every case to behave as a child of God that I may live & that I may dye under ye Smiles of Gods Countenance through faith in a mediator whom I would love above all.[44]

It is important to stress that Ryder does mention the word *credit*—the subject is not off-limits in the diary. What is striking, given the emphasis in recent historiography, is that his concerns about credit were comparatively insignificant.

Even the social situations that may have damaged Ryder's reputation leave him relatively unshaken in the diary. The diary records a dispute in the fall of 1757 between, on one side, Ryder and a distant kinsman by marriage, John Darnton, and, on the other, their coreligionist, Joseph Sigston.[45] A fragmented piece of information given in a note at the back of one of the diary volumes indicates that Ryder and Darnton took a trip to nearby Dalton "to be an Evidence for Mr Darnton paying 25 pound to Joseph Sigston." Darnton gave the seventy-one-year-old Sigston two bills, but Sigston refused to take the second of the bills, claiming he would have "nothing but specie."[46]

Ryder and Darnton rode back to Leeds with the matter unsettled. When we turn to the entry in the main body of the journal written on the day the episode occurred (November 30, 1757), we read:

> This day after some business in the forenoon, In the afternoon I heard both Good and Evil, I was desired into company upon a speciall occasion a little out of town with a man who had made a profession, and some part of life behaved somewhat plausibly, but this afternoon I thought he both talked & acted very strangely, I could scarcely have Imagined to have heard & seen so much in any man, at least in any man who professed the Gospell.[47]

Later entries confirm that Sigston was the strangely acting man here "who made a profession" (i.e., a Dissenter).[48] They also reveal that members of the community met to discuss "a very different piece of work" and to "make alterations with many . . . upon ye most equitable terms." The matter at hand was clearly the dispute between Sigston and Darnton, which threatened to become a lawsuit. Ryder was sullen on noticing the connection between breaches of "unity in nation, country, house, or family" but hopefully recorded a sermon delivered "very apt to the purpose," which must have targeted Sigston and Darnton, both of whom sat in Call Lane's pews.[49] Yet in spite of the minister Whitaker's attempts at reconciliation, Ryder alludes to increased tension.

What is important with respect to the question of self-perception are not these obscure details but what Ryder wrote about the event next, namely, nothing. Given the threats to Ryder's reputation that the matter posed—and even more the threats posed to his close friend Darnton—we should expect some handwringing in the diary. But instead of being any more anxious than he was already, Ryder was relatively nonchalant and incredulous in the entries surrounding the dispute, and then the episode fades from the journal. Reputation was unquestionably important. And we should pay careful attention to the relationship between credit and self-perception, not to mention self-control, but we should be just as careful not to dismiss the role of religion with respect to economic behavior. Diligence and frugality and virtually every other aspect of commercial behavior were of supreme inward importance to Ryder precisely because of their soteriological consequences. What in the first instance gave shape to Ryder's economic outlook, self-image, and the image he projected to others was a spiritual struggle he waged daily in the privacy of his journal to stay poised between damming extremes.

CONCLUSIONS

So what, then, can Ryder's record of self-perception tell us about the role of religion with respect to economic behavior? In some ways the answer is close to what Weber proposed a century ago in his *Protestant Ethic and the Spirit of Capitalism*.[50] It is true that the evidence unearthed in the century since Weber wrote his famous essay no longer supports the simple equation of "Calvinism" with the doctrine of predestination.[51] In the early modern British Isles, and notwithstanding the rifts over predestination that research continues to suggest made civil war more likely, the overarching theological principle held by Puritans, if not by most committed Protestants, was the related concept of "providence," by which God was thought to maintain an active presence in even the tiniest and most obscure of earthly affairs.[52] But if we plug into Weber's thesis the idea of providentialism and the watchfulness it demanded, the perfect storm of Protestantism and Capitalism, which was Joseph Ryder, does support Weber's claims about the affinity between "the virtues cultivated by Calvinism . . . [and] the restrained, strict, and active posture of capitalist employers of the middle class."[53] The cautions the other case studies in this book make against the application of Weber's insights to Europe as a whole nevertheless also need to be heeded. But here again "watching" may be the keyword. Where the Reformed churches in Scotland, Switzerland, and the Low Countries had a relative abundance of preachers and external disciplining mechanisms like the consistory, English Calvinists, from the late sixteenth century on, depended on voluntary techniques of discipline. These were driven by a tradition of "practical theology" that authorized and encouraged lay readers to conduct their own searches for signs of providence and their salvation.[54] The intense sort of watchfulness Ryder embodied (and which made English Calvinists as a whole distinctive within the European Reformed community) was, in other words, an outgrowth of a particularly English religious situation.[55] It may well be this prescribed watchfulness that sets godly English merchants apart from, for example, Amsterdam merchants in the seventeenth century who were more quickly amenable to whatever religion fit their business interests; it may also be this watchfulness that gives the basic story Weber outlined ongoing relevance in early modern England.

Ryder was, in any case, far from abandoning his religiosity for the sake of profits or a diminution of the spiritual anguish that was brought on by either commercial success or failure. He instead maintained his defenses against Satan, poverty, and worldliness by living a life of careful moderation, which required a delicate and ongoing balancing act. Let us listen, one last time, to Ryder giving us a self-portrait as even his prose seems to search for equilibrium:

> This Day Yields but an uncomfortable reflection upon consideration of too much Indifferency In Religion, For Hearing of ye Conversation of a Good man being always pleasant, & I my self at Times Inclining to be so, I took something of Freedom this way. Yet calling things over again I found it as I though [*sic*] something Difficult to be Chearfull without too much Levity, or to be Sad & pensive without remains of too much discontent and perplexity, And Thought if God was pleased to Grant me a Sweet medium I might hereby be Enabled to go on my way with rejoicing.[56]

No shortage of advice about how to achieve the "sweet medium" of both his psychological state and business life came from religious experience. Thomas Whitaker recommended self-alignment between poverty and riches and condemned not wealth and inequality in and of themselves but the vices to which "affluent circumstances too frequently led men . . . pride, luxury, voluptuousness, tyranny and oppression of the poor, forgetfullness of God."[57] Success was laudable, Whitaker told his prospering congregation time and again, as long as one properly utilized the bounty of Providence. A minister in nearby Wakefield "preacht [moderation] to us in our pursuit after earthly things and moderation in practice."[58] And the Bible was of course the wellspring of such advice. "Remove far from me vanity and lies," runs Proverbs 30:8–9; "give me neither poverty nor riches; feed me with food convenient for me; Lest I be full, and deny thee, and say, Who is the LORD? or lest I be poor, and steal, and take the name of God in vain." Diary-writing too assisted a watchful eye in search of equilibrium. And not just for Ryder. The middling ethos pervades self-writing in early modern Britain.[59] Staying in the middle offered protection from the spiritually barren states of both poverty and abundance, and diaries were the ideal technologies for such self-maintenance. As Ryder told his diary, the reading and writing of which offered self-given advice, those "in the middle station [are] perhaps more happy than either of the others, for fullness is very apt to make us unmindful of God . . . [the] very poor are too apt to envy those above them, and to quarrel with providence."[60] Hence, too, the importance of charity, which Ryder distributed both from his funds and those collected at Call Lane. Charity permitted the redirection of the surplus that might entail too much upward mobility and assuaged

Ryder's troubled mind. In prosperous years he wrote, "Oh that I may be enabled to use ye World so as not to abuse it, & to be as charitable as opportunity & ability will allow."[61]

But practicing charity and occupying the middle class did not automatically bring psychological relief. Giving away money did not answer the spiritual question of whether charitableness was authentic or mechanical; being in the middle was easier to imagine than to quantify and confidently recognize. Persistent throughout Ryder's life was, rather, his suspicion of his own motives, and this should draw our attention to a polarity shift in the self-perception of early modern godly capitalists in Britain. In the simplest terms, Ryder found self-loathing where Smith's rational agent found self-love. This tells us not just about Ryder and others like him; it also helps to put a face on the abnormality assumed in Smith's free-market psychology. Ryder was just the sort of person whose vain self-perception Smith saw a need to spiritually decriminalize. Watchful clothiers may have been the backbone of the protoindustrial economy in places like Leeds. But it was by telling the last wave of early modern capitalists that their loathsome view of themselves was almost exactly misperceived that the first wave of political economists could more easily construct a psychological model suited to their vision of modern capitalism.

Notes

1. A keyword search of "self-perception" and "self perception" in the *Eighteenth-Century Collections Online* database yields no hits; under a definition of "self-" the *Oxford English Dictionary* records a use of "self-perception" in Ralph Cudworth's 1678 *The True Intellectual System of the Universe.*
2. Adam Smith, *The Theory of Moral Sentiments* (London 1759), 259.
3. Adam Smith, *The Theory of Moral Sentiments, Volume II* (London 1790), 173, 178. On the revisions Smith made to his text, see the first chapter of D. D. Raphael, *The Impartial Spectator: Adam Smith's Moral Philosophy* (Oxford: Oxford University Press, 2007).
4. For an overview of the Enlightenment's moral redefinition of wealth, a project Smith was only one of many to undertake, see Roy Porter, *The Creation of the Modern World: The Untold Story of the British Enlightenment* (New York: W. W. Norton, 2000), 383–96; the authoritative fuller statement on the subject remains Albert O. Hirschman, *The Passions and the Interests: Political Arguments for Capitalism Before Its Triumph* (Princeton: Princeton University Press, 1977).
5. On the other hand, we do possess much eighteenth-century personal writing of an economic nature that evinces little religious expression and

much diary writing of a spiritual nature, especially from an earlier period, that shows less concern with commerce. For the former, see John Smail, ed., *Woollen Manufacturing in Yorkshire: The Memorandum Books of John Brearley, Cloth Frizzer at Wakefield, 1758–1762* (Leeds: Yorkshire Archaeological Society, 2001); S. D. Smith, *"An Exact and Industrious Tradesman": The Letter Book of Joseph Symson of Kendal, 1711–1720* (Oxford: Oxford University Press, 2002); K. H. Burley, "An Essex Clothier of the Eighteenth Century," *Economic History Review* 11 (1958): 289–301; Julia de Lacy Mann, "A Wiltshire Family of Clothiers: George and Hester Wansey, 1683–1714," *Economic History Review* 9 (1956): 252. For the latter, see two classic monographs based on spiritual diaries: Paul Seaver, *Wallington's World: A Puritan Artisan in Seventeenth-Century London* (Stanford: Stanford University Press, 1985); and Alan Macfarlane, *The Family Life of Ralph Josselin, A Seventeenth-Century Clergyman: An Essay in Historical Anthropology* (Cambridge: Cambridge University Press, 1970).

6. Maxine Berg, *The Age of Manufactures, 1700–1820: History, Innovation and Work in Britain* (London: Routledge, 1994), 208.
7. Steven Burt and Kevin Grady, *The Merchants' Golden Age, Leeds 1700–1790* (Leeds: S. Burt, 1987), 3; John Rule, *The Vital Century: England's Developing Economy, 1714–1815* (London: Longman, 1992), 101–2.
8. Daniel Defoe, *Writing on Travel, Discovery, and History,* ed. W. R. Owens and P. N. Furbank, vol. 3, *A Tour Thro' the Whole Island of Great Britain*, Volume III, ed. John McVeagh (London: Pickering & Chatto, 2001), 73.
9. The figures come from Burt and Grady, *The Merchants' Golden Age*, 3, 7; for more on Leeds see Herbert Heaton, *The Yorkshire Woollen and Worsted Industries from the Earliest Times Up to the Industrial Revolution*, 2d ed. (Oxford: Oxford University Press, 1965); E. P. Thompson, *The Making of the English Working Class* (London: V. Gollancz, 1963); R. G. Wilson, *Gentlemen Merchants: The Merchant Community in Leeds, 1700–1830* (Manchester: Manchester University Press, 1971); "The Supremacy of the Yorkshire Cloth Industry in the Eighteenth Century," in N. B. Harte and K. G. Ponting, eds., *Textile History and Economic History: Essays in Honour of Miss Julia de Lacy Mann* (Manchester: Manchester University Press, 1973); Pat Hudson, *The Genesis of Industrial Capital: A Study of the West Riding Wool Textile Industry, c.1750–1850* (Cambridge: Cambridge University Press, 1986); and John Smail, *Merchants, Markets, and Manufacture: The English Wool Textile Industry in the Eighteenth Century* (New York: St. Martin's Press, 1999). Although wool is the relevant commodity with respect to Ryder, it is important to note the expanding variety in Leeds' eighteenth-century economy; on this subject, see W. G. Rimmer, "The Industrial Profile of Leeds, 1740–1840," *Publications of the Thoresby Society* 14 (1968): 130–57.

10. On Leeds and "protoindustrialization," see Pat Hudson, "Proto-industrialization in England," 49–66, and Sheilagh C. Ogilvie and Markus Cerman, "The Theories of Proto-industrialization," 1–11, in *European Proto-industrialization*, Ogilvie and Cerman, eds. (Cambridge: Cambridge University Press, 1996). For an important challenge, although one that does not apply to the West Riding, see Donald C. Coleman, "Proto-industrialization: A Concept Too Many," *Economic History Review* 36 (1983): 435–48. On Leeds' population see R. G. Wilson, "Georgian Leeds," in *A History of Modern Leeds*, ed. Derek Fraser (Manchester: Manchester University Press, 1980), 24. On the issue of growth more generally, see Pat Hudson, ed., *Regions and Industries: A Perspective on the Industrial Revolution in Britain* (Cambridge: Cambridge University Press, 1989), which should be read with her "Capital and Credit in the West Riding Wool Textile Industry, c.1750–1850"; on the slower rate of change and the decline alluded to here see, from the same volume, Marie B. Rowlands, "Continuity and Change in an Industrialising Society: The Case of the West Midlands Industries" and Brian Short's "The De-industrialization Process: A Case Study of the Weald, 1600–1850."
11. On spiritual diary writing, see Tom Webster, "Writing to Redundancy: Approaches to Spiritual Journals and Early Modern Spirituality," *Historical Journal* 39, no. 1 (1996): 33–56; Michael Mascuch, *Origins of the Individualist Self: Autobiography and Self-Identity in England, 1591–1791* (Cambridge: Polity Press, 1997); and Margo Todd, "Puritan Self-fashioning: The Diary of Samuel Ward," *Journal of British Studies* 31 (July 1992): 236–64. Much insight into the form and meaning of these texts can also be found in Seaver, *Wallington's World* and Macfarlane, *The Family Life of Ralph Josselin*.
12. West Yorkshire Archives Service, Sheepscar, MS GA/B27. On colored woolen cloth, see also Heaton, *Yorkshire Woollen and Worsted Industries*, 286–7 and Smail, *Merchants, Markets, and Manufacture*, 23. I am also indebted here to conversations with John Smail, whose expertise on the wool industry has helped me to limit the possible business activities in which Ryder would have been engaged. For a nuanced view of eighteenth-century family life that accords with Ryder's domestic experience, see Naomi Tadmor, *Family and Friends in Eighteenth-Century England: Household, Kinship, and Patronage* (Cambridge: Cambridge University Press, 2001).
13. See Stephen Kalberg's excellent edition and translation of Max Weber, *The Protestant Ethic and the Spirit of Capitalism* (Los Angeles: Roxbury Publishing, 2002), to which subsequent citations of this text refer.
14. Borthwick Institute, York, Leeds Wills, 1700–1830, "Will of Joseph Ryder of Leeds (1695–1768)." Ryder alludes to his retirement from trade when he writes of delivering his "last cloth" on May 1, 1756, but he nevertheless continued to dabble in the cloth business for the next decade.

15. John Rylands Library, Deansgate: Unitarian MSS Q/6 "Diary of Joseph Ryder" (henceforth JRD), July 4, 1737.
16. JRD May 20, 1740; Mar. 25, 1741.
17. For example, JRD June 29, 1745: "This Day I had severall strangers at my house being our Publick fair, and they were desirous to be looking at our new conveniencies and I found watchfullness very necessary lest any thing of [H]ezekiahs temper should too much prevail, that while I am showing any one ye comfortable settlement I have I should grow proud as tho' I had anything which I had not receiv'd [by grace]."
18. Heaton, *Yorkshire Woollen and Worsted Industries*, 290 n1.
19. Ryder took his trip in August and September 1744.
20. Leeds City Library, reel 36, item 3724.
21. JRD, July 28, 1748; on the changing meaning of Presbyterianism in the early eighteenth century, see C. Gordon Bolam et al., *The English Presbyterians: From Elizabethan Puritanism to Modern Unitarianism* (Boston: Beacon, 1968), 160–74.
22. The following information can be gleaned from the diary itself, but I am also indebted here to a useful summary in Herbert McLachlan, "Diary of a Leeds Layman, 1733–1768," *Transactions of the Unitarian Historical Society* 4, no. 3 (1929–30): 248–67.
23. The unspecific cause of "old age" is given as Ryder's cause of death in the Leeds parish register. See "The Register of the Parish Church of Leeds," *Publications of the Thoresby Society* 25 (1917, 1918, 1920, 1922): 289.
24. The historiography of Dissent in the eighteenth century awaits a book-length study to update Michael R. Watts, *The Dissenters* (Oxford: Oxford University Press, 1985). In the meantime see John Seed's "The Spectre of Puritanism: Forgetting the Seventeenth Century in David Hume's History of England," *Social History* 30, 4 (2005): 444–62; and "History and Narrative Identity: Religious Dissent and the Politics of Memory in Eighteenth-Century England," *Journal of British Studies* 44, 1 (2005): 46–63; also see the articles dedicated to Dissent and Parliamentary debate in a special edition of *Parliamentary History* 24, 1 (2005).
25. The urtext of watching is Isaac Ambrose's *Media: The Middle Things, in Reference to the First and Last Things* . . . (London, 1650).
26. Ambrose, Media, 45.
27. JRD, Oct. 14, 1744.
28. John Calvin, *Commentary on the Book of Psalms*, trans. James Anderson (Edinburgh: Calvin Translation Society, 1843), vol. 1, xxxvi.
29. See the entries for "vain" and "vanity" in the OED.
30. JRD, Apr. 19, 1741.
31. JRD, July 1, 1733.
32. Smith, *Theory of Moral Sentiments*, Volume I (London, 1790), 122.
33. JRD, Apr. 19, 1741.
34. Defoe, *Writings on Travel, Discovery, and History*, 73.
35. JRD, August 22, 1758.

36. JRD, Aug. 26, 1733.
37. JRD, Oct. 11, 1735.
38. JRD, July 1, 1734.
39. JRD, December, 13, 1734.
40. On credit in the West Riding, and from which much of the following discussion draws, see Hudson, *Genesis of Industrial Capital*, 140–42, and John Smail, "The Culture of Credit in Eighteenth-Century Commerce: The English Textile Industry," *Enterprise and Society* 4 (2003): 299–325.
41. Craig Muldrew, *The Economy of Obligation: The Culture of Credit and Social Relations in Early Modern England* (Basingstoke: Macmillan, 1998); Alexandra Shepard, "Manhood, Credit and Patriarchy in Early Modern England c. 1580–1640," *Past and Present* 167 (2000): 75–106; Liz Bellamy, *Commerce, Morality, and the Eighteenth-Century Novel* (Cambridge: Cambridge University Press, 1998).
42. Muldrew, *Economy of Obligation*, 2.
43. JRD, Apr. 10, 1766.
44. JRD, June 27, 1749.
45. On the family connections, see *Publications of the Thoresby Society* 25, 262. Also see Wilson, *Gentlemen Merchants*, 76, 244, 245.
46. On Sigston's age and for a record of other Dissenters in Leeds, see my 2005 Brown University dissertation, "The Watchful Clothier: The Diary of an Eighteenth-Century Protestant Capitalist," appendix 2. The back matter regarding the Sigston affair appears in volume 27.
47. JRD, Nov. 30, 1757.
48. See JRD, Dec. 3, 1757 and Dec. 5, 1757.
49. Public Record Office, London, RG4/3674.
50. This argument is considered at greater length in Margaret C. Jacob and Matthew Kadane, "Missing, Now Found in the Eighteenth Century: Weber's Protestant Capitalist," *American Historical Review* 108 (2003): 20–49.
51. See Hartmut Lehmann and Guenther Roth, eds., *Weber's Protestant Ethic: Origins, Evidence, Contexts* (Cambridge: Cambridge University Press, 1993); and Philip Benedict's *Christ's Churches Purely Reformed: A Social History of Calvinism* (New Haven, CT: Yale University Press, 2002).
52. For a recent statement on the importance and divisiveness of predestination in the early Stuart period, see David R. Como's "Predestination and Political Conflict in Laud's London," *Historical Journal* 46, no. 2 (2003): 263–94; and *Blown by the Spirit: Puritanism and the Emergence of an Antinomian Underground in Pre-Civil-War England* (Stanford: Stanford Univeristy Press, 2004). On providence, see Alexandra Walsham, *Providence in Early Modern England* (Oxford: Oxford University Press, 1999).

53. Weber, *Protestant Ethic and the Spirit of Capitalism*, 89. I consider the adaptability of this concept to Weber's thesis more fully in my "La vigilanza e L'etica protestante di Weber," in *Contemporanea. Rivista di storia dell'800 e del'900* 9, 2 (2006); suggestive too is Kaspar von Greyerz's contribution to Lehmann and Roth, *Weber's Protestant Ethic.*
54. The libraries of Huguenot in France reveal that European Calvinists could nevertheless be interested in the English production of this literature, but it was far from a national preoccupation in France. See my "Les bibliothèques de deux théologiens réformés du 17e siècle, L'un puritain anglais, l'autre pasteur huguenot," *Bulletin de la Sociètè de l'Histoire du Protestantisme Français* 147 (2001): 67–99.
55. This discussion of the peculiarities of the English Reformed tradition is indebted to Benedict's *Christ's Churches Purely Reformed*, 317–29, and Patrick Collinson's *Godly People: Essays in English Protestantism and Puritanism* (London: Hambledon, 1983), passim.
56. JRD, Apr. 11, 1734.
57. JRD, Nov. 15, 1735.
58. JRD, Sept. 12, 1750.
59. Michael Mascuch, "Social Mobility and Middling Self-Identity: The Ethos of British Autobiographers, 1600–1750," *Social History* 20, 1 (1995).
60. JRD, Apr. 13, 1767.
61. JRD, Feb. 2, 1739–40.

Index